# Ageing and Popular Culture

As the 'grey market' perpetuates the quest for eternal youth, the biological realities of deep old age are increasingly denied. Until now, social theorists have failed to assess the cultural implications of continued population ageing. *Ageing and Popular Culture* is the first book to trace the historical emergence of stereotypes of retirement and document their recent demise. Its argument is that, although modernisation, marginalisation, and medicalisation created rigid age classifications, the rise of consumer culture has coincided with a postmodern broadening of options for those in the Third Age. With an adroit use of photographs and other visual sources, Andrew Blaikie demonstrates that an expanded leisure phase is breaking down barriers between mid- and later life and that biographical and collective visions of ageing need to be reconciled. At the same time, 'positive ageing' also creates new imperatives and new norms with attendant forms of deviance. While babyboomers may anticipate a fulfilling retirement, none relish decline. Has deep old age replaced death as the taboo subject of the late twentieth century? If so, what might be the consequences?

ANDREW BLAIKIE is Senior Lecturer in the Department of Sociology at the University of Aberdeen. He is the author of *Illegitimacy, Sex and Society* (1993) and has published extensively on historical and contemporary aspects of family formation, social perceptions, and the life course.

# Ageing and popular culture

Andrew Blaikie

CAMBRIDGE
UNIVERSITY PRESS

PUBLISHED BY THE PRESS SYNDICATE OF THE UNIVERSITY OF CAMBRIDGE
The Pitt Building, Trumpington Street, Cambridge CB2 1RP, United Kingdom

CAMBRIDGE UNIVERSITY PRESS
The Edinburgh Building, Cambridge, CB2 2RU, UK
http: //www.cup.cam.ac.uk
40 West 20th Street, New York, NY 10011–4211, USA    http: //www.cup.org
10 Stamford Road, Oakleigh, Melbourne 3166, Australia

First published 1999

Printed in the United Kingdom at the University Press, Cambridge

Typeset in Plantin 10/12pt   [CE]

*A catalogue record for this book is available from the British Library*

*Library of Congress cataloguing in publication data applied for*

ISBN 0 521 55150 1 hardback
ISBN 0 521 64547 6 paperback

# Contents

# Illustrations

# Preface

In the jacuzzi at a leisure club I attend, one of the older swimmers once asked me what I did for a living. I told her I was a sociologist. 'Oh, yes, and what do they do?', she intoned. It took some restraint not to respond 'Watch people sitting in hot tubs', but I bit my lip and nobody fled the scene. In fact, I have never been an ethnographer. However, my curiosity about my fellow human beings has led me to formulate ideas about what they do with their lives on the basis of casual observation. This, of course, is a hit-and-miss process, and many aspects of later life, particularly those not evident in public places, or hidden away in institutions, are simply invisible. Nevertheless, like many who have reached a stage of adulthood where they are wondering what their futures may hold, I have detected changes in the presentational styles of old age: these ladies are not like I remember my grandparents when they were sixty-five, some forty years ago. But, then, forty years ago I was hardly old enough to appreciate ageing in the way I do today. Through engaging in a disquisition on ageing and popular culture I would like to think that I am attempting to focus interest by unearthing more knowledge than is apparent from superficial spectatorship. Yet social knowledge is contextual, its differing resonances depending not only on when it is written and read and by whom, but also on the age of both writer and reader.

Perhaps it is a necessary quality of the supposed 'objectivity' of scholarship, but rarely do academics write about topics of which they have first-hand personal experience. Later life is a case in point, although Britain has particularly honourable exceptions in Margot Jefferys, Peter Laslett, and Michael Young.[1] I need then to begin with a

---

[1] M. Jefferys (ed.), *Growing Old in the Twentieth Century* (London: Routledge, 1989); P. Laslett, *A Fresh Map of Life: The Emergence of the Third Age* (London: Weidenfeld and Nicolson, 1989); M. Young and T. Schuller, *Life After Work: The Arrival of the Ageless Society* (London: HarperCollins, 1991). Jefferys has also produced a reflexive personal account (M. Jefferys, 'Inter-generational relationships: an autobiographical perspective', in A. Jamieson, S. Harper, and C. Victor (eds.), *Critical Approaches to Ageing and Later Life* (Buckingham: Open University Press, 1997), pp. 77–89), as have North American

disclaimer: I am not old. I am not long into mid-life, and, while I wish for many more years, at the same time I do not wish to grow old if that involves any major constriction of opportunity. This book arises from that contradiction. Why is it that this babyboomer, born in the middle of the twentieth century – a potential pensioner – wishes to remain forever young or, at least, non-aged, and what may be the implications, assuming I am typical of my generation?

Karl Mannheim reminds us that generations are 'self-consciously formed by relatively unifying historical experiences'.[2] It follows that, whilst I am ill equipped to form judgements about later life since I have yet to arrive there, my own socially and historically located fears and expectations of it will necessarily colour any world view that I may have. Because of this I shall say comparatively little concerning 'experience', be this in the sense of skills and knowledge accumulated over time, or the lived reality of being old.[3] However, I will attempt to trace the lineages of the current situation, to account for how the cultural climate surrounding ageing from mid- to later life came into being. To that extent, this history is, first, a genealogy of knowledge in the Foucauldian sense: rather than attempting to furnish an empirical history of old age, it interrogates a number of discourses about ageing and tries to establish the links between them. Secondly, as a sociology, it elaborates some of the connections between power, discipline, surveillance, and control, essentially the impact of such discourses upon older people and society more generally.[4]

But there is also a more personal accommodation. It has been conjectured that people become experts in the study of ageing because this allows them to distance themselves from their own fears of decline and mortality. Arguably, indeed, such 'gerontophobia' explains some of the present predicament of the so-called ageing enterprise, the industry that has developed on the back of our ageing population.[5] Although this position has many detractors, perhaps we are all guilty of some measure

gerontologists Wilma Donahue, Bernice Neugarten, and Matilda White Riley. However, as one discussant points out, here the list ends (W. A. Achenbaum, 'Critical gerontology', in Jamieson, Harper, and Victor, *Critical Approaches*, pp. 16–26 (p. 24)).

[2] M. Featherstone and A. Wernick, 'Introduction', in M. Featherstone and A. Wernick (eds.), *Images of Aging: Cultural Representations of Later Life* (London: Routledge, 1995), pp. 1–15 (p. 13).

[3] On the definition and relevance of experience as pertaining to old age, see B. Bytheway, 'Progress report: the experience of later life', *Ageing and Society* 16 (1996), 613–24.

[4] M. Foucault, *Power/Knowledge: Selected Interviews and Other Writings, 1972–1977*, ed. C. Gordon (Brighton: Harvester, 1980).

[5] C. L. Estes, *The Aging Enterprise* (San Francisco: Jossey-Bass, 1979); B. S. Green, *Gerontology and the Construction of Old Age: A Study in Discourse Analysis* (New York: Aldine de Gruyter, 1993).

of repression or displacement. Equally cynically, others have pointed out that, whereas in 1967 a politician could be cited remarking of old age that 'the subject has no glamour', by the 1980s, 'the astute careerist might be well advised to specialise in "the elderly" as soon as possible'.[6] The motives of the researcher, or cultural interpreter, thus require scrutiny. By way of an apologia, I simply offer the following account.

In the mid-1980s I was endeavouring to complete a thesis about unmarried motherhood in nineteenth-century Scotland, whilst living from a series of by-employments as a part-time tutor and lecturer. Like many in such a limbo, I was prepared to turn my hand to any kind of work for which I considered myself qualified, and, when a job arose as a Research Officer in the Social History of Old Age, I did not have to think for long before applying for the post. I was successful, and for the next two years embarked on a process of familiarisation that was to lead, again opportunistically, to employment as Lecturer in Gerontology, with a brief this time not to research but to run a programme of courses for mature students in adult and continuing education. I thus fell into ageing by accident, rather than by design. By the end of the decade I had become well entrenched in the professional domain of British social gerontology. However, a creeping unease dogged me. I felt something of a charlatan: many of those I taught were older than myself and, unlike them (mostly nurses and social workers), I had no practical working experience with older people. Moreover, though sympathetic, I did not feel the sense of mission shared by so many advocates for the cause of anti-ageism. I reasoned that my anxiety stemmed from having to see 'old age' as a social problem, and that, if I could only recognise another less judgemental vision, I would be better able to justify my role. 'Object-ivity' would never do, but recourse to the sociology of knowledge persuaded me that it was important to ask how 'ageing' has been constituted, both at the level of disciplinary and political discourse, and in everyday life.

From where I stood as a thirtysomething, the theorisation of the life course suggested a means of exploring this issue in ways that incorpo-rated the subjectivity of my personal engagement with ageing, in dialogue with students and researchers whose cultural, cohort, and professional situations positioned them differently. Consequently, I enjoyed the luxury of creating a masters' programme in Life Course Development as a fertile testing ground for host of projects, ranging from developmental psychology through financial management to social policy, that had as a lowest common denominator a concern with

---

[6] R. Means and R. Smith, *The Development of Welfare Services for Elderly People* (London: Croom Helm, 1985), pp. 362–3.

persons in mid- and later life, and, as a conjoint aim, the better under-standing of the processes constructing the context in which these people found themselves. With hindsight, I think we were naive to expect that some kind of holistic vision could emerge from such a disparate range of encounters. Indeed, in my writing since then, I have found myself colluding willingly with positions that openly disavow the search for any monolithic meaning in ageing. During the past seven years I have vacated social gerontology for a more general role as a sociologist, and learned more to appreciate the impact of consumer culture, particularly its visual referents, on our interpretation of the ageing body and under-standing of the life course. In the research presented here I have reflected on my changing interests since 1985. If there is an overarching theme it is the necessity to question the legitimacy of grand theory. What sociologists or gerontologists might choose to replace this with is an enormous question that I can address only briefly and rather elliptically. Nevertheless, I hope the flavour of that search becomes evident in course of the book.

The journey down these few years has been forked with many productive excursions, and a number of acknowledgements are in order. Social gerontologists are gregarious beings and I have benefited in countless ways from working in a number of committees, in particular the British Society of Gerontology, the Association for Educational Gerontology, the Centre for Health and Retirement Education, and the Centre for the Study of Adult Life. My colleagues, both at Birkbeck College, London, and in the University of Aberdeen, have provided the sustaining collegiality that is so important from one day to the next. And the students I have taught – encountered is perhaps a more apt term, for I have often learned from them – have been a constant stimulus, both in my home institutions and elsewhere. Age Concern England, the King's Fund Institute, and the Royal College of Art (DesignAge) have gener-ously invited me to speak, and the BBC and Open University to broad-cast. Through the kindnesses of colleagues who invited me to Denmark, Finland, Iceland, Norway, Sweden, Switzerland, China, and the USA, I also have been able to test out ideas on a number of international audiences. I hope in this largely British and sometimes esoteric work they will find something that chimes in with their own intellectual preoccupations and with cultural issues of ageing in their different communities. Against this, I have to say that great zones of territory remain untouched. For example, this book makes no reference to ageing in the developing world – a massive oversight in any work that purports to discuss 'culture', but one that others will surely rectify.

I should like to thank both the ESRC and the Nuffield Foundation for funding which enabled the research in chapters 2, 6, and 7 to be undertaken, and several publishers for permission to reproduce parts of the following articles in adapted form: Whiting and Birch Ltd for 'Age consciousness and modernity: the social reconstruction of retirement', *Self, Agency and Society* 1, 1 (1997), 9–26 (in chapter 3); 'Images of age: a reflexive process', *Applied Ergonomics* 24, 1 (1993), 51–7, copyright with kind permission from Elsevier Science Ltd (in chapter 4); 'Photographic memory, ageing and the life course', *Ageing and Society* 14, 4 (1994), 479–97 (chapter 5), and 'Beside the sea: visual imagery, ageing and heritage', *Ageing and Society* 17, 6 (1997), 629–48 (chapter 7), with thanks to Cambridge University Press; 'Photographic images of age and generation', *Education and Ageing* 10, 1 (1995), 5–15, and 'Representations of old age in painting and photography' (with Mike Hepworth), in A. Jamieson, S. Harper, and C. Victor (eds.), *Critical Approaches to Ageing and Later Life* (Buckingham: Open University Press, 1997), pp. 102–17 (in chapter 6).

Archival research was conducted in numerous locations. It would be invidious to single out particular individuals for their good guidance – all were more than helpful and gave generously of their time and enthusiasm. To those anonymous referees who read the initial proposal for this book and one who subsequently read the full manuscript and proffered sage advice I am most grateful. Finally, I should like to add particular thanks to two colleagues, co-authors, and friends without whom several of the ideas discussed here could never have developed or flourished: John Macnicol and Mike Hepworth. Their abiding faith has borne me more than they know.

# 1 Introduction: foreign land

> The trouble is that old age is not interesting until one gets there, a foreign country with an unknown language.[1]

Jeanne Calment died as I was completing this book in the summer of 1997: she was 122. The oldest known person was interesting precisely because of her prodigious chronological achievement, and, in 1996, presumably for reasons of both novelty and posterity, a pop CD featuring her voice was released. A pensioner already when Hitler invaded France, and a grandmother since the 1920s, as a teenager she had met Van Gogh. Her accumulated biography may fascinate, but her longevity alone lent her a unique power: she could speak with the authority of one who was there about a time before anyone else living was born. All other sources of history are fixed – texts, images, voices even can be manipulated in the here-and-now, but the original datum remains a dead utterance. However, with Mme Calment we had a lifeline, literally her lifeline, tenuously connecting past and present. Where knowledge is power, her experience rendered her God-like. She was a time-traveller.

Although she was proud of her feat, less lofty considerations excited the oldest woman in the world: 'A week before her 121st birthday, Jeanne Calment is agitated. "I hope you've remembered to get my shampoo", she tells nursing staff in a commanding tone. "And my jewellery. I'll be needing it for the photographs. What colour dress shall I wear? I always take so much pleasure from photographs."'[2] Doubtless part of that pleasure lay in the immortality achieved via the transfer to celluloid, the moment captured forever. This offers a great irony, for photography, nowadays an ultimately democratic medium, allows us all a certain fame or, at least, a mark of recognition that will transcend our lives. History and imagery, then, are closely interwoven not only in the

---

[1] J. Ford and R. Sinclair, *Sixty Years On: Women Talk About Old Age* (London: Women's Press, 1987), p. 51.
[2] A. Sage, 'Six score and one', *Observer Review*, 18 February 1996, 8.

portraits of the great and good, but also in the genealogies that we call family albums. In between lie all the anecdotes, narratives, texts, and icons of our age, the memoirs of statesmen, policy documents, caricatured silhouettes on road signs warning drivers of 'elderly people' in the vicinity, or perceptions of whole civilisations as ageing populations. In England and Wales there are almost ten 100th birthday parties every day and the number of British centenarians is growing by 8 per cent per year. By 2000, that statistic might include the Queen Mother, whilst in the next century more than a third of the affluent world – though not just its affluent elders – will be over sixty. Yet the fact remains that we are not especially interested in later life – except as a coda to social history – until we get there; and when we do we find ourselves disorientated by the crossing to a new land. If the past is a foreign country, so too is the future.

The last British press photograph of Mme Calment before her death is striking because in it she nonchalantly holds a cigarette from which a wisp of blue smoke emanates.[3] In a shocking reversal of the *memento mori* image associating smoking with lung cancer, she cocks a snook at death. She has been lucky, we say. She has cheated the cathartic blows life brings. Is her survival unfair, immoral even? Or would we all like to get away with it, enjoy life without being reminded of our responsibilities to temper pleasure with dutiful moderation? By contrast, the oldest man in Britain is a Scots farmer who, at 108, 'puts his longevity down to three factors: a bowl of porridge every day, never going to bed on a full stomach, and hard work'.[4] It seems that we cannot observe such icons without reading into them a host of cultural messages about how life should and should not be led. Images act as catalysts for sociological inquiry.

In an effort to explain the dialogue between perceptions and social change, this study takes popular culture as its central theme. Defining this project is not easy, for, as Raymond Williams indicates: 'Culture is one of the two or three most complicated words in the English language ... mainly because it has now come to be used for important concepts in several distinct intellectual disciplines.'[5] Sociology and history are key among these, and I do not intend a long disquisition on the interpretation of the term in either. I simply understand culture to mean the human creation and use of symbols. Whereas popular culture

[3] J. Turney, 'The age of the oldie', *The Times Higher Education Supplement*, 23 May 1997, 18–19 (p. 19).
[4] 'After 108 years, three days still make all the difference', *Herald*, 22 August 1997, 2. The writer William Burroughs, notorious for his low-life drug addiction and sexual waywardness, died in the same week as Mme Calment at the age of eighty-three.
[5] Raymond Williams, *Keywords* (London: Flamingo, 1983), p. 87.

conventionally emphasises phenomena that evolve within the general population, as opposed to the media, my interpretation focuses on the dialogue and dialectic between everyday perceptions, policy, media, and academic attitudes, and the lived realities of ageing.[6] The symbols and signs that we understand as images form the backdrop to a contest for meaning. These are not the preserve of older people alone, nor are they just a fabricated set of stereotypes or ideological poses claiming control over definitions. Rather, the popular understanding of ageing is a negotiated process, albeit one that is rarely at the front of our minds because it happens to us all. I shall return to the theme of popular culture later in this chapter. First, however, something requires to be said concerning the sociological stance underpinning the argument.

## Sociology: structure, agency, and ageing

It is useful to distinguish between theories proposing that behaviour and attitudes are determined by changes in political, economic, and social structures, and phenomenological approaches examining the emergence of consciousness in everyday life. Thus, I begin by examining two related, but often opposed approaches: social constructionism and symbolic interactionism. Social constructionists reject the view that ageing is simply 'natural', a pre-given essence, arguing that each individual's experience is to a high degree moulded by socio-cultural factors. 'Old age' has had varying connotations according to historical periods, and differs between cultures. Similarly, factors such as material conditions during childhood or lifetime health behaviours – themselves class-related – are likely to have differential impacts upon longevity. Symbolic interactionists meanwhile contend that 'social life depends on our ability to imagine ourselves in other social roles'.[7] Blumer proposed that 'human beings act towards things on the basis of the meanings that the things have for them' and that these meanings arise out human interaction.[8] Thus, rather than inhering in objects (or subjects) themselves, the meanings we attach to them emerge from social processes. These processes and the motives that inform them are distinguished by our use

---

[6] While 'popular culture' is sometimes taken to refer to the monolithic, trivial experiences of the subordinate 'masses', I see it as a negotiated definition between sets of meanings that vary according to one's vantage point: for example, although 'from above' policy perceptions clearly differ from 'from below' pensioner perspectives, there exists sufficient common ground for 'old age' to be jointly recognised if differently interpreted.

[7] N. Abercrombie, S. Hill, and B. S. Turner, *The Penguin Dictionary of Sociology*, 3rd edn (Harmondsworth: Penguin, 1994), p. 421.

[8] H. Blumer, *Symbolic Interactionism: Perspective or Method* (Englewood Cliffs, NJ: Prentice Hall, 1969), p. 2.

of communication through symbols. It follows that the ways we describe the world form our understanding of it; hence the prime significance of labelling, stereotypes, and images to the interpretation of ageing.

Among constructionist theories, the political economy perspective has been especially influential. Political economy is a conflict theory contending that social inequalities are grounded in the economic organisation of society, specifically capitalism.[9] This approach sees retirement levels fluctuating over time as a result of politically driven labour force requirements, and posits the structured dependency of older people collectively on the rest of society as a consequence of limited and unequal access to resources, particularly income.[10] As chapter 2 will indicate, the argument has proven particularly useful in establishing the parameters fencing in the experience of later life in twentieth-century Britain.

Fennell *et al.* are justifiably critical of the tendency to 'describe the activities and lifestyles of older people, rather than consider linkages between ageing and the social, political and economic structure', for great swathes of writing still report empirical studies in which theory is absent or unacknowledged.[11] However, through its stress on social structure, political economy runs the risk of reifying 'society', or 'retirement', as something 'out there' to which the individual must accommodate or resist. It limits the scope for individuals, or groups, to construct their own meanings and destinies. 'Structures' in themselves are not replete with social meaning, since older people (indeed, all of us) have identities and views which are immersed in tangible, personally experienced relationships. It follows that meanings and motives can be understood fully only at the micro-level, and, while the more persuasive studies drawing on the political economy perspective have incorporated this requirement, another more overtly sociological tradition has also emerged. Here context has been the watchword.

Attempts to contextualise ageing focus on the centrality of human awareness. Thus, although such external factors as the state of the economy may impinge upon everyday life, it is the ways in which these influences are interpreted that are of prime significance. Any notion of

---

[9] C. Phillipson, *Capitalism and the Construction of Old Age*, ed. P. Leonard (London: Macmillan, 1982; Critical Texts in Social Work and the Welfare State), is the best-known British exposition.

[10] G. Fennell, C. Phillipson, and H. Evers (eds.), *The Sociology of Old Age* (Milton Keynes: Open University Press, 1988), pp. 52–5. For a review of literature on the political economy of old age, see M. Minkler and C. Estes (eds.), *Critical Perspectives on Aging: The Political and Moral Economy of Growing Old* (Amityville, NY: Baywood Press, 1991).

[11] Fennell, Phillipson, and Evers, *Sociology of Old Age*, p. 41.

'society' beyond that actively constructed *in situ* is an abstraction. Thus, although from a political economist's perspective the analysis of old age should concentrate on the construction and distribution of roles (political and economic as well as social), there is a complementary need for exploration centred on how social relationships are constituted through *social* encounters. Such thinking pervades ethnographic studies of old age subcultures, some of which are discussed in chapter 8.

In aiming to describe the life-world – the taken-for-granted everyday reality of ordinary older people – phenomenologists identify typifications, that is, languages and routines based on shared assumptions through which the social fabric is maintained. Such theorists stress agency, the ability of individuals to act independently – albeit intersubjectively – of any overarching social structure. Thus, their main demerit lies in neglecting the one concept seen as crucial by the political economists.[12] Neither macro-level social constructionism nor interactionist and ethnographic micro-studies are entirely satisfactory: the former risks portraying action as overdetermined by external forces, while the latter ignore these selfsame constraints. How, then, can we resolve the dualism of structure and agency, whereby, to paraphrase Karl Marx, ageing people make their own histories, but not under circumstances of their own making? The answer would appear to lie in theorising a dialectic between the life-world and the social structure.[13]

For Berger and Luckmann, the social construction of reality relies upon a three-stage process: first, people create culture; secondly, their cultural creations become realities, which through time are taken for granted as natural and inevitable; thirdly, this reality is unquestioningly absorbed as valid by ensuing generations.[14] Thus ageing is made to appear self-evident, an inevitable aspect of the human condition, when, in fact, it is also a profoundly sociological – and historical – construct. Such unexamined taken-for-grantedness helps to explain why ageism is by no means always obvious to all affected by it. Two significant inferences might be drawn from this formulation: first, each individual is

---

[12] Ethnomethodology presents an extreme position whereby actions and utterances have meaning only within the context of their occurrence. The difficulties of this closed approach are demonstrated by linguistic studies of ageing where older people use language in different ways depending on the presence or absence of non-aged persons.

[13] A. Giddens, *Central Problems in Social Theory* (London: Macmillan, 1979), has devised the concept of structuration to emphasise the interdependence rather than opposition of structure and agency. He argues that social structures do not so much repress individual endeavour as provide resources on which action is based; actions, in turn, create structures. Whilst this may be an elegant formulation, it fails to explain the determining force behind the dialectic of historical transformation.

[14] P. Berger and T. Luckmann, *The Social Construction of Reality: A Treatise in the Sociology of Knowledge* (Harmondsworth: Penguin, 1991).

born and socialised into a ready-made cultural environment; secondly, the time of our birth will to a degree condition the ways we perceive things. World views are thus partially inherited and generationally distinct at the same time. Several strands in the present work derive from this observation, among them the emphasis on the differing attitudes and experiences of successive cohorts of elders (as manifest, for example, in the 'time-signatures' discussed in chapter 8), and, at the same time, the need to interpret continuities as well as disjunctions within individual life courses. This last point is crucial if we are to understand both how people make sense of their own ageing and how they act on the basis of these interpretations.

## Life courses, world views, fresh maps

Whilst perceptions and evaluations of age are socially created, the ageing process itself is ultimately a biological one. Medical and cultural knowledges may be applied to extend or enhance the experience, but death will come to us all (although this does not negate the cultural significance of the manifold constructions through which, individually and collectively, we may attempt to deny or indeed celebrate the inevitability of mortality). Like every organism, the body goes into a state of irreversible decline following maturity. What is contentious is not this physiological fact, but how the social frame impinges upon it. 'Maturity' itself is a term capable of many and varied definitions and the biological is but one of these. Thus whilst stages of physical advancement can easily be gauged from visible signs of growth and puberty, childhood and adolescence are flexible social categories varying through time and across cultures. The seven-year-olds who were regarded, according to Ariès, as miniature adults in early modern Europe would be classified as children today.[15] 'Adolescence' was a term coined as late as 1904, and what we now clearly recognise as 'youth culture' would have been difficult to discern before the Industrial Revolution. Equally, the subdivisions of later life are malleable because they are and have been similarly dependent upon social and cultural developments. For example, menopause is a biological process particular to females, but the 'mid-life crisis' is a historically recent, specifically Western concept appertaining to both men and women. Because such classifications have a significant impact, psychologically, economically, and socially, upon the ageing individual, life course perspectives begin from the standpoint of the individual passing through them.

[15]  P. Ariès, *Centuries of Childhood* (Harmondsworth: Penguin, 1962).

Inputs from developmental psychology derive largely from the Jungian claim that many individuals find themselves at a turning point in mid-life, and that 'we cannot live the afternoon of life according to the program of life's morning ... Whoever carries into the afternoon the law of the morning ... must pay with damage to his soul.'[16] While the difficulty of managing this transition has been popularly linked with the notion of 'mid-life crisis',[17] Erikson states that each stage of life includes a series of appropriate tasks to be fulfilled before moving on to the next phase. Thus, he argues, adult life sees a conflict between 'generativity' (producing and piloting the next generation and/or leaving an imprint of worth to society) and stagnation, which must be resolved prior to seeking the late life goal of 'ego-integrity', that is 'an assured sense of meaning and order in one's life and in the universe, as against despair and disgust', which can only be achieved by accepting personal limitations, not least that one is mortal.[18] While lifespan developmental psychologists have recognised the significance of early life experiences for how individuals deal with the changes of later life, so too gerontologists have latterly acknowledged the principle of contingency – 'to understand people in late life it is necessary to see them in the context of their whole life history'.[19] The legitimacy of studying older people without also interrogating their earlier lives has become somewhat strained. Although 'elderliness' is generally denoted by physical appearance, cognitive and social changes often move along separate trajectories: a person may look old but retain strong mental alertness and possess 'youthful' social attitudes. Alongside shared factors like structured dependency, which tend to collectivise the experience of later life, we must set the contention that as each individual ages so the stock of their differentness from the next person increases – the older the cohort, the greater is the degree of diversity and individuality to be expected. Hypothetically, people who have lived longer will have had more time in which reflect and act upon a broader range of experiences than younger

[16] C. G. Jung, 'The transcendent function', in H. Read, M. Fordham, G. Adler, and W. McGuire (eds.), *The Structure and Dynamics of the Psyche*, 2nd edn, vol. VIII of *The Collected Works of C. J. Jung*, 20 vols. (London: Routledge and Kegan Paul, 1972), p. 396.

[17] See E. Jacques, 'Death and the mid-life crisis', *International Journal of Psychoanalysis* 46 (1965), 502–14.

[18] E. H. Erikson, *Identity and the Life Cycle: A Reissue* (New York: W. W. Norton, 1980), p.103.

[19] J. Bond, R. Briggs and P. Coleman, 'The study of ageing', in J. Bond and P. Coleman (eds.), *Ageing in Society: An Introduction to Social Gerontology* (London: Sage, 1990), pp. 17–47 (p. 27); L. Sugarman, *Life-Span Development: Concepts, Theories and Interventions* (London: Methuen, 1986), provides comprehensive coverage of the field.

people. At the same time variations according to class, race, gender, and culture are also likely to have become more entrenched.

The disruptive impact upon family patterns of economic recession, unemployment, and employment changes during the 1980s has led to fresh interest in gender and generational aspects of domestic and work relationships. As a guide to interpretation, developmental psychology is of limited value since concentration on individual experience necessarily restricts its utility as a sociological tool. However, a second approach, life course analysis, offers considerable attractions. Life course analysis has roots in the research of historical demographers in the United States, particularly Tamara Hareven, whose work focuses on the synchronisation, or otherwise, of 'family time' and 'historical time'.[20] Historical time is linear (rather than cyclical) and chronological, both in terms of individual lives ('when I was five', 'when I was forty-five') and in relation to the broad sweep of historical events (the Depression, the Second World War, the Sixties, the Nineties). Meanwhile, it has long been recognised that the family follows a cycle or sequence of stages through which individuals pass as they age. Thus as one's family career develops one's roles and responsibilities, as child, young adult, parent, and grandparent will differ. Moreover, the economic wellbeing of the family unit, as well as its social stability, will be affected as its composition alters over time. Changes in technology (Taylorism, Fordism, mechanisation, computerisation), the business cycle and policy – including retirement pensions – and the organisation of the labour force mean that one's work career, and family network, will be affected, in turn, by 'industrial time'. The sequences of industrial change will impact upon kinship obligations, forcing adaptations, for example, in who cares for children and older relatives. A contemporary instance would be the rise of female participation in the micro-components industry following their husbands' being made redundant from heavy manufacturing jobs. Does this entail a rise in male domestic work? Or are alternative arrangements made to look after young children or elderly kin outside the home? Or does a double burden fall upon women who must be both earners and domestic carers?

It would seem logical to add a further temporality, that of 'cultural time'. Cultural time would refer to prevalent values and attitudes, reflected in changes in age-appropriate behaviours – the styles, lifestyles, and hairstyles conventionally felt to match different age groups.

---

[20] T. K. Hareven, 'Family time and historical time', *Daedalus* 106, 2 (1977), 57–70; T. K. Hareven (ed.), *Transitions: The Family and the Life Course in Historical Perspective* (New York: Academic Press, 1978).

'Acceptable' age-norms of dress, sexuality, pastimes, and bodily appearance clearly vary according to one's location in historical time.

These four axes of family, historical, industrial, and cultural time form trajectories that interact to contextualise the ageing process, yet I know of no single study that exploits such complementarity, nor of any attempt to merge life course analysis with lifespan developmental psychology. The virtues of applying such a model would be manifold: it addresses the interaction of micro- and macro-level factors; it provides a relational perspective that moves beyond unitary, age-based definitions of the subject; and it theorises relationships between life-stages, thus facilitating biographical research. However, the scale of such a task is awesome, and the present analysis, while hinting at the resonances for each stage and temporality, concentrates mainly upon cultural time.

Explaining shifts in cultural norms is not simply a matter of accounting for changing fashions. An important thread in my discussion concerns the challenge to 'traditional' cultural values which have imbued attitudes to ageing. The dominance of the work ethic, an orientation towards youthfulness, and belief in notions of 'progress' (however defined) can only be detrimental to those who have retired, are no longer young, and are thereby 'outdated'. Arguably, however, such views are being eroded as consumerist values come to outweigh production-based ideals, leisure becomes a stronger currency, and the modernist, ever novel promise of capitalism gives way to a preference for niche markets and recycling of 'heritage'. Chapter 3 considers the implications for a metamorphosis of social consciousness as postmodernity succeeds modernity, whilst chapters 7 and 9 in particular consider the ways in which memories, collective and personal, evoke both continuities and discontinuities in social patterns.

Whatever the cultural changes wrought by production and consumption patterns, the twentieth century has seen a monumental demographic transformation. By 2000 half the British population will be over fifty. Not until the 1920s did the proportion attaining age sixty exceed 10 per cent, but since then it has doubled.[21] This secular shift has occurred throughout the developed world as a result partly of a distant cause, namely the massive reduction in infant mortality and improvements in child health. Expectation of life after fifty was rather slower to increase than the expectation at birth, but this too has shown a steady increase, particularly for women, who can now expect to live an average thirty years beyond fifty, as against twenty at the turn of the century. Old age has become progressively feminised because the further one moves

---

[21] Laslett, *A Fresh Map*, pp. 49–50.

up the age scale, the greater the fraction of the population who are female. However, a parallel transformation has occurred with the emergence of retirement – until recently an overwhelmingly male experience – for, whereas nearly three-quarters of men aged sixty-five and over were still in paid work in the 1880s, by the 1980s less than 3 per cent remained in full-time employment.[22]

The implications of these trends are sufficiently significant to require a major rethinking of the life course, or what Laslett refers to as *A Fresh Map of Life*. This is explored in chapter 3, but it is germane here to outline its crucial element – the rise of the Third Age. The emergence of retirement has coincided with the increase in numbers of people living beyond what has come to be considered 'retirement age'. Thus, there are now more people than ever before spending a long phase of their lives in a non-work environment:

Male expectation of life in Britain implies that a man who is to leave work at fifty-five can look forward to spending as much time in retirement as he will spend in employment as early as his mid-thirties, twenty years more at his job and twenty years after he has left it. The corresponding figures for women are even more striking because they live longer and are expected to retire earlier.[23]

For Laslett, the First Age broadly coincides with childhood, and the Second with adulthood and earning. The next, or Third, Age is generally bounded by the period between workending and the Fourth Age of 'dependence, decrepitude, and death'. Thus, a division between Third and Fourth Ages effectively bisects the conventional category 'old age'. Whereas decline as one aged may once have been gradual, the shape of the biological survival curve now reflects an abbreviation of the Fourth Age, so that following a long period of relatively good health, final illness is more and more likely to be steeply compressed into the very last years of life, beyond age eighty-five.[24] While both retirement age and the onset of 'final decline' or 'terminal drop' vary according to individuals, aggregate patterns reveal remarkable social changes. Nevertheless, Laslett insists that the expansion of the Third Age must be measured qualitatively since it 'can only be experienced in the company of a nationwide society of those with the disposition, freedom, and the

[22] A. Blaikie and J. Macnicol, 'Ageing and social policy: a twentieth-century dilemma', in A. M. Warnes (ed.), *Human Ageing and Later Life* (London: Edward Arnold, 1989), pp. 69–82 (p. 69).

[23] Laslett, *A Fresh Map*, p. 90. Provisions towards the equalisation of state pensionable ages for men and women in the UK are currently being enacted.

[24] Ibid., pp. 4, 56–7. The phrase 'compression of morbidity' and the rectangular survival curve – so called because a long plateau of cumulative population survival suddenly dips, thus approximating a right angle – are explained in J. F. Fries and L. M. Crapo, *Vitality and Aging: Implications of the Rectangular Curve* (San Francisco: W. H. Freeman, 1981).

means to act in the appropriate manner'. This brings us back to the
question of world views, since particular attributes, including the existence of widespread cultural norms, expectations, and wherewithal are
necessary qualifications for Third Age membership. Acting in 'the
appropriate manner' is central to Laslett's notion of the Third Age as
the 'era of personal fulfilment' at a personal level and, collectively, a
stage of cultural development where older people act as 'trustees for the
future' of society.[25] He argues that, although Britain has been numerically a Third Age society since 1950 – the point when over half the
people reaching twenty-five could statistically expect to reach age
seventy – the nation lags far behind in achieving his desired cultural aim.
Appreciative of this mismatch, the present analysis indicates where and
why the gap is closing and where and why it is not.

Intriguingly, the 1940s and 1950s were also the formative period of
social gerontology. To what extent, therefore, has the discipline succeeded in shadowing the emergence of a Third Age?

### Gerontology as discourse

Gerontology, particularly in North America, is characterised by a
rhetoric of holism, whereby the different theories and methods of
biomedicine, psychology, and the social sciences are somehow supposed
to converge around the central concern of old age. Despite crossover
plenaries at major international conferences, the research evidence of
such fusion is slight; rather, gerontology could be said to suffer from
'physics envy'.[26] Compared to most sciences, and, indeed, social
sciences, it is an immature area. Many researchers have thus sought
legitimacy through emulation of the established 'hard' sciences. This
has led to the 'scientisation' of theory and methods in general, while
social gerontology has been a poor relation to medical and psychological
aspects of investigation.

In his perorations on handbooks about ageing, of which there are now
several in the USA, Achenbaum is critical of 'multidisciplinary incanta-
tions'. Statements of the requirement for understanding human ageing
from a number of disciplinary viewpoints simultaneously are also legion
in the UK; however, research rarely delivers on such a promise, whilst
consensus over aims has not promoted theoretical clarity: 'If historical,
political, and economic features are as important as biological, psychological, and social factors in examining the contexts of the ageing
process, why are they so underrepresented?' This is not helped by 'the

---

[25] Laslett, *A Fresh Map*, pp. 77, 196.
[26] Achenbaum, 'Critical gerontology', p. 16.

mix of science and advocacy that colours much research on ageing' whereby gerontology pretends to be both value-free and value-based in the same breath.[27]

Until the 1960s the social study of ageing was dominated by a 'social problems' perspective concerned with policy and welfare needs. However, it has been suggested that the influence of cultural movements thereafter and political organisation amongst older people (the Gray Panthers in particular) have influenced a shift towards approaches which question assumptions made by the non-aged. The very coining of the term 'ageism' testifies to this.[28] Since the 1970s interest has grown in the social construction of ageing, in lived experience, and in normal as against pathological ageing. There is now a clear division between gerontology as a branch of biology which 'treats aging as a genetically programmed process' and social gerontology. Nevertheless, sociologists agree that 'despite these changes, gerontologists are still concerned with social rather than sociological questions'.[29] Pensions, older people, and retirement represent objective social problems rather than subjects for investigation in their own right and on their own terms.

Moreover, the historical ascendancy of gerontology presents analytical problems of its own. Any sociological study of 'old age' or 'the elderly' must acknowledge that these are social constructs formulated within a disciplinary context. 'Old age' and 'the life course' are labels which are deployed to classify people. And, as Katz points out, discourses on ageing are also disciplinary in the sense that they aid the process of regulation and control of older people.[30] There are parallels here with Foucault's analysis of madness, which argues that the criteria used to label individuals changed over time according to shifting ways of thinking and writing about insanity. More than ideologies, these discourses had real effects, not only because alternative rationales were precluded, but also because thinking was translated into action – real 'mad' people were incarcerated.[31] Gerontological research, like all discourse, demands the conceptual integration of 'islands of knowledge',[32] yet, claims Achenbaum: 'We are in a phase of being data rich and theory poor … An investigator's first research on ageing usually

[27] W. A. Achenbaum, 'One United States approach to gerontological theory building', *Ageing and Society* 9 (1989), 179–88 (182, 184).

[28] R. Butler, *Why Survive?: Being Old in America* (New York: Harper and Row, 1975).

[29] Abercrombie, Hill and Turner, *Penguin Dictionary*, pp. 11, 182.

[30] S. Katz, *Disciplining Old Age: The Formation of Gerontological Knowledge* (Charlottesville, VA, and London: University Press of Virginia, 1996).

[31] M. Foucault, *Madness and Civilization* (London: Tavistock, 1971; orig. published 1961).

[32] J. E. Birren and V. L. Bengtson (eds.), *Emergent Theories of Aging* (New York: Springer, 1988), p. ix.

begins with a microtheory derived from a subpart of the discipline in which the investigator was trained ... [Gerontology is a] land of many islands with few bridges between them.'[33] Again, to borrow from Foucault, the present analysis is underpinned by a quest to derive an 'archaeology of knowledge' about ageing – to indicate the context-bound origins of the accretion of meanings piled layer upon layer over one another as older moral understandings have been superseded by the apparent rationality of scientific interpretation. If such a historical brief reveals discontinuities, so too the disciplinary domains it interrogates – gerontology and, rather cursorily, geriatrics – represent a connectivity between areas of theoretical endeavour that strain the 'archipelago' metaphor. As chapter 2 indicates, geriatrics as an 'expert' discourse had the effect of moving persons labelled 'senile' into 'homes', while, more generally, the policy agenda for 'old age' eventually stipulated the retirement pension for all above a certain age. Regarding discourses as all-encompassing can, however, lead to an effacement of lived reality:

The emphasis on discourse assumes cultural effects that may be more apparent than real.

Far from suffering the effects of surveillance and medicalisation, many elderly people in modern society have suffered from neglect and loneliness, not to mention physical hardship and poor health. And it might be argued that far from being over-regulated and subject to powerful forms of surveillance, older people have all too often been marginalised and left to fend for themselves ... A more balanced view would need to bring into account the changing *experience* of growing old.[34]

## Discourse as gerontology

Paradoxically, one way out of the dilemma posed by a positivist faith in quasi-scientific 'facts' (medicalised models) versus an adherence to the veracity of contextual accounts (which may be meaningful but are infinite in their variety) may be via discourse analysis. Discourses are social constructs in that they constitute mechanisms and boundaries through which identities may be interpreted. It follows that all items

[33] J. E. Birren, 'My perspective on research on aging', in V. L. Bengtson and K. W. Shaie (eds.), *The Course of Life: Research and Reflections* (New York: Springer, 1989), cited in W. A. Achenbaum, 'Images of old age in America, 1790–1970: a vision and a re-vision', in Featherstone and Wernick, *Images of Aging*, pp. 19–28 (p. 20).

[34] M. Bury, Review of Katz, *Disciplining Old Age, Ageing and Society* 17 (1997), 353–5 (pp. 354–5). Foucault has been criticised for 'giv[ing] us history as a subject-less structure, and one in which men and women are obliterated by ideologies' (E. P. Thompson, *The Poverty of Theory and Other Essays* (London: Merlin Press, 1978), p. 387, n. 34).

contained within a discourse, be these people, bodies, utterances, memories, images, or policy documents, may be read as 'texts' or 'narratives'. The research task then becomes one of searching for internal consistencies or coherence within and between texts, rather than measuring these against some objective external truth. Far from making claims about authenticity, interpretation is concerned with situating individual cultural phenomena within a larger world view in order to establish their 'documentary meaning'.[35] Put this way, discourse analysis has great appeal when applied to visual sources. As with content analysis, which attempts to quantify data rather than evaluate, there is the problem of classifying material according to a set of categories or textual elements which are pre-determined or created by the researcher. However, when, as in chapter 5, one discourse (that of social gerontology) is ranged against another (photographic representation of older people), contradictions emerge that alert us to the dangers involved in privileging any singular interpretation.

## The postmodern turn

Other juxtapositions reflect the development from undifferentiated mass society (modernity) to an increasingly subtle commodity culture in which individuals choose their identities (postmodernity). As the culture industries, especially the popular media, have become more sophisticated, so individual lives have become personal 'projects' revolving around 'lifestyles' which can be bought in the market place. At the same time the notion of an integral, coherent self has been fragmented so that identity can change at different stages in the life course. There is thus a tension between the biographical idea of a continuous developing self and the postmodern notion of the multiple, situational self. These changes signify movement from a status system organised around production to one based on consumption. And, in so far as older people are regarded as consumers of leisure, rather than persons who have retired from production, the shift has been a liberating one.

Where does this leave the interpreter? Bauman points out that 'comment on our daily experience cannot be more systematic than the experience itself'.[36] One does not have to endorse postmodernism as an analytical view to accept that contemporary culture thrives on pastiche, self-conscious irony, and relativism. It might be argued that any attempt to analyse ageing in the final quarter of the twentieth century can result

---

[35] See K. Mannheim, *Essays on the Sociology of Culture* (London: Routledge and Kegan Paul, 1956).
[36] Z. Bauman, *Thinking Sociologically* (Oxford: Basil Blackwell, 1990), p. 19.

only in a crisis of representation, either because theories are too categorical and falsely stereotype 'the old', or, on the contrary, because our reflexivity reduces the 'otherness' of ageing, thus rendering gerontology superfluous.[37] But this does not mean that the representations one can discern are without fascination for the sociologist whose role it is to elucidate complexity, not to simplify life. Although social science has sometimes been delegated the task of undermining ideologies, I prefer to pursue a more humanistic quest for meaning.[38] Perceptions need to be deconstructed rather than demoted. In this sense, my arguments are driven more by Weberian sociology than by critical gerontology.

### A time for age?

Pilcher points out that 'like class, ethnicity, and gender, age is a social category through which people define and identify individuals and groups within society. Age is both an important part of how we see ourselves and how others see us', not least because it 'acts as an important basis for the distribution of social prestige ... [a]ccess to power, material resources, and citizenship'.[39] To the extent that it acts as an organising principle, ageing may be understood either by reference to perspectives that emphasise structural organisation of society at the macro-level (theories of cohort and generation, functionalist and political economy approaches), or interpretative, processual theories, concerned with individuals and the role of meanings, including lifespan developmental psychology and interactionist sociology.[40] Studying the recent history of old age requires a combination of macro- and micro-level approaches, although, since motivations are rarely recoverable save by oral accounts and popular literature (both of which present methodological minefields), scholars have tended to concentrate on textual, policy-related materials that inevitably produce rather schematic accounts of what the powerful did, or wished to do, to *the* elderly as an objectified social category.

In the popular media, a vision which pictures old people as a passive and pathological problem group characterised by dependency has been partially eclipsed by 'positive ageing' messages about the hedonistic joys of leisured retirement. Thus, a recent study of the adventurous freedoms of retirement on the road in recreational vehicles (RVs) begins by

---

[37] See Jamieson, Harper, and Victor, *Critical Approaches*, p. 185.
[38] J. Habermas, *Towards a Rational Society* (London: Heinemann, 1971)
[39] J. Pilcher, *Age and Generation in Modern Britain* (Oxford University Press, 1995), p. 1.
[40] Ibid., p. 29.

castigating academics for failing to grasp contemporary realities: 'If students gained their understanding of old age only by reading the contents of gerontological journals, they would assume it is a bleak and hopeless time of life.'[41] This is reflected in the social construction of emotions, where romance (and sexual pleasure) are devalued, whilst loneliness is lent a spurious appropriateness as the master-emotion of later life.[42] When the old were the 'deserving poor', there was little demand to overturn the structures of society. However, as the experiences of today's ThirdAgers begin to resemble those of adolescence, why have we not seen the emergence of a new band of folk devils (and the release of pent-up *Sturm und Drang* this implies) to complement the moral panic over the 'burden of dependency'?

## Ageism and cultural studies

The oft-heard, oxymoronic statement that 'the elderly are a heterogeneous group' exemplifies our paradoxical understanding of old age through the twentieth century. We have categorised and classified a social phenomenon and in the process labelled all old people, yet we have latterly recognised the necessity to deconstruct the monolithic disregard for human diversity resulting from such perception, policy, and practice. There exists a tension 'between the pull towards oversimplifying stereotypes of youth and age and the opposite pull towards the discovery of increasing complexity and differentiation'.[43] Inevitably, in its historical and historiographic concerns, this project acknowledges a more general stricture (for 'women' substitute 'older people') that sometimes, 'one cannot study the experiences of women as a group, but one can study a popular conception of women, since it treats all women alike'.[44] This vision of homogeneity often provokes offence, the point being the use of the definite article: discussing elderly people is fine, elderliness being a qualification referring to their condition (they are persons who happen to be elderly), but to talk of *the* elderly is to create a category of people definable by their elderliness alone (they can possess no existence independent of their elderliness, and are thus considered 'not fully human'). According to such a position, 'elderly' is acceptable

---

[41] D. A. Counts and D. R. Counts, *Over the Next Hill: An Ethnography of RVing Seniors in America* (Peterborough, Ont.: Broadview Press, 1996), p. 16.
[42] M. Hepworth, 'Ageing and the emotions', *Journal of Educational Gerontology* 8, 2 (1993), 75–85.
[43] Featherstone and Wernick, 'Introduction', p. 9.
[44] L. J. Rupp, *Mobilizing Women for War: German and American Propaganda, 1939–1945* (Princeton University Press, 1978), p. 5.

when used as an adjective, but not when used as a noun.[45] However, the noun 'elder' appears to create no such problem.

Ageism needs locating. The reasons behind discrimination are frequently economic, but the capacity to maintain oppression is primarily psychological. Ageism is both institutionalised in the social structure – legally, medically, through welfare, education, and income policies – and internalised in the attitudes of individuals. In a capitalist society people are valued on economic terms, and, whilst young dependants – children – are regarded as potential assets, older people are not. It has been argued, therefore, that the structured dependency of 'the elderly' as a group, which developed with the emergence of retirement, has generated accompanying forms of legitimation: ideological supports have been provided through biological reductionism (rights denied because of disability, frailty, or failing health), psychological explanations (dependency reflects child-like behaviour and status), and social justification (old people want to disengage from society).[46]

According to this perspective a constructed consensus disguises major variations in interest between different groups of pensioners, particularly between those who rely on the public sector and those who have private pensions. Class differences persist into and may be exacerbated by old age. We need also to recognise and assess the double jeopardy of ageism and sexism as this applies to women as well as the triple jeopardy faced by ethnic elders.[47] In the context of all the rhetoric about 'care in the community', the relative balance between family support and state assistance is also significant, as is the distinction made between the 'young old' and 'old old'. Expert classifications made by scientists and bureaucrats sometimes ramify, at other times contradict, popular perceptions. Although retirement communities in many cases (Sun Cities, for instance) reflect voluntary self-segregation, to extrapolate that old age *per se* is subculturally distinct would be to denigrate attempts made by the Gray Panthers and many others to stress age-integration and interdependency across all age groups. Nevertheless, political expressions from older people highlight the requirement to balance social constructionist perspectives, imbued with notions of surveillance and control, with human agency arguments emphasising self-determination.

While both sociologists and gerontologists have generally stressed

[45] Fennell, Phillipson, and Evers, *Sociology of Old Age*, p. 7, discuss 'the stigmatising use of adjectives as nouns'.
[46] P. Leonard, 'Editor's Introduction', in Phillipson, *Capitalism*, pp. xi–xiv.
[47] C. Itzin, 'The double jeopardy of ageism and sexism: media images of women', in D. B. Bromley (ed.), *Gerontology: Social and Behavioural Perspectives* (London: Croom Helm, 1984), pp. 170–84; A. Norman, *Triple Jeopardy: Growing Old in a Second Homeland* (London: Centre for Policy on Ageing, 1985).

constructionism, the cultural studies tradition has placed great emphasis on the efforts of minorities to make their own cultures. The former have said a good deal about old age, but the latter have been extraordinarily quiet. There is still a reticence among sociologists to include ageing with the now conventional grouping of class, race, ethnicity, and gender among the key organising principles of social life. Gerontologists, meanwhile, tend to discuss old age, or ageing after retirement, rather than adopting a life course perspective that acknowledges the implications of earlier experiences for later developments. As a consequence, the academic discussion of age *in itself* is seen as marginal to a range of issues (gender differentiation, unemployment, equal opportunities) considered more pressing, both culturally and as regards social policy.

Nevertheless, cultural studies perspectives could provide useful inroads. For example, the feminist insight that public and private forms of culture are not sealed against one another has informed the ways in which 'a girls' magazine like *Jackie* ... picks up and represents some elements of private cultures of femininity by which young girls live their lives'. Such material tends to be instantly evaluated as 'girls' stuff' and trivial. Yet its has been argued that what is occurring is a re-appropriation among the targeted readership of elements first borrowed from their own culture.[48] Whether readers are so pro-active or whether they are more passive consumers, such popular literature forms a bedrock of their socialisation to modern adolescence. An analysis of older women's periodicals might reveal a similar story. Pick up your weekly edition of *People's Friend* and the cover nearly always depicts a country scene. Look inside, and you can read regular features called 'The Farmer and His Wife' and 'From the Manse Window', and holiday features on the Yorkshire Dales or Royal Deeside. There is rarely a city street in sight, not even in the advertisements. The fact that incontinence aids and chair lifts predominate among the latter is sufficient to remind us that 'The Famous Story Paper for Women' is mostly marketed at old ladies. But why should rural romance be so readily associated with such a social group? From the vantage point of today's elderly reader stuck in her inner city tenement or tower block, one can see why such values might appear comforting in a world of muggings, theft, and the 'breakdown of the fabric of society', the apparent collapse of the mores of community. The magazine retails a vision of an alternative world, in which justice and right prevail and everyone lives happily ever after. Above all it rekindles nostalgically their roots in former places of safety. Like *Jackie*, *People's Friend* publicly provides raw materials – be these fashion

---

[48]  R. Johnson, *What Is Cultural Studies Anyway?*, CCCS Occasional Paper General Series, SP No. 74, University of Birmingham (1983), p. 23.

features, advice on relationships, escapist fantasies, or ideologies – on which readers reflect in order to construct their private lives. Indeed, the letters page and readers' photos are representations of this process in action.

The pastimes of older people provide much food for thought, but this requires to be matched by a ready eye for linking empirical observation with social theory. For example, relatively large numbers of working-class older women appear not only to enjoy watching all-in wrestling, but to invest considerable amounts of emotional energy in following each bout. The great semiotician Roland Barthes once argued that professional wrestling is a spectacle, rather than a sport, in which justice is played out in the ring: in the end, the good guy wins and the bad guy gets his come-uppance.[49] Could it be that the reason such theatre appeals to impoverished older women is that, when they have seen little justice in their own lives, to see the enactment of just deserts provides the catharsis that has otherwise eluded them? Psychiatrists would call this abreaction, but how might sociologists investigate further?

One reason why analysis of how older people make their own cultures has been lacking is because youth has occupied centre stage in both popular culture and sociological investigation since the 1960s. As the potential workforce, adolescents constitute future parents, producers, and consumers. Thus their styles of rebellion, resistance, and spending have been of critical interest. Until very recently little enthusiasm was shown for investing in the consumption potential of older people since they lacked both productive and reproductive capacities. We know that this has now changed, yet aside from cataloguing the efforts of political campaigns, we still know very little about old age cultures of discontent. If anything, popular journalists have stolen a march on academics here. Take, for example, a 1992 *Newsweek* article that notes how 'the generation that refused to grow up is growing middle aged ... Baby boomers, by sheer force of numbers, have always made their stage of life the hip stage to be in', then proceeds to muse over the consequences, concluding with the remark of a New York management consultant that 'the whole concept of "retirement" should be retired'.[50]

---

[49] R. Barthes, 'The world of wrestling', in R. Barthes, *Mythologies* (St Albans: Paladin, 1976), pp. 15–25.

[50] M. Beck, 'The new middle age', *Newsweek*, 7 December 1992, 50–6 (50, 56). There are no 'ageing' counterparts of the classic text on youth, S. Hall and T. Jefferson (eds.), *Resistance Through Rituals* (London: Hutchinson, 1976), the discussion of 'lads' subcultures in P. Willis, *Learning to Labour* (Aldershot: Saxon House, 1977), or of A. McRobbie's analysis, 'Working-class girls and the culture of femininity', MA thesis, University of Birmingham, 1977, reprinted in A. McRobbie, *Feminism and Youth Culture: From Jackie to Just Seventeen* (Basingstoke: Macmillan, 1991), pp. 35–60.

Whilst interest in the future drives such speculation, any cultural sociology of ageing must be historical. History helps us to understand the past as well as to trace the lineages of the present, but the alliance with sociology depends more especially upon three conceptual foci: first, sociology is concerned with both the transition to capitalism and, arguably, into late or post-capitalism, as historical processes; secondly, sociology focuses on the constraints imposed by particular social contexts upon individual life histories; thirdly, sociology shares with history a concern with empirical patterns of interaction between human agency and social structure.[51] Given the preceding discussion, in explaining the contemporary popular culture around ageing it seems logical that an approach which can embrace both large-scale transformations in social policy and micro-level shifts in commonsense understandings might be the most plausible.

## The framework of this study

In Britain the average expectation of life at birth in 1900 was fifty-three. As we reach 2000 it is in the high seventies. The most dramatic increases have been among the over-85s, but whilst the million or so persons soon likely to inhabit deep old age present the state (as they do governments throughout the developed, and increasingly also developing, world) with a major resource burden because of the declining health status of many of their number, this group remains proportionately slight. It is the huge rise in numbers living on not just into retirement – itself a twentieth-century invention – but now expecting to experience retirement as an expanded and active life course stage that is my main concern. The issue is deftly stated as follows:

Almost everyone used to work until they dropped. Now, just as life expectancy rises, we are moving people out of work earlier. How will we understand the shape of a life if paid employment takes up 35-odd years out of, say, 95? What are all these people going to do?

We have hardly begun to address this question. We have created a cult of youth which shows no signs of abating just because youth is on the wane: we are all old people pretending to be kids. Until we overcome this cultural lag between the facts of age structure and our preferred images and values, we will not begin to sort out how the brave new world of the old might look.[52]

This book aims to construct a series of reference points by which a sociology of ageing appropriate to these matters might be anchored. Peter Laslett's *A Fresh Map of Life* offered a major re-interpretation of

---

[51] P. Abrams, *Historical Sociology* (Shepton Mallet: Open Books, 1982).
[52] Turney, 'The age of the oldie', 18–19.

the life course and carried the message that it was time for Western societies to wake up to the social realities of population ageing.[53] But what factors were responsible for the invisibility of such a mass social phenomenon in the recent past? Chapter 2 examines the influence that particular readings of the recent history of ageing have had upon social thought while opening up the cultural construction of age for debate. The connections between popular perceptions and political questions are explored by looking at ageing in earlier times and considering problems with method, and in particular modernisation theories. In the past two decades much re-evaluation of the 'golden age of senescence' hypothesis has occurred, such that the once conventional wisdom that older people enjoyed high status in extended families in pre-industrial society has been fundamentally challenged. This chapter considers the historical analysis of the position of older people in the past by considering three filters through which understanding has percolated: modernisation, marginalisation, and medicalisation. The emergence of age-graded systems of classification as part of the bureaucratisation of the social system is considered from the point of view of its impact on high policy issues (retirement pensions), industrial questions (management of the workforce), and altered popular perceptions of age-appropriateness. In the same way that different discourses may be ranged against one another as an analytical aid, it is important to appreciate the value of triangulation: comparing the fruits of different approaches to the same issues in the hope that a nuanced picture of social reality will emerge. For example, when considering retirement in the interwar era, both 'from above' discussions amongst policymakers and social researchers and 'from below' attitudes struck by pensions campaigners are analysed, while popular cultural perceptions of ageing from tabloid cartoons and respondents in social surveys are also included. Thus the focus shifts between national and international concerns about population and resources and local, personal, and peer group apprehensions of ageing.

Despite major shifts in the position of older people in Western society during the first half of the twentieth century, accounts of the emergence of retirement have ignored the role of old age pressure groups, preferring arguments which emphasise structured dependency rather than human agency. Following the birth of welfare states, the stress remained on social investigation of pensioners in the community and frail elderly persons in institutions. Crucially, the development of appropriate ethics for managing ageing populations relies both on the images held by

---

[53] Laslett, *A Fresh Map.*

policymakers and on the role and impact of elders within the process. With the crumbling of the postwar consensus in both Europe and North America and the rise in age consciousness, older people have become more vocal and their interests more visible. However, the self-image presented by retired persons' associations frequently contradicts social images of older people held by non-pensioners. The shift from regarding old age as poverty-ridden and assistance-driven to seeing retirement as a generalised condition of leisure aspiration is not one that directly parallels the egalitarian concerns of politically active lobbyists. We are forced to look elsewhere for enlightenment.[54]

Although the retirement pension and the costs of health care remain abiding concerns, a trend towards recreational and educational issues indicates growing awareness of later life as a period of cultural as well as economic diversity. This line of reasoning is initially pursued in chapter 3, then in more depth in chapter 8. Both chapters discuss the impact of population ageing upon popular culture, with special reference to the growing age consciousness exemplified by the emergence of the Third Age as a social phenomenon of the later twentieth century. The proportionate expansion of the population over pensionable age was far greater in the first half of the present century than it has been since, but institutionalisation of retirement and the stereotyping of old age rendered later life far less visible an experience than it has now become. The recognition that retirement now involves a period of up to thirty-five years of life after work prompts a sociological re-evaluation of this increasingly significant phase in the life course of most people. Policy-based studies emphasising the structured dependency of 'the elderly' are perhaps less germane than ethnographic approaches focusing on biography, community, and the presentation of self. The 'chronological bonds' which once bound people to age-appropriate behaviours are loosening as popular perceptions begin to stress the expectation of an extendible mid-life phase.

Arguably, as the Third Age expands in both quantity and quality, deep old age ('the Fourth Age of decrepitude and senility') suffers from yet more distancing, stigmatisation, and denial. Positive ageing is in part a response to population ageing by marketers anxious to stimulate demand. As consumer culture targets the 'grey market', positive ageing becomes conditional on the possession of sufficient income, cultural

---

[54] I have acknowledged the particular salience of political economy in the 'expert' analysis of the late nineteenth and earlier twentieth centuries, when old age was first conceived as a national social problem, because a cultural picture of later life can be derived only by reconstructing the policy environment. However, such a perspective is rather less significant in dealing with the contemporary cultural landscape, where, fortunately, other sources abound.

capital, and mental and physical health. Thus, while the phase of active adulthood expands to embrace many more seniors, stronger taboos form around those in poverty, those whose pastimes lack positive cultural resonances, and those suffering from disability and diseases such as Alzheimer's.

Chapter 4 considers the significance of Hollywood, television, and market models on the popular imagery of ageing as a process that is increasingly problematic for a global culture of consumerism that emphasises continuing youthfulness. The motion picture industry heralded a reworking of popular understanding of the relationship between the body and the self. From the 1920s onwards film stars codified a set of assumptions about youthful beauty. Increasingly the outer, visible body came to express 'personality' (in contradistinction to the Victorian idea of authenticity being dependent upon inner character formation). Slogans such as 'looking good, feeling great'[55] and 'it is normal to re-invent oneself'[56] express a readiness to seek accessible modes of rejuvenation such as anti-wrinkle creams, facelifts, and liposuction in the service of that youthful ideal of the 'performing self'. In particular, role models like Jane Fonda and Joan Collins demonstrate that 'glamour no longer has its sell-by date'.[57] Meanwhile the reality of population ageing means that advertisers are beginning to accommodate the notion that more potential consumers will be older and are beginning to redesign products accordingly. While the ergonomics of in-car comfort and easy-to-hold cutlery represent adaptations in line with physical changes, so too most elders demand fashion products that do not differentiate between themselves and younger people. Thus, while images of ageing reflect the social obsession with youth and physical health, older people modify the imagery in line with their needs and aspirations as their numbers, and spending power, increase. In their turn, image makers and market leaders influence social understandings and expectations of age-appropriateness, both for older people and future generations (themselves) in later life. Changing stereotypes of ageing are reviewed through an examination of postcards and cartoons while content analysis of selected magazines, including those aimed at people in mid- and later life, is used to provide a sharper instrument for reflecting significant transformations. These studies lead to the identification of style as the current keyword as personal fulfilment becomes an

---

[55] M. Hepworth and M. Featherstone, *Surviving Middle Age* (Oxford: Basil Blackwell, 1982), p. 90.

[56] J. Deitch, *Post Human* (New York: Distributed Art Publishers, 1992), p. 27.

[57] A. Blaikie, 'Ageing and consumer culture: will we reap the whirlwind?', *Generations Review* 4 (1994), 5–7 (6). Cf. M. Kenny, 'Sex appeal has its sell-by date', *Daily Mail*, 28 February 1991, 32.

ever-more realisable goal. Although such a development signals an expansion of individual possibilities in later life, such potential is constrained by overarching structures of social power. For example, pre-retirement and mid-life planning courses (with titles like *Coping with Change*[58]) assume that the individual makes adjustments within an agenda of retirement and redundancy that is broadly imposed upon him or her and that pensions are determined by external policy factors. Nevertheless, in the past fifteen years this pattern has shifted towards one where greater choice but also greater risk predominate, leaving older people perhaps less dependent but no less vulnerable.

Remaining with the theme of imagery, the discussion in chapters 5, 6, and 7 uses photography as an example of the ways in which the growing visual awareness of the body allows for a range of interpretations according to salient social factors. While the collusion of age-stereotyping and nostalgic views of the past has resulted in ageing people becoming symbols of a lost or disappearing world, photographic images can also be used therapeutically as a source from which older people (and younger) might reconstruct their identities. Such work represents one example of the ways in which a sense of self can be affirmed through biographical methods. However, the limits of reconstruction are also significant. Like any source through which memories may be evoked, photographs present illusory and selective images. In raising questions about how visual sources may be treated, chapters 5 and 6 suggest a cautious but positive evaluation: on the one hand, images have no meaning independent of the layers of cultural resonance that frame them; at the same time, and partly because of this, family therapists, reminiscence workers, and artists find that photographs have a catalytic value in prompting individuals to reassess their lives.

Chapter 7 is a case study of the relationship between ageing, the seaside, and heritage in which photographs and other visual referents are seen to be crucial resources for the construction of moral communities reflecting aspirations to return to an imagined past.

Under modernity the quest for belonging encounters a series of contradictions emphasising the fragility of such collective endeavours. Chapters 8 and 9 explore the tensions between the ageing individual and society. Chapter 8 focuses on the everyday world of later life as depicted in ethnographic and community studies. At what points does age matter and how do individuals and groups manage the transitions and crises of mid- and later life? If, as Thompson *et al.*'s detailed interviews suggest, older people do not feel old, then what are the

[58] A. Coleman and A. Chiva, *Coping With Change: Focus on Retirement* (London: Health Education Authority, 1991).

implications of having a young mind trapped within an ageing body?[59] Featherstone and Hepworth's concept of the 'mask of age' is considered as one attempt to understand this dilemma.[60] But if people are able to disguise their true age by means of cosmetic procedures, then does this act to camouflage the realities of ageing? And what happens when bodily betrayals (incontinence, mobility problems, dementias) force acceptance? The discussion examines some ways in which older people experience the status passages that signify movement from Third to Fourth Age. Whereas the shift from adulthood to retirement can be approached in ways similar to the upheavals of youth (adolescence and 'middlescence' both being characterised by liminality and identity crises), later transformations (entry into institutional care, living with dementias, dying) involve issues of communication breakdown between the older person and significant others. Important new work is beginning to interpret the uses of language both amongst older people and between them and their carers. Also, while the medical classification of 'confusion' implies failure to communicate, ethnographic studies have shown that such categorisation can inhibit understanding of the mechanisms of coping being developed by 'confused' older people. The meanings attached to home, family, and social network are critical to the preservation and reworking of identity. Clubs, friendship circles, grandparenthood, maintaining links with kin, and drawing upon the survival strategies used to deal with past transitions are considered in a range of settings, urban and rural, in which ageing individuals must adjust to changed social circumstances. Experiences of retirement migration and segregated living are also discussed.

A central question, given the constraints of economy, culture, and society, is: what motivates people to age as they do? For this reason I have chosen to conclude with a chapter that problematises biography. Biographies link personal understandings to specific actions. By definition they shift emphasis away from overarching theories towards contextualised ways of seeing. As members of particular cohorts, individuals provide insight into the cumulative experience of their age group, and indeed of their class-, race-, gender-, and place-bound cultures, but they also offer examples of discontinuity and difference. The suggestion that secularised modern societies are characterised by rootlessness and cultural amnesia renders problematic notions of

---

[59] P. Thompson, C. Itzin, and M. Abendstern, *I Don't Feel Old: The Experience of Later Life* (Oxford University Press, 1990).

[60] M. Featherstone and M. Hepworth, 'The mask of ageing and the postmodern life course', in M. Featherstone, M. Hepworth, and B. S. Turner (eds.), *The Body: Social Process and Cultural Theory* (London: Sage, 1991), pp. 371–89.

memory, home, and community as repositories of meaning and identity for ageing individuals. Alongside the possible severance from a sense of the past lies a disruption of the orderly progression through predictable life-stages. But while it may be true that more people are living through a healthy, active retirement, thus stretching the bounds of mid-life, bleak reminders of the final phase of life continue to haunt us. This ghost of the future fuels a pursuit of agelessness which is also a retreat from the encounter with old age. The tension between continuity over time (at both social and personal levels) and fragmentation is the central pivot on which the conceptual argument hinges in chapter 9. Our understandings of ageing and the lived experience of it are socially constructed such that we regard the progress of individuals through time as a linear process guided by a series of 'markers' (stages marked by particular conventions and expectations). Whereas modernity has emphasised and made rigid these signposts and stages (via such formal impositions as mandatory retirement ages and informal expectations such as, say, dress codes), we are latterly witnessing a turn towards an apparently greater freedom of choice for the individual as these 'chronological bonds' are loosened. This may be characterised as a shift from the fixed life cycle which saw human ageing as akin to that of other animals (the 'ages of man') to the life course as an altogether more flexible entity dependent upon individual ways of negotiating a route through life. The conclusion thus sets biographical issues in the context of the contemporary shift from modernist social order to postmodern fragmentation. Contemporary contexts of social interaction challenge one's sense of fixed identity, and Kaufman's notion of 'the ageless self' runs up against the idea of self as malleable and multifaceted. Ageing is presented as a diverse phenomenon, first because this counterbalances the anachronistic, stereotyped assumption that all older people are alike and, secondly, to challenge the orthodoxy of grand narratives or one-explanation theories. However, underlying the diversity of ageing experiences are important historical continuities, not least pervasive economic inequalities between generations, and the bodily decrements of deep old age.

To reiterate: my reading of 'popular culture' is one that relates to cultural phenomena emanating from within the ageing populace, rather than simply mass media portrayals. While aiming to understand the interaction between the two, I am also concerned to explore the ways in which people manage their identities within a changing social system; hence the focus on the self and communication. Of course this does not mean that I am eschewing the requirement to provide a sustained theoretical thread. Nevertheless, one of the points I am trying to make is that ageing is about social and cultural variety, and that it is unhelpful to present an argument that appears overly deterministic and 'closed'. This is precisely the problem that has dogged gerontological theory-building in recent decades as a series of master-narratives have rather unsuccessfully succeeded one another. One thing we ought to have learned from Max Weber is that 'social life and individual action are grounded in meaning: yet meaning is always and everywhere a cultural construct'.[61] And, while culture is ubiquitous, it is also remarkably malleable, not to say elusive.

[61] B. Martin, 'The cultural construction of ageing: or how long can the summer wine really last?', in M. Bury and J. Macnicol (eds.), *Aspects of Ageing: Essays on Social Policy and Old Age* (Egham: Department of Social Policy and Social Science, Royal Holloway and Bedford New College Social Policy Papers No. 3, 1990), pp. 53–81 (p. 54).

## 2 The history of old age: popular attitudes and policy perceptions

### Introduction

Before examining the contemporary culture of ageing, it is necessary to outline the historical frame of reference. The further one goes back in time, the thinner becomes the concrete evidence of the ageing experience 'on the ground', and the more one is forced to rely upon the imaginative readings of historians. However, for the modern industrial period since 1750, it is possible to interrogate a number of interpretations with an eye on their methodological and factual limitations. This chapter questions assumptions of a 'lost golden age' of senescence and considers how and why opinions vary over the changing status of older people in modernising Western societies. The stereotyping of old age in the earlier part of the twentieth century is linked to the impact of political issues, in particular the effects of an increasingly bureaucratic ordering of the population by age classifications which highlighted pensioners (a new category) as a 'burden' on society. The analysis aims to tease out significant strands in the political discourse – population panics, the political economy of retirement, vocabularies of obligation or 'deservingness', and medicalisation – that have continued to inform ideologies of age in the half-century since the British welfare state began. It is argued that this focus on the emergence of old age as a social problem has had important repercussions for popular perceptions of later life.

### A distant mirror

The recent ageing of Western populations has prompted considerable academic enquiry. However, historians have been slow to recreate the lost social worlds of the aged. While a clutch of scholars is beginning to refine our understanding of the more recent past in North America and Europe, for less modern times only one major study exists.[1] We know

---

[1] G. Minois, *History of Old Age: From Antiquity to the Renaissance* (Cambridge: Polity Press, 1989). Whilst French studies have characteristically been concerned with the long

precious little of the mentalities of the ancient world, and, in a pre-literate epoch, much of the documentation on which more recent histories might be based is lacking – quantifiable parish records or qualitative social surveys are wholly absent. Older people show up in the record only when they are a problem, and with average life expectancies scarcely reaching mid-adulthood, they were generally too scarce to be more than a curiosity. Indeed, Thompson *et al.* observe that 'because death was such a central concern in the past, the history of death is much more fully studied than the history of living old people'.[2] We are therefore forced to rely upon syntheses of literary imagery, anthropological overview, and philosophical exegesis. For example, Minois suggests a perceptible worsening in the position of Palestinian elders – from patriarchs to degraded old men – through a study of Old Testament texts; the accursed and pathetic old age of the tragedies is compared with the Greek cult of youth; the medieval virtue of a healthy old age is contrasted with the symbolism of Christian art – a strange amalgam of signs of sagacity (white hair) and sin (withered skin). In Merovingian and Carolingian times, older people could expect to live as long as we do but remain absent from the record because they played a negligible social role and relied on their families for care.

In emphasising the virtues of youth, great literature provides a broadly pessimistic picture of age:

The celebration of youth is a persistent strand in European culture. When the unhappy Mignon in Goethe's *Wilhelm Meister* tries on her angel costume, she pictures heaven as a state of restored youthfulness which will last forever. The binary opposite symbol is old age as *memento mori*. In Western culture there are few images of old age as an unequivocally enviable state. It may be associated with the wisdom of experience and the detachment of those who, in an age of faith, perhaps anticipate a more fully spiritual existence once the chrysalis of the earthly body is thrown off; yet the sunken cheeks, withered dugs, and frosted locks are always deployed as symbolic reminders that old age is the threshold of death – the cold 'winter season', the Sphinx's three-legged creature. The inescapable tragedy of physical and mental decay is one of the staple poetic and visual messages of serious art, and the prospect of old age is not one which has appealed to western artists, writers, or even theologians, while folk Christians have usually shared Mignon's belief – the resurrection of the body had better be the body in its prime rather than its decay.[3]

Nevertheless, it would be wrong to assume that in the pre-industrial past old people were always a small minority, or always treated

---

term, studies of the United States tend to begin with American independence in the 1770s.
[2] P. Thompson, Itzin, and Abendstern, *I Don't Feel Old*, p. 22.
[3] B. Martin, 'The cultural construction', p. 62.

negatively. For example, the youth-selective mortality of the Black Death allowed for a reassertion of the relatively old within their family hierarchies as wealth and power regrouped in their favour. Older men were held in greater respect by warrior societies, where they could bathe in their reflected triumphs, than in agrarian circles where the indigent peasant had little to look back on and still less to offer the coming generation, hungry for his land. Economic powerlessness is frequently invoked as a barometer of status, yet, in an age before retirement came to specify a social *rite de passage*, culture and religion were also highly significant. Negative and positive perceptions often coexisted in the past, as they do in the present. Minois claims the Romans' rejection of constricting simplification and categorisation helped to preserve the dignity of older people since people 'criticized individuals, but not the age group, and so safeguarded the complexity, the contradictions, and the ambiguity of old age, both its miseries and its grandeur', whilst Spencer refers to the 'ambivalence that accompanies the increasingly liminal status of old age'.[4] An ambiguity in attitudes towards old age appears to be the only consistent historical factor one can isolate, and, as we shall see, such ambiguity has frequently been cultivated to suit political ends. Nevertheless, by medieval times the image of the ages of man as a series of steps ascending from infancy to a podium in early adulthood, plateau-ing through mid-life, followed by a descent through the later stages, had emerged to form a metaphor which persisted for centuries.[5]

Because of the increasing availability of comparative sources, the past two centuries provide a more fertile field of research.[6] At the same time, the debates about perceptions are all the more vexed. A sociologist comments that 'when we look to professional historians for an understanding of the significance of old age in the past . . . we need to remain sceptical . . . many of their sources are . . . the words of the established, the powerful, and famous, many reflecting personal anxieties about later life rather than changing cultural values and institutional regulations'.[7] With the development of an empirical social history of old age (as against cultural speculation) the relationships and views of the common

---

[4] Minois, *History of Old Age*, p. 112; P. Spencer, 'The riddled course: theories of age and its transformation', in P. Spencer (ed.), *Anthropology and the Riddle of the Sphinx: Paradoxes of Change in the Life Course* (London: Routledge, 1991), pp. 1–26 (p. 24).

[5] J. Burrow, *The Ages of Man: A Study in Medieval Writing and Thought* (Oxford: Clarendon Press, 1986).

[6] See P. Thompson, Itzin, and Abendstern, *I Don't Feel Old*, p. 43: 'Most of even the best material is second-hand, typically refracted through the rewording of prejudice and interviews . . . It is only for the last century and a half that a direct picture becomes a convincing possibility.'

[7] B. Bytheway, *Ageism* (Buckingham: Open University Press, 1995), p. 17.

people – particularly in such fields as household formation, marriage, labour force participation, and welfare arrangements – have begun to surface.[8]

## Pre-industrial origins

Ultimately, the onset of old age has always been a personal issue. As Peter Stearns avers in his study of French society, 'in the final analysis we have to let ageing begin when people think it begins. This involves arteries and an immense amount of history.'[9] However, as social beings we are each influenced by societal attitudes and our socio-economic position as much as we are affected by our biological and mental states. Both individually and collectively, ageing is a cultural state of mind. Although the term 'culture' implies things non-economic, *mentalités* do have material effectivity. The current conception of time, for example, has been part and parcel of the development of the modern life course, bound by chronological stages. Furthermore, the values shared by most contemporary Western states and enshrined in public policies can have profound effects upon the status of older people. As Martin notes: 'The problem with a culture which at the symbolic level emancipates elderly and young alike from ancient obligations is that it severs them from traditional rights and statuses at the same time.'[10]

A good deal of gerontological inquiry falls within the framework of modernisation theory, one of the key issues being the impact of industrialisation and urbanisation on the status of the aged. An initial model, hypothesising a decline in the function and status of old people, congruent with the transformation from an agrarian to an industrial economy, was proposed by Burgess in 1960.[11] Cowgill and Holmes argued that four simultaneous processes operated since c. 1850 to shatter traditional society and thus transform the status of the aged: the development of modern health technology has contributed to the ageing of the population, creating thereby pressures for retirement and curtailing their income; modern economic technology, in creating new occupations and transforming old ones, has further exacerbated job losses amongst older workers; urbanisation has attracted rural youth to the cities, 'thus breaking down the extended family in favour of the nuclear, conjugal unit'; finally, mass education and literacy have undermined the

[8] E.g., M. Pelling, 'Old age, poverty, and disability in early modern Norwich: work, remarriage, and other expedients', in M. Pelling and R. M. Smith (eds.), *Life, Death, and the Elderly: Historical Perspectives* (London: Routledge, 1991), pp. 74–101.

[9] P. N. Stearns, *Old Age in European Society* (London: Croom Helm, 1977), pp. 16–17.

[10] B. Martin, 'The cultural construction', p. 74.

[11] E. W. Burgess (ed.), *Aging in Western Societies* (University of Chicago Press, 1960).

mystique of age.[12] While such a before-and-after model relies upon the myth of a lost golden age of senescence, subsequent debate has revolved about the question of whether or not low status is associated with modernisation *per se*.

'The people of early America', asserts Fischer, 'exalted old age; their descendants have made a cult of youth.'[13] The authority of old people in primitive societies lay in their function as transmitters of the wisdom of experience from one generation to the next. When, however, this usefulness was outlived, they became a burden.[14] Prior to 1770 the aged were venerated, godly, but between 1770 and 1820 the development of equality amongst family members displaced the generational hierarchy. From then on the old became a symbol of disdain. Achenbaum adopts a similar approach, arguing that, prior to 1865, the old were seen to possess valued insights about healthful longevity and served as guardians of virtue; they could 'actively serve others in many capacities' and 'synthesise and share vital lessons garnered from the past and present ages'. Thereafter, however, these roles became increasingly obsolescent. Achenbaum claims that cultural ageism was an independent variable, claiming that 'ideas have a life of their own' and that the rise of ageist attitudes after the American Civil War was not directly connected to 'actual demographic, occupational, or economic conditions'.[15] Whatever the case, differences in dating between Fischer's and Achenbaum's studies do not affect their fundamental agreement over what changed.[16]

---

[12] D. O. Cowgill and L. Holmes (eds.), *Aging and Modernization* (New York: Appleton-Century-Crofts, 1972); D. O. Cowgill, 'The aging of population and societies', *American Association of Political and Social Science* 415 (1974), 1–18, quoted in D. H. Fischer, *Growing Old in America* (New York: Oxford University Press, 1977), p. 21.

[13] Fischer, *Growing Old*, p. 4.

[14] L. W. Simmons, *The Role of the Aged in Primitive Societies* (New Haven, CT: Yale University Press, 1945). This social anthropological view of primitive society, and by implication the pre-industrial position of older people in the West, has been challenged by N. Foner, *Ages in Conflict: A Cross-Cultural Perspective on Inequality Between Old and Young* (New York: Columbia University Press, 1984). The differentiation between the 'merely elderly' and 'really aged' none the less remains as an observational criterion: ' "a point is reached in aging at which any further usefulness appears to be over and the incumbent is regarded as a living liability ... All societies differentiate between old age and this final, pathetic plight." But the *criteria* on which classifications are made are not universal' (C. Haber, *Beyond Sixty-Five: The Dilemma of Old Age in America's Past* (Cambridge University Press, 1983), pp. 1–2).

[15] W. A. Achenbaum, *Old Age in the New Land: The American Experience Since 1790* (Baltimore and London: Johns Hopkins University Press, 1978), p. 24. See also W. A. Achenbaum, 'The obsolescence of old age in America, 1865–1914', *Journal of Social History* 8 (1974), 48–62.

[16] Fischer, *Growing Old*, pp. 21–3, discusses imprecision over the periodisation of change in terms of varying stresses employed in different disciplines: Parsonian sociologists emphasise changes in family structure; economists focus on occupational change and the rise of retirement systems; and intellectual historians concentrate on rhetorical

Both note the social dichotomy rent between a useful, venerable old age and an obsolescent, despicable senescence.

These are, of course, generalisations that ignore differences between different groups and individuals. Stone and others have noted that, in pre-industrial America, respect for the elderly depended on wealth and property possessed, not simply longevity.[17] Meanwhile, Thomas argues that in early modern England age differences, though significant, 'did not cancel out those of class and sex'. In civic life, 'important offices were normally assumed by the solidly middle-aged: "grave and sad men who are above the levities of youth, and beneath the dotages of old age"'. While the power of patronage allowed the upper class to travel 'through life on a fast stream', for most manual workers old age meant 'first to move to lighter (and lower-paid) work, then a decline to abject dependence'.[18]

In popular mythology respect for elders has been tied to family care. However, critics have attacked the conventional wisdom that older people enjoyed high status in extended families in pre-industrial society. While Greven and Demos have argued that respect in the past depended upon property,[19] Quadagno indicates how the decline of the rural English household as a productive unit affected work opportunities and the living arrangements of older people.[20] Small farmers could guarantee physical security through control over land inheritance but this did not confer the respect of their children, who, apparently, frequently despised them openly. There is thus no necessary link between the

debates amongst specific communities of interest. The debate in social psychology, meanwhile, vacillates between 'activity theorists' who stress the imposition of segregation and alienation *upon* older people elderly through 'unnatural retirement', and 'disengagement theorists' who contend that normal ageing involves an active process of social withdrawal.

[17] L. Stone, 'Walking over grandma', *New York Review of Books* 24, 8 (1977), 110–16.

[18] K. Thomas, 'Age and authority in early modern England', *Proceedings of the British Academy* (1976), 205–48 (205, 212–13, 240). See also Haber, *Beyond Sixty-Five*, p. 60: 'To be poor and outcast in America was not to be venerated but rather despised.' Stearns, *Old Age*, takes the view that in France the old have always been treated with unmitigated disdain.

[19] P. Greven, *Four Generations: Population, Land, and Family in Colonial Andover, Massachusetts* (Ithaca, NY, and London: Cornell University Press, 1970); J. Demos, *Past, Present, and Personal: The Family and the Life Course in American History* (Oxford University Press, 1986).

[20] J. Quadagno, *Aging in Early Industrial Society: Work, Family and Social Policy in Nineteenth-Century England* (London: Academic Press, 1982). J. Demos, 'Old age in early New England', *American Journal of Sociology* 84 (1978), 248–87, describes patterns of partial retirement, with people working in assorted part-time jobs as in Britain. See also H. Chudacoff and T. K. Hareven, 'Family transitions into old age', in Hareven, *Transitions*, pp. 217–43.

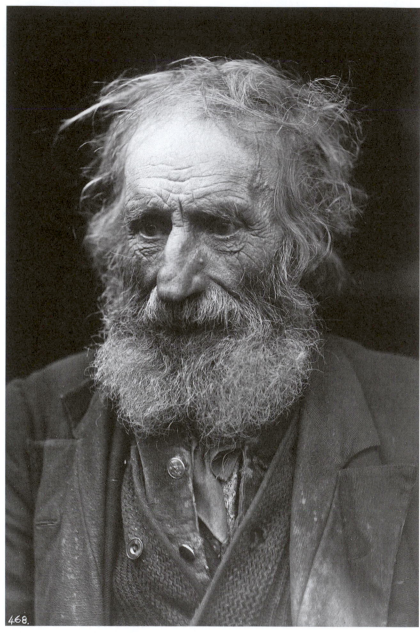

1    The face of the past. Photograph taken 1876–80 by Frank Meadow
Sutcliffe, Hon.FRPS (1853–1941). © The Sutcliffe Gallery, Whitby.

various elements of status.[21] Demographers have concentrated on specific issues such as the relationship between dependency and family size. Laslett, for example, has shown that old people in pre-industrial England were no more likely to be living with their married children than they are today; so, too, maintains Wrigley, both the early modern peasant (with land to pass on) and the twentieth-century pensioner possess a security in old age that the elderly, displaced through the demands of early industrial capitalism, did not have.[22] More older people appear to have lived alone before and after industrialisation than during it.

Cultural historians have emphasised the ability of powerful intellectual and political forces to mould popular opinion. Haber inaugurates a critical history of geriatrics, pointing to its simultaneous reliance on advances in scientific medicine and cultural prejudices. Urbanisation and industrialisation eroded patriarchal authority, as the tightly knit family and landholding structure on which elder power was based crumbled. Consequently, the life-stage of such individuals became 'the subject for countless tracts' by doctors, statisticians, social reformers, and others, reliant upon their rising expert, professional status to sustain a negative, senescent image of ageing in order to segregate dependants. This quasi-professional categorisation was engineered via a 'bureaucratic approach ... classifying their recipients primarily according to age'. A path was thus cleared for institutionalisation, medicalisation, and severance from society via an 'expanding notion of dependent superannuation', specifically the first mandatory retirement programmes.[23]

Consequently, Haber continues, 'In the nineteenth century ... although most aged persons remained employed and independent, their last stage of life was often portrayed as one of disease and dependence.'[24] By the turn of the century, when G. Stanley Hall began to theorise 'senescence' as a counterpoint to adolescence, the prevailing image was one of surviving the shipwreck: 'Many of those who attain advanced years are battered, water-logged, leaky derelicts without cargo or crew, chart, rudder, sail, or engine, remaining afloat only because

---

[21] Quadagno, *Aging*, pp. 205, 12.

[22] P. Laslett, 'The history of aging and the aged', in Laslett, *Family Life and Illicit Love in Earlier Generations* (Cambridge University Press, 1977), pp. 174–213; M. Anderson, *Family Structure in Nineteenth-Century Lancashire* (Cambridge University Press, 1971); E. A. Wrigley, 'Reflections on the history of the family', *Daedalus* 106 (1977), 71–85.

[23] Haber, *Beyond Sixty-Five*, pp. 4, 5, 81.

[24] Ibid., p. 173, referring to W. A. Achenbaum and P. Stearns, 'Old age and modernization', *Gerontologist* 18 (1978), pp. 307–12.

they have struck no fatal rocks or because the storms have not yet swamped them.'[25]

The Industrial Revolution had freed older people from the early modern bonds of family and locality. But a secular re-evaluation of age as scientific problem had superseded ancient religious views. The stage was set for a fresh 'curriculum' in which old age became a problem requiring the intervention of government and, increasingly, trained professionals.[26]

### Ageing in the earlier twentieth century: vocabularies of explanation

A tradition of empiricism in British social research can be traced in the detailed Victorian studies of Henry Mayhew, Charles Booth, and Seebohm Rowntree, each of whom provided important information on the living conditions of older people in their time. Although their works had a marked impact on the social surveys of the interwar years (discussed pp. 47–9 below), and, indeed, upon Townsend's monumental work in the late 1950s, the invisibility of old age from the broader historical record continued into modern times.[27] In 1965, Townsend and Wedderburn noted that: 'Between 1901 and 1947 the numbers of persons in Britain who were aged sixty-five and over grew from under 2 to 5 millions. Yet in that period very little information on the problems of the aged was published. It is an extraordinary fact . . . there was a dearth of published information and, apparently, of interest too.'[28] In so far as it appeared to resist analysis by contemporaries, ageing was a socially opaque issue.[29]

This era began with the advent of old age pensions in 1908 and ended with the imposition of the retirement condition in 1948. However, the

---

[25] T. R. Cole, *The Journey of Life: A Cultural History of Aging in America* (Cambridge University Press, 1993), p. 212, quoting G. S. Hall.

[26] Cole, *Journey of Life*, p. 22. For an overview of recent studies in the history of ageing, see D. Troyansky 'Historical research into ageing, old age and older people', in Jamieson, Harper, and Victor, *Critical Approaches*, pp. 49–62. On American historiography, see C. Haber and B. Gratton, *Old Age and the Search for Security: An American Social History* (Bloomington: Indiana University Press, 1994).

[27] Peter Townsend acknowledges this in the introduction to P. Townsend, *The Last Refuge: A Survey of Residential Institutions and Homes for the Aged in England and Wales* (London: Routledge and Kegan Paul, 1962; abridged edn, 1964), p. 14. See also P. Townsend, *The Family Life of Old People: An Inquiry in East London* (London: Routledge and Kegan Paul, 1957; Harmondsworth: Pelican, 1963).

[28] P. Townsend and D. Wedderburn, *The Aged in the Welfare State* (London: G. Bell and Sons, 1965), p. 10.

[29] See P. Laslett, 'Gregory King, T. R. Malthus and the origins of English social realism', *Population Studies* 39, 3 (1985), 351–62.

long interval between these historic milestones saw any consideration of later life heavily outweighed by the major issue of unemployment. In and around the Depression years pensioners endured at least as much as workers, but their marginality to the nuclear family, on which the nation's livelihood depended, meant that despite their protests – and these were more volatile than is generally supposed – the definitive icon of the era was the hunger march, not the pensioners' rally.

Although the details of policy debates in the interwar years need not detain us here,[30] the ideologies of social policy developed then have been fundamental in framing old age ever since. Rather than reflecting the experiences of older people, these illuminate the 'vocabulary of motive' pursued by the policymakers who sought to persuade others of the acceptability of their actions by employing particular terminologies and classifications.[31] The elements of this vocabulary were three-fold: first, the social problems of ageing had to be presented as demographically induced; secondly, justifying the removal of older people from the labour market depended on claims about the capabilities of older minds and bodies to continue in work; thirdly, the obligation for the state rather than the family to support the aged required the deployment of 'burden of dependency' arguments.

### Population panics

We are up against something fundamental, something vast and almost terrifying in its grim relentless development. We cannot expect to muddle through.[32]

In 1899, Rowntree had written in the concluding sentence to *Poverty* that 'the dark shadow of Malthusian philosophy [had] passed away'.[33] But, forty years on, a new spectre was haunting British social investigation. By the 1930s the demographic transition, largely a result of falling fertility and infant mortality rates since the 1870s, prompted press speculation about 'a future Britain with deserted cities and idle factories while the spa towns were clogged up with pensioners in bath chairs ... industrial retardation, spiralling welfare costs, a lack of economic enterprise, higher taxation ... and a decline of "creativity" and energy in the national psyche'.[34] The combined effect of birth control and

---

[30] For a discussion, see A. Blaikie, 'The emerging political power of the elderly in Britain, 1908–1948', *Ageing and Society* 10, 1 (1990), 17–39.

[31] See C. W. Mills, 'Situated actions and vocabularies of motive', *American Sociological Review* 5, 6 (1940), 904–13.

[32] R. M. Titmuss and K. Titmuss, *Parents Revolt: A Study of the Declining Birth-Rate in Acquisitive Societies* (London: Secker and Warburg, 1942), p. 56.

[33] B. S. Rowntree, *Poverty: A Study of Town Life* (London: Nelson, 1901), p. 361.

[34] Blaikie and Macnicol, 'Ageing and social policy', p. 74.

population ageing was a demographic panic led by influential academics, behind which lurked a convenient scapegoat: in the face of mass unemployment and the drift towards war older people had become victims of their own survival.

The success of health reforms led Cambridge economist Enid Charles to write that 'we need no longer take an alarmist view of changes in the quality of population'. Instead, she argued, age-structure was becoming critical: whereas, in 1935, 12.45 per cent of the population of England and Wales was aged sixty and over, by the year 2000 this would rise to 46.49 per cent. Such explicit quantification quickly gave rise to panic-forecasting over the economic implications of an increasing dependency ratio.[35] The pathological tenor of Richard Titmuss and Kay Titmuss's prediction that the country would soon need to produce 'armchairs and bedroom slippers instead of children's foods' while an ageing society would 'lose the mental attitude that is essential for social progress' and present 'the mournful aspect of ... deserted and derelict areas, [with] houses uninhabited and equipment unused' verged on the hysterical.[36] They continued: 'The future will have to be planned and this ... will require greater intelligence, courage, power of initiative, and qualities of creative imagination ... qualities ... not usually to be found in the aged.'[37] This negative social imagery pervaded political thinking. While Titmuss and Titmuss talked of a 'process of the domination of old age and its interests [that] has already been developing for some years',[38] Conservatives argued that young men were needed both to defend a threatened Empire and as the mainstay of British industry. Meanwhile, radicals latched on to the dangers of a society governed by an inherently reactionary gerontocracy in which social mobility at the younger ages would be stunted:

Old people are more and more tending to dominate our social institutions: for example, of 558 MPs in the House of Commons who reveal their ages two in five received their education before the Boer War (38 per cent are sixty years of age and over one MP in eight is aged seventy and over). In the party which calls itself progressive one in five of 147 Labour MPs are aged seventy and over ... The average age is 55.2, whilst for titled MPs the average is 58.4 ... Clearly we do not lack ripe experience and Victorian memories, but are these the gifts we require to build a New Social Order?[39]

---

[35] E. Charles, *The Menace of Under-Population: A Biological Study of the Decline of Population Growth* (London: Watts & Co., 1936; orig. published as *The Twilight of Parenthood* (1934)), pp. 36, 43, 143.

[36] Titmuss and Titmuss, *Parents Revolt*, p. 27.

[37] Ibid., p. 46.    [38] Ibid., p. 47.

[39] Conservative Party Annual Conference Report, 1937, pp. 37–43.

The threat was not restricted to the British experience, and in 1948 the great French demographer Alfred Sauvy claimed that 'the danger of an eclipse of Western civilisation owing to lack of replacement of its human stock cannot be questioned'.[40]

Underlying such fears was an impressionistic and untested set of assumptions about the mental and physical deficiencies of older people. If the adjectives used to describe population ageing were wholeheartedly gloomy, the associated ageism was ripe with illogicalities. Whilst the poverty of the aged was constantly being reiterated, it was predicted that their consumption would sap resources. Thus, whilst Parliamentarians claimed that 'our grandfathers and grandmothers are afraid to eat too much lest they should be taking the bread out of the mouths of their grand-children',[41] Titmuss and Titmuss averred that 'the demand for basic necessities, such as bread, will diminish as the need for semi-luxurious old age rises'.[42]

The effects of improvements in health care had been visible for some time. In 1934, for example, it had been commented in Parliament that: 'expectation of life is greater now than it ever has been … Today, women of fifty have not the haggard appearance they used to have twenty years ago.'[43] Such greater longevity occasioned much negative speculation as to its potential effects. By 1948, the research organisation Political and Economic Planning was remarking that an elderly population was unlikely to be 'adventurous or vigorous in the social and political spheres'.[44] The next year, the Royal Commission on Population reported:

Older people excel in experience, patience, in wisdom and breadth of view; the young are noted for energy, enterprise, enthusiasm, the capacity to learn new things, to adapt themselves, to innovate. It thus seems possible that a society in which the proportion of young people is diminishing will become dangerously unprogressive.

Alternatively, commented the Ministry of Labour,

---

[40] A. Sauvy, 'Social and economic consequences of the ageing of Western European populations', *Population Studies* 2, 2 (1948), 115–24 (123).

[41] Ellis Smith, MP (1938), quoted in N. Branson and M. Heinemann, *Britain in the Nineteen Thirties* (London: Weidenfeld and Nicolson, 1971), p. 229.

[42] Titmuss and Titmuss, *Parents Revolt*, p. 46; United Kingdom, Parliament, *The Final Report of the Royal Commission on Population*, Cmd. 7695 (1949), p. 113, stated that: 'The old consume without producing which differentiates them from the active population and makes them a factor reducing the average standard of living of the community.'

[43] United Kingdom, Parliament, House of Commons Debates (Hansard), vol. 286, col. 449, 1934 (Debate on Retiring Pensions).

[44] Political and Economic Planning, *Population Policy in Great Britain* (London: PEP, 1948), p. 84.

With improved health and advances in the social services, people now live longer than they used to; and they are healthier and fitter at a higher age. There is evidence that continuance in employment helps the retention of health and active fitness; the break in the normal routine on retirement often results in physical and mental "ageing".[45]

It seems that older people were damned at every turn.

History repeated itself in the 1980s, with a resurgence of population panic. In 1981 a symposium – tellingly entitled 'The Impending Crisis of Old Age' warned that a particularly serious problem which is 'already casting an unmistakable shadow over the National Health Service [is] the marked increase in the numbers of the very elderly and frail people which will occur in Britain in the next twenty years'.[46] Similarly, in 1986, Pifer and Bronte wrote:

Few Americans realise that their country is in the midst of a demographic revolution, that, sooner or later, will affect every individual and every institution in the society. This revolution is the inexorable aging of our population. By the middle of the next century, when this revolution has run its course, the impact will have been at least as powerful as that of any of the great conquest and subsequent closing of the frontier, the successive waves of European immigration, and the development of our great cities ... the post-World War II baby boom, the civil rights and women's movements, the massive influx of women into the paid labour force, the revolution in sexual mores, the decay of many of our large urban centers. All these developments have had a profound effect on our nation, but the aging of the population will certainly have equal, if not greater, impact if some startling but quite possible demographic projections materialise.[47]

Since then, provocative scholarly critiques, crystallised in the title of the volume *Workers Versus Pensioners*, have become the fodder of speculative journalism.[48] A *Sunday Times* article with the headline 'Justice in an ageing world' led with the sensationalist statement: 'All over the developed world, the recently retired are enjoying a golden age. Though

---

[45] United Kingdom, Parliament, *Final Report of the Royal Commission on Population*, p. 121, and United Kingdom, Ministry of Labour and National Service, *Employment of Older Men and Women* (London: Minister of Labour and National Service, 1952), p. 4, both cited in P. Johnson, *The Economics of Old Age in Britain: A Long-Run View, 1881–1981*, CEPR Discussion Paper No. 47 (London: CEPR, 1985), pp. 11–12.

[46] R. F. A. Shegog (ed.), *The Impending Crisis of Old Age* (Oxford: Nuffield Provincial Hospitals Trust/Oxford University Press, 1981), p. 11; the UK Department of Health and Social Security pamphlet *A Happier Old Age* (London, HMSO, 1978), p. 7, speaks of the 20 per cent rise in the over-65s between 1966 and 1976 as being a 'dramatic increase', yet between 1911 and 1951 their numbers rose by 160 per cent.

[47] A. Pifer and L. Bronte (eds.), *Our Ageing Society: Paradox and Promise* (New York and London: W. W. Norton & Co., 1986), p. 3.

[48] P. Johnson, C. Conrad, and D. Thomson (eds.), *Workers Versus Pensioners: Intergenerational Justice in an Ageing World* (Manchester: CEPR/Manchester University Press, 1989).

governments everywhere are trimming back on welfare, so far most cuts and extra contributions have fallen on the young and early middle-aged; their pensioner-parents have preserved their benefits largely intact.'[49] Articles of the 'More pensioners will depend on fewer workers' type have since become legion. And from such emotive reports one might gain the impression that the 'welfare generation' is not only reaping its rewards, but that its adult children are suffering in the bargain. The frightening political arithmetic all too easily colludes with an ideology regarding individual older people as agents in a fiscal conspiracy as 'Twilight of Parenthood' discourses are again evoked to explain a fertility level that has dwindled to 1.8 children per couple.[50]

### The political economy of retirement

Ambiguous, sharply opposed claims for the capabilities or deficiencies of 'the elderly' have been deployed according to political and economic convenience. During the interwar Depression older workers were considered less efficient than younger, less adaptable to changing processes of production and rapid technological change, and the most dispensable in times of slump.[51] In the later 1920s 'enfeeblement' justified their removal from the labour force on grounds that their relative frailty stunted productive capacity. Conversely, in the years of postwar austerity and the 'never-had-it-so-good' period of the 1950s, their wisdom, commitment, and reliability were emphasised as labour shortages became manifest. In a climate of reconstruction concerted attempts were made to persuade older operatives to stay in work, attempts, indeed, which praised their enhanced physical capabilities.

Such flexibility is graphically evident in the writings of Seebohm Rowntree, who in 1931 claimed:

it is one of the sources of our industrial weakness to-day that men whose powers are thus waning are often excessively unwilling to resign one shred of their

---

[49] P. Wilsher, 'Justice in an ageing world', *The Sunday Times*, 9 July 1989, Section F, 1.

[50] W. Brass, 'Is Britain facing the twilight of parenthood?', in H. Joshi (ed.), *The Changing Population of Britain* (Oxford: Blackwell, 1989), pp. 12–26. See also C. Phillipson, 'Inter-generational relations: conflict or consensus in the 21st century', *Policy and Politics* 19 (1991), 27–36; N. Wells and C. Freer (eds.), *The Ageing Population: Burden or Challenge?* (London: Macmillan, 1988).

[51] It was considered only reasonable that 'broken-down old men', well able to withstand idleness, should become redundant, otherwise the younger unemployed might 'go to pieces'. The flaws in such a calculus were largely ignored. In December 1929, the *Birmingham Post* reported a suicide letter signed 'Frank Thornby, aged 62', with the footnote 'Out of employment ... The younger men get the jobs' (C. Phillipson, *The Emergence of Retirement*, University of Durham, Department of Sociology and Social Administration, Working Papers in Sociology No. 14 (University of Durham, 1977), pp. 24–6, 32–5.

authority, and may even tend to become more arbitrary as they become less convincing. Their increasing limitations make it impossible for them to understand that their accustomed door of service to humanity is gradually closing before them. They still endeavour pathetically to fling it wide, as of old – instead of turning to the open door.[52]

By 1947, he had sharply reversed his views:

the [Nuffield] enquiry pointed clearly to the fact that many old people can render valuable service in industry – service which should be made full use of in view of the crucial importance of increasing the total volume of wealth produced by the nation ... Employers who have a fixed retiring age for their employees should consider whether, in view of the present and prospective shortage of manpower, such a policy is in the national interest.[53]

These varying imputations of character and capability resemble the gerontological debates between disengagement and activity theorists that subsequently occurred in the United States, and which are discussed in chapter 3. However, against this continuing preoccupation with 'fitness for work', the logic of pensions policy was rather inelastic. Over the course of a century retirement emerged as a fixed rite of passage, determined by chronological age, where once it was once gauged more flexibly according to the physiological and mental capacity of the individual. The proportion of the British population aged sixty-five and over has trebled. Meanwhile, the proportion of men over sixty-five in employment has fallen from three-quarters in 1881 to just one-tenth by 1981. Recent estimates calculate that only about 3 per cent are working full-time and about 4 per cent half-time.[54] This transformation is partly due to an increasingly specialised division of labour and shake-out of elderly workers; but it has also been a product of greater prosperity and higher living-standard expectations, giving rise to a desire for retirement.[55] Neo-Marxists regard the imposition of mandatory retirement as part of the process of social engineering whereby elderly

---

[52] B. S. Rowntree, 'Growing old usefully: an Easter message for the middle aged', *Birmingham Gazette*, 2 April 1931, Rowntree Papers, ART 16/2, Borthwick Institute of Historical Research, University of York.

[53] B. S. Rowntree, 'The care of the aged', *Industrial Welfare* (1947), 46–50 (50). (Note that the same people are addressed as 'middle aged' in 1931, but 'the aged' in 1947.) By the mid-1980s, when recession struck again, employees aged thirty-five at a television assembly plant in Wales were offered early retirement, on the grounds that younger workers were faster, fitter, and less resistant to change (W. Tyler, 'Structural ageism as a phenomenon in British society', *Journal of Educational Gerontology* 1, 2 (1986), 38–46 (42)).

[54] L. Hannah, *Inventing Retirement: The Development of Occupational Pensions in Britain* (Cambridge University Press, 1986), p. 123; M. Abrams, 'Changes in the life-styles of the elderly, 1959–1982', in United Kingdom, Central Statistical Office, *Social Trends No. 14* (London: HMSO, 1984), London, pp. 11–16 (p. 14).

[55] Hannah, *Inventing Retirement*, documents the increase in occupational pension schemes.

people were marginalised into a condition of 'structured dependence'. By contrast, in the UK it is now clear that trade union and labour movement demands for pensions to be dependent on the employee's ending work heavily influenced Beveridge's thinking, while, in the United States, Graebner argues that legislation reflected the gathering strength of the union movement, who saw in a nationalised system a means of curbing the control of employers' private pensions schemes.[56] Gratton goes further, asserting that 'it was the working class, not the efficiency experts, who carried the pension campaigns'.[57]

Despite this revisionism, accounts of the emergence of retirement pensions have ignored the role of old age pressure groups, preferring arguments which emphasise structured dependency rather than human agency. However, analysis of the two main campaigning organisations – the National Conference on Old Age Pensions (NCOAP), active from 1916 to 1926 and the National Federation of Old Age Pensioners' Associations (NFOAPA), from 1938 onwards – reveals that older people repeatedly sought to win concessions that would offer them a real choice between an 'honourable retirement', financed via adequate pensions, and the opportunity to remain in the labour market if they so wished.[58]

Focusing moral invective on the 'penalty on thrift', whereby such things as Post Office savings, or proceeds from selling allotment produce led to cuts in individual pensions, the NCOAP argued for the universal 'acknowledgement of citizenship on reaching the qualifying age without a poverty test or an inquisition into means'. Dignity could be restored only by removing the 'pauper taint' through a 'system of personal thrift organised by the state'.[59] Composed largely of trade union and friendly society affiliates aiming to defend the 'respectable aged Britisher' they sought to articulate the 'passive protest' of the older people on whose behalf they spoke. However, their interests were at variance with those of the mass of poor pensioners for whom saving was not an option. It was not until the late 1930s that a representative group drawn from the ranks of pensioners themselves came to prominence. The NFOAPA invoked a militant brand of constituency and Parliamentary lobbying

---

[56] J. Macnicol and A. Blaikie, 'The politics of retirement, 1908–1948', in Jefferys, *Growing Old*, pp. 21–42; W. Graebner, *A History of Retirement: The Meaning and Function of an American Institution, 1885–1978* (New Haven, CT: Yale University Press, 1980).

[57] B. Gratton, 'The new history of the aged: a critique', in D. Van Tassel and P. N. Stearns (eds.), *Old Age in a Bureaucratic Society: The Elderly, the Experts and the State of American History* (Westport, CT: Greenwood Press, 1986), pp. 3–29 (p. 18).

[58] Blaikie, 'Emerging political power'.

[59] National Conference on Old Age Pensions (NCOAP), Reports and Pamphlets, 4 November 1922, p. 5; NCOAP, *Review of Ten Years' Progress* (London: NCOAP, n. d. [1927]), pp. 3–4.

and mass petitions, using its mouthpiece *The Pensioner* to pillory the government through Orwellian budgetary calculations, satirical cartoons, and abrasive editorials. Compared with the generation of 1850 whose 'silent suffering' had no direct voice, this working-class movement represented the first literate generation who had during their life course 'acquired trade union habits and organisation'.[60] Their greater self-consciousness ensured that, if, in the later Victorian era, the 'aged poor' were merely a shambling column marching in the great army of the impoverished, by the middle of the twentieth century 'pensioners' were a distinctive social group with specific needs acknowledged by the state.

Such 'from below' history indicates the potential political power of an age group that has become an ever larger proportion of the electorate. However, since the membership of that group is highly diverse, there is no evidence of pensioners voting en bloc. Older people tend to behave conservatively in that they vote now as they did when they first entered work. Thus their current predicament is less significant in determining preferences than lifelong convictions rooted in a wide range of ideologies and circumstances.[61]

### Family obligations and family patterns

The so-called burden of dependency has fluctuated over time. Although the scale of welfare dependency may be unprecedented, historical demographers maintain that in many periods in the pre-industrial past the dependency ratio of elderly to non-elderly population was high. In supporting older people the family and the collectivity (usually the parish) have accompanied rather than opposed one another.[62] However, statutes upholding the social obligation of households to look after their elderly members have been written into English welfare legislation for four centuries, and at times when collective funds have been stretched family-orientated solutions have been advocated.[63]

If the development of pensions in the earlier twentieth century saw the state coming to play a larger role in provision, during the recent

---

[60] Branson and Heinemann, *Britain in the Nineteen Thirties*, pp. 226–7.

[61] Reasons for the failure of increased representation to deliver policy change are examined in Blaikie and Macnicol, 'Ageing and social policy', pp. 77–9. A number of further issues remain unresolved, not least the question of when older people first objected to their portrayal, rather than simply to the lack of coverage given to their needs and demands.

[62] J. E. Smith, 'Widowhood and ageing in traditional English society', *Ageing and Society* 4, 4 (1984), 429–49.

[63] R. M. Smith, 'The structured dependence of the elderly as a recent development: some sceptical historical thoughts', *Ageing and Society* 4, 4 (1984), 409–28 (422–3).

recession the pendulum has swung back to a higher proportion of private responsibility.[64] The 1980s promotion of 'Victorian values' – private and voluntary charity, self-help, and the 'return' to a system of informal care and unpaid support – meant that, defined against the artificiality of institutions, family care was regarded as 'natural', with women the 'natural' carers. However, the momentum of social change responsible for creating large numbers of elderly people has also operated to decrease the availability of the traditional carers. Smaller family sizes, increased divorce rates, and growing numbers of working women have all acted to separate adult women, functionally and geographically, from their ageing parents.[65]

Nevertheless, today less than 5 per cent of all persons above pensionable age are living in communal establishments, including hospitals and psychiatric units, whereas at the turn of the century around 6 per cent inhabited poor law institutions. Research into pre-modern households has indicated a consistent desire among older people to retain autonomy: 'a place of your own, with help in the home, with access to your children ... within reach of support', an arrangement now generally styled 'intimacy-at-a-distance'.[66] In 1851, only 8 per cent of households contained three or more generations, while the proportion is somewhere around half that today. Thus, throughout recent history the vast majority of older people have remained in the community where they have lived independently. Whilst most lived in couples, since 1961 the numbers living alone rapidly doubled such that, by 1981, 43 per cent of older people resided in private households in the company of another pensioner and 30 per cent lived alone; by 1994, the latter proportion had risen to 39 per cent.[67]

In that lower fertility today means smaller numbers of siblings and other relatives, there is less scope for laterally extended families. However, the family has begun to develop in two fresh dimensions. First, with a rise in divorce rates, new networks of step-kin have arisen;

[64] Controversially, D. Thomson, 'The decline of social welfare: falling state support for the elderly since Victorian times', *Ageing and Society* 4, 4 (1984), 451–82, argues that the welfare state has brought a lessening of collective support for dependent elderly. However, D. Hunt, 'Paupers and pensioners: past and present', *Ageing and Society* 9, 4 (1990), 407–30, strongly disputes D. Thomson's findings and conclusions.

[65] Spatial separation is more marked in some areas than others, owing to labour market differences and the fact that the phenomenon is more likely to be characteristic of middle-class families (where parents may also have relocated after retirement) than working-class ones.

[66] Laslett, 'The history of aging and the aged', p. 213.

[67] M. Anderson, 'The emergence of the modern life-cycle in Britain', *Social History* 10 (1985), 69–88; United Kingdom, Office of Population Censuses and Surveys, *General Household Survey 1994* (London: HMSO, 1995), tables 2.31 and 6.3 (figures for 65+ age-group: 33 per cent of men and 62 per cent of women aged 75+ lived alone).

secondly, with increased life expectancy, three- and four-generation families are growing rapidly, prompting new sociological dilemmas:

The 'beanpole family' is the family of the future ... Adults in the fifties or even sixties will have parents still living. Their children will have grandparents alive when they too have children ... less clear is the way these new-style families will manage mutual care. One scenario has fit grandparents looking after working mothers' and fathers' children, to everyone's benefit ... How many 'Thirdagers' will want to tie themselves down for a fresh bout of child-rearing? Will they be living close enough to the children? Will they be looking after their own, still older, parents instead?[68]

### Surveying social standards

The complexity of emerging attitudes is illustrated in a bulletin published by the social reporting organisation Mass-Observation in 1948 and simply entitled *Old Age*.[69] Respondents talked of:

*a very real fear of senile decay; two in five dread mental debility; and as many as seven in ten are afraid of undermining their physical powers* [emphasis in original] ... there is always the fear of being a burden, of elapsing into a second childhood and of being a perpetual drag on the young ... only one in five anticipates it as a pleasant time ... It is true that it can be a time of vigorous activity ... On the other hand, old age can be a time of senile decay ... And others prefer death to a decay in life.

A 23-year-old metallurgist claimed he was 'often irritated in the presence of old people, particularly those whom I regard as inferior to myself in knowledge and experience. They claim to know better because of their age whereas often they are hopelessly and patently out of date.' Meanwhile, a retired railway official commented: 'I am one of those old chaps who knew when to give up – whilst I could still enjoy my leisure. I have several hobbies – conchology, thunderstorm observation, reading, etc. – and am never bored or without occupation. The difficulty with most old people is that they do not know how to occupy themselves and so obviate becoming a burden or a nuisance, or both, to other people.'

There was anxiety about institutionalisation. 'In 1948', began the *Bulletin*, 'Mr Bumble's workhouse still casts its shadow.' One woman in her thirties felt 'a great dislike for the old-fashioned workhouse and the

---

[68] Turney, 'The age of the oldie', 19. M. Anderson, 'The emergence of the modern life-cycle', 70, notes that, 'while the average woman of the 1970s could expect to live twenty-five years after the birth of her last grandchild, a woman of the middle of the eighteenth century could expect to die twelve years before her last grandchild was born'.

[69] Mass-Observation, *Bulletin*, New Series, No. 21 (1948). Subsequent references are from this source.

new Rest Homes. For the people who have to go in such places I feel sorry. For myself, while I had six pennies and the gas laid on, I would take that way out before entering one.' The pamphlet closed by stating that:

Aesthetically, too, old people sometimes offend. They cannot help their physical failings, 'double-chin, wrinkles, knobbly, misshapen limbs', but there is no need to disregard the aesthetic proprieties. As one 36-year-old housewife writes: 'I shall see to it that I smell nice and dress in pastel shades, keep flowers always by me and not be, as one old lady who terrified me as a child, an old lady dressed always in black, who smelt musty like the grave, and always reminded me of a fat spider ready to grab me.'

At one point a strong plea is made for greater humanitarian awareness: 'But no reform, Utopian or not, will avail while our attitude is wrong. What the old want, many people argue, is not more utilitarian comforts, but more sympathy. The human touch is needed to rescue them from the efficient clicking of the State machine.'

In the later twentieth century retirement is increasingly concerned with consumption. However, during the first half of the twentieth century, the simple poverty of most retirees meant that welfare issues took the floor. However, by contrast with the plethora of postwar studies, the interwar years were curiously deficient in research into ageing. Poverty surveys using or adapting Rowntree's life cycle model saw old age as largely peripheral to the nuclear family with children. In 1930, however, Priscilla Dodds, research assistant to the New Survey of London, interviewed several dozen East London pensioners about living conditions, domestic budgets, and attitudes towards various forms of support. As the Departmental Committee on Old Age Pensions (1919) had revealed, many subsisted on low-protein diets. Most knew few other old folk, and some were visited only by sons and daughters, on whom they partly depended; many had bought no new clothes in over ten years; and some were 'inclined to plead poverty to all enquirers', frightened that any disclosure might disqualify them from receiving full pensions. Pensions were rarely deemed satisfactory although many stated they 'would rather starve' than rely on the parish.

The flavour of Miss Dodds's remarks, meanwhile, resembled that of a Relieving Officer in the weighing up of motives and indexing of approval and disapproval:

Miss S. seemed to be rather a grubby woman. Her clothes were very, very untidy, not very clean and not too well cared for. She said, however, that she always took care to go out looking neat, and that I must not judge her by her morning clothes as she had just got up . . . She said that she always buys a 1s 8d bottle of Guinness each week, as when you get old you must have nourishing things. I rather wondered whether she drinks ... as there was a large bottle of beer on the table.[70]

The means test extended the control functions of political economy into the private, domestic sphere, intruding into the minutiae of household management, dress, and personal habits.[71] Older people who had worked all their lives were considered 'deserving' claimants for relief. However, within this classification, some were considered more deserving than others. As we have seen in the propaganda of the NCOAP an ethical apartheid, hinging around self-help, thrift, and respectability, was internalised in the belief system of old people themselves, not least as a criterion for making class distinctions. For example, an old lady interviewed in Greenwich in 1929 remarked:

There ought to be a system where the deserving poor get enough to live on without having to go to the Public Assistance Committee with the thriftless part of the community ... the people who have been thoroughly hard-working all their lives find it very hard to swallow their pride and have to go down to the parish just as the lower types do. They are often told they do not need relief as they are neatly dressed.[72]

It appears that the struggle for dignity amongst the old became an excuse for an official meanness of vision. The *New Survey* remarked: 'On the whole it is satisfactory to know that while most will struggle to keep away from public assistance, they will not, in the last resort, allow their pride to starve them.' Similarly, the complacency of those detailed to arrange slum clearance could be breathtaking:

Old people can well be left in the slums longer than those with young families. They are settled in their habits and common use has made them negligent or tolerant of their surroundings ... they have lived in worse conditions and will take no great harm from spending the last of their days there.[73]

The image here is one of apathetic victims waiting out their sentence. As Rowntree put it: 'they do get an occasional ounce of tobacco, or a glass

---

[70] H. Llewellyn Smith, *The New Survey of London Life and Labour*, 9 vols. (London: P. S. King and Son, 1932), vol. III, Appendix, pp. 457–68 (p. 459).

[71] For a development of the Malthusian ideas behind social – as against political – economy, see G. Procacci, 'Social economy and the government or poverty', *Ideology and Consciousness* 4 (1978), 55–72.

[72] *New Survey of London*, 1930–5 original MSS, British Library of Political and Economic Science, London. A popular anecdote from Islington recalls relief being refused to women carrying shopping bags on the grounds that they were visible evidence that they could afford to buy their own food (Clio Co-operative video *Let's Not Forget: Women's Memories of Islington* (London: Clio Co-operative, 1984)).

[73] Llewellyn Smith, *New Survey*, p. 209; H. Quigley and I. Goldie, *Housing and Slum Clearance in London* (London: Methuen, 1934), pp. 142–43, quoted in J. Stevenson, *Social Conditions in Britain Between the Wars* (Harmondsworth: Penguin, 1977), p. 206.

of beer, but only by suffering a little more from cold or undernourishment. A poor, drab ending to a life.'[74]

There was just one bleaker finale. Those who could no longer manage in the community were moved into residential care.[75] Thomson has revealed that, as other categories of paupers were sectioned off for separate treatment in specialised institutions, 'the workhouse became, more by default than design, the institution of the aged'.[76] After the 1940s only the labels changed: 'inmates' became 'residents', 'institutions' became 'hostels', as former workhouses were converted into geriatric units. Inside public assistance institutions 'people slept in large dormitories, sat on hard chairs, looked out on cabbage patches diversified by concrete, were separated according to sex, and, except one day a week, could not pass the gates without permission'.[77] Clearly these bastilles were very much in line with both Goffman's total institution and Foucault's panopticon with all their implications for surveillance and control.[78] As geriatrics became the theory, such homes became the domain for the working out of practice.

Stearns has commented that 'of all the silent groups yet uncovered by historians ... the elderly, as a group, remain the most inarticulate'.[79] In Britain, certainly, popular press coverage confirmed Fielding's dictum that 'the sufferings of the poor are, indeed, less observed than their misdeeds; not from any want of compassion but because they are less known'.[80] In 1909, the year following the introduction of the first state pensions, the *News of the World* ran a story under the headline 'Pension

---

[74] B. S. Rowntree, *Poverty and Progress: A Second Social Survey of York* (London: Longmans, Green and Co., 1941), quoted in Phillipson, *The Emergence of Retirement*, p. 18.

[75] Despite the claim that five-sixths of aged earners were men, the number of older men in poor law institutions was twice that of older women. One explanation advanced was that: 'senile old men who cannot look after themselves properly are felt as a more troublesome burden on the house-hold of younger people than old women who often give domestic help in various ways. Hence the old men are more properly sent to an institution where they can be properly looked after. More old women than men live solitary lives, as is to be expected, since the women would as a rule be better able ... to manage for themselves' (Llewellyn Smith, *New Survey*, pp. 204, 190–1, 194).

[76] D. Thomson, 'Workhouse to nursing home: residential care of elderly people in England since 1840', *Ageing and Society* 3 (1983), 43–69 (47).

[77] N. Roberts, *Our Future Selves* (London: George Allen and Unwin, 1970), p. 26; see also Lord Amulree, *Adding Life to Years* (London: Bannisdale Press, 1951), pp. 12–17, and Means and Smith, *Development of Welfare Services*.

[78] K. Williams, *From Pauperism to Poverty* (London: Routledge, 1981), argues that the regulatory programme monitored pauperism (a moral programme) rather than poverty (an objective indicator of need).

[79] Stearns, *Old Age*, p. 12.

[80] H. Fielding, *Proposal for Making an Effectual Provision for the Poor* (London: A. Millar, 1753), quoted in P. Golding and S. Middleton, *Images of Welfare: Press and Public Attitudes to Poverty* (Oxford: Basil Blackwell, 1982), p. 1.

fraud – first conviction under new act',[81] yet newspaper reviews of the *New Survey of London* devoted at best a token sentence to the chapter on old age. When 1,275,000 applications were lodged for the new supplementary pensions of 1940 (within the first three months of availability) instead of the expected maximum of 400,000, *The Times* leader thus talked of 'a remarkable discovery of secret need'.[82]

Historical relationships within and between families are not easy to research, and informal transfers of income between generations are notoriously difficult to gauge.[83] If pensioner poverty was generally obscured, the important role of older women within the extended family was largely invisible,[84] while those living outside the household hearth were still more hidden. Consider, for instance, George Orwell's surprise in 1933:

Two or three of the lodgers were old-age pensioners. Till meeting them I had never realised that there are people in England who live on nothing but the old-age pension of ten shillings a week. None of these old men had any other resource whatever. He said: 'Well, there's ninepence a night for yer kip – that's five and threepence a week. Then there's threepence on Saturday for a shave – that's five an' six. The you 'as a 'aircut once a month for sixpence – that's another three 'apence a week. So you 'as about four an' fourpence for food an' bacca.'

He could imagine no other expenses. His food was bread and margarine and tea – towards the end of the week dry bread and tea without milk – and perhaps he got his clothes from charity.[85]

While inadequate pensions and a climate of high unemployment ensured that the majority faced 'the weary monotony enforced by life around the poverty line', this bland portrayal masked wide variations.[86] On the Isle of Wight, J. B. Priestley discovered quite another category of

---

[81] 'Pension fraud – first conviction under new act', *News of the World*, 7 February 1909, cited in Golding and Middleton, *Images*, p. 36.

[82] A. Deacon, 'Thank you, God, for the means-test man', *New Society*, 25 June 1981, 519–20 (520).

[83] The privacy legally enjoyed within the family home presents a barrier to investigation. For example, while journalists have latterly exposed abuse of the residents by staff, elder abuse in families has rarely been uncovered. But, as is now becoming clear, we are misguided if we think that every small household is necessarily a happy one. See S. Biggs, C. Phillipson, and P. Kingston, *Elder Abuse in Perspective* (Buckingham: Open University Press, 1995).

[84] See, however, E. Roberts, *A Woman's Place: an Oral History of Working-Class Women, 1890–1940* (Oxford: Basil Blackwell, 1984), pp. 175–81.

[85] G. Orwell, *Down and out in Paris and London* (Harmondsworth: Penguin, 1971), pp. 119–20.

[86] Phillipson, *The Emergence of Retirement*, pp. 20–1. In the 1940s, as in the 1890s and 1990s, the proportion of people of pensionable age in Britain at or below subsistence level was around one-third. See Blaikie and Macnicol, 'Ageing and social policy', pp. 75–7.

retiree: 'elderly gentlefolk tucked away in charming old manor houses or converted farms ... keep[ing] open house for young male relatives on leave from the East'.[87] Meanwhile, an undercurrent that was to become a tidal wave was just discernible as the spread of compulsory retirement among the middle class 'began to generate a new more generalised culture of retirement, a more widespread conception of retirement as a period of usable leisure'.[88]

## Postwar medicalisation

The paucity of interwar studies is rendered more stark by Townsend and Wedderburn's further observation that, 'Suddenly, in the late forties and fifties ... the problems of old age were discovered ... the trickle of carefully documented studies became a modest stream, slightly preceding the floodwaters of interest and research in the subject which were released in the United States in the mid-1950s.'[89] If anything, this understates the volume and impact of American research in the early 1940s and early 1950s, especially the work of such central figures in the social sciences as Parsons and Havighurst,[90] but we can state with some confidence that prior to the Second World War the particular concerns of old age had not been considered a subject for much serious social investigation.

This was to change quite suddenly. Under Beveridge's guiding hand, the National Insurance Act (1946) established a system of flat-rate universal pensions in Britain. In 1947 the Centre for Policy on Ageing was founded, the Gerontological Society of America met for the first time, and, under the auspices of the Nuffield Foundation, Rowntree's study of old age was published.[91] *Old People* comprehensively examined incomes, housing, living conditions, recreation, and social life. However, like many of the surveys that were produced in the following twenty years, it now marginalised later life not by ignoring it, but by focusing on the specific conditions of those over pensionable age – the 'problems of the elderly'. In 1943 an audience of older US professionals had been lectured on the requirements of their fellow citizens: 'If they cannot be given real lives, they must have proxy ones ... Nine million people today ... need schools, recreation centers, arts and crafts centers,

---

[87] J. B. Priestley, *English Journey* (London: Gollancz, 1934), pp. 20–1.
[88] P. Thane, *Ageing and the Economy: Historical Issues*, CEPR Discussion Paper No. 16 (London: CEPR, 1984), pp. 6–7.
[89] Townsend and Wedderburn, *The Aged in the Welfare State*, p. 10.
[90] See chapter 3, pp. 60–1.
[91] B. S. Rowntree, *Old People: Report of a Survey Committee on the Problems of Ageing and the Care of Old People* (London: Nuffield Foundation/Oxford University Press, 1947).

sheltered work shops, adult playgrounds, marriage brokers, social clubs.'[92] In the 1950s a similarly restricted agenda was advocated in Britain, as anxiety over the detrimental health effects of abrupt work-ending ('retirement impact') led to such schemes as the Employment Fellowship (formerly Winter Distress League) sheltered work-rooms where 'elderly workers could be employed for two hours a day, on small assembling and packing jobs'.[93]

Another significant turning point came with the growth of geriatrics as a distinct branch of medicine. In a number of guises geriatrics had been active in Europe since the middle of the nineteenth century, and in the 1930s Marjorie Warren had instigated an innovatory British approach to the medical treatment of the aged, demonstrating, for example, that stroke victims could be rehabilitated. However, as a modern subject with a specific identity, British geriatrics began with Sheldon's classic survey *The Social Medicine of Old Age* published in 1948.[94]

Sheldon's study pioneered a method for evaluating clinical, social, preventative, and remedial needs *in the community*. Thus, from the outset geriatrics was more closely involved with the social circumstances of its patients than any other branch of medicine. In the thinking of those who have followed Michel Foucault, this expanded clinical role and accompanying extension of surveillance rendered it a discipline of social regulation.[95] Since many older people have traditionally chosen not to use medical services, under-reporting of illness has been counteracted by screening and the extension of the medical gaze to incorporate social and environmental circumstances – hence the remark of one geriatrician that 'individuals discovered in the community must be supervised for life'.[96] In assessing geriatric patients, the division between 'normal' and 'abnormal' changes has become critical. In the early days, this was a matter for speculation and subjective evaluation. But this methodological difficulty has now been 'reformulated as a problem of

[92] G. Lawton (ed.), *New Goals for Old Age* (New York: Columbia University Press, 1943), p. 32, cited in Cole, *Journey of Life*, p. 224.

[93] S. Harper and P. Thane, 'The consolidation of "old age" as a phase of life, 1945–1965', in Jefferys, *Growing Old*, pp. 43–61 (p. 57).

[94] D. Armstrong, *Political Anatomy of the Body: Medical Knowledge in Britain in the Twentieth Century* (Cambridge University Press, 1983), p. 85; Stearns, *Old Age*, pp. 80–118; J. H. Sheldon, *The Social Medicine of Old Age* (London: Nuffield Foundation/Oxford University Press, 1948).

[95] Armstrong, *Political Anatomy*, p. 85, remarks that 'geriatrics was a speciality born directly of the survey'.

[96] F. Anderson, *Practical Management of the Elderly* (Oxford: Basil Blackwell, 1967), p. 55, cited in Armstrong, *Political Anatomy*, p. 92.

clinical strategy'.[97] Conventional distinctions made between health and disease assume that diseases exist as separate entities; however, this is not so for geriatric medicine. Instead, for the Foucauldians, older people are being colonised via the use of medicine to treat essentially social ailments. In 1948 it was claimed that one-third of the elderly patients in a Birmingham infirmary were in hospital for social rather than medical reasons. Ever since, some have argued that geriatric intervention diverts attention from environmental or economically induced problems. Clearly, ageing is a physical process and we would be foolish to assume that by demonstrating the problematic character of geriatrics we were also demonstrating its dispensability. Without it many people would clearly suffer far more than they do.[98] However, medicine remains central to the fundamental contradiction of a 'modern society on the one hand vaunting longevity as one of its major technological and moral achievements, while on the other hand showing itself to be less than well prepared to meet the personal and cultural needs of an ageing population'.[99]

### Coda: old age and modern memory

Medicalisation completes the triangular frame of the conceptual edifice on which the recent history of old age has been built, the other supports being modernisation and marginalisation. In much social history older people have been objects of the gaze of others (politicians, medics, reformers, and investigators) rather than subjects speaking for themselves.[100] However, oral historians have made attempts to rectify this, and the pathbreaking works of Blythe, Elder, Thompson et al., and Bertaux and Thompson stand out.[101] As chapter 8 indicates,

[97] Armstrong, *Political Anatomy*, p. 88.
[98] M. R. Bury, 'Social constructionism and the development of medical sociology', *Sociology of Health and Illness* 8, 2 (1986), 137–69.
[99] K. Morgan, 'A good time to be old', *Listener*, 8 October 1987, 5–6 (5). It is a salutary thought that in Britain three-quarters of people over the age of seventy-five receive drugs and one-third take between four and six drugs at any one time, while up to 15 per cent of hospital admissions into geriatric units are thought to be due to drug-induced diseases (C. Phillipson, 'Drugs and the elderly: a critical perspective on the Opren case', *Critical Social Policy* 3, 2 (1983), 109–16 (109)). With such a ready market in the geriatric field, it comes as no surprise that large drug companies should be willing to sponsor major gerontological projects and international conferences.
[100] P. Thane, Review of Haber and Gratton, *Old Age*, *Generations Review* 5, 2 (1995), 16.
[101] R. Blythe, *The View in Winter: Reflections on Old Age* (Harmondsworth: Penguin, 1979); G. H. Elder, *Children of the Great Depression* (University of Chicago Press, 1974); P. Thompson, Itzin and Abendstern, *I Don't Feel Old*; D. Bertaux and P. Thompson, *Between Generations: Family Models, Myths, and Memories* (Oxford University Press, 1993).

ethnographic studies have drawn on memories, collective and personal, in explaining scripts, strategies, and ways of seeing among today's elders. Reminiscence also provides a fruitful route to interpretation, both of past events and of the effects of those events upon today's older people. For example, Coleman refers to recorded accounts of the Second World War, often told by women, 'of "war as a thief" which had taken away their house, their livelihood, and their family as it had previously been constituted'.[102] Alternatively, Elder *et al.*'s studies of veterans from that war, and from Korea and Vietnam, point to certain gains for some in dexterity and self-esteem.[103] A guiding theme in research adopting life course perspectives has been that past crises can provide learning experiences informing coping strategies later in life, and chapter 9 stresses the deep significance of cohort and continuity of self.[104] Nevertheless, as Michael Ignatieff eloquently explains, the structure of modern bureaucracy works against any sympathetic appreciation of the expressive, non-instrumental needs of older people:

My encounters with them are a parable of moral relations between strangers in the welfare state ... Their needs and entitlements establish a silent relation between us. As we stand together in line at the post office, while they cash their pension cheques, some tiny portion of my income is transferred into their pockets through the numberless capillaries of the state ... They are dependent on the state, not upon me, and we are both glad of it. Yet I am also aware of how this mediation walls us off from each other ...

The political arguments between left and right over the future of the welfare state which rage over these people's heads almost always take their needs entirely for granted. Both sides assume that what they need is income, food, clothing, shelter, and medical care, then debate whether they are entitled to these goods as a matter of right, and whether there are adequate resources to provide them if they are. What almost never gets asked is whether they might need something more than the means of mere survival.[105]

Discerning such intangible matters as the human resources deemed sufficient to enjoy a reasonable quality of life is no simple task, but one which – as I hope will become apparent – cannot be ignored.

[102] P. Coleman, 'Last scene of all', *Generations Review* 7, 1 (1997), 2–5 (2); M. P. Bender, 'Bitter harvest: the implications of continuing war-related stress on reminiscence theory and practice', *Ageing and Society* 17, 3 (1997), 337–48.

[103] G. H. Elder and E. C. Clipp, 'Introduction to the special section on military experience in adult development and aging', *Psychology and Aging* 9 (1994), 3–4.

[104] S. di Gregorio, 'Understanding the "management" of everyday-living', in C. Phillipson, M. Bernard, and P. Strang (eds.), *Dependency and Interdependency in Later Life: Theoretical Perspectives and Policy Alternatives* (London: Croom Helm, 1986), pp. 327–37; S. di Gregorio, '"Managing" – a concept for contextualising how people live their later lives', in S. di Gregorio (ed.), *Social Gerontology: New Directions* (London: Croom Helm, 1987), pp. 268–84.

[105] M. Ignatieff, *The Needs of Strangers* (London: Chatto and Windus, 1984), pp. 9–11.

## Conclusion

This brief overview has aimed to identify the ambiguities in our understanding of ageing and to locate old age within the popular and political cultures of particular Western societies in the past. It is clear that simply to assume that 'in the past' all elders bathed in the light of a lost golden age, or conversely that all old people were poor in the old days, is a flawed misconception. Accordingly, although some aspects of modernisation, such as technological change and the rise of bureaucracy, are undoubtedly evident, modernisation theory suggests an overly linear transformation in attitudes to ageing. The roles and statuses of older people in the family, employment, and civil society more generally have always been multifaceted. The values placed on these have fluctuated according to political processes which have accentuated economic priorities and thus acted to marginalise older people into a position of structured dependency. Nevertheless, such age differentiation has not gone unchallenged, and it would be wrong to regard chronological age as necessarily disempowering.

Paul Johnson has observed that: 'Today, as with the Edwardian debate over Old Age Pensions and the concern after the Second World War with the shifting age structure of the population, the resurgence of interest in old age owes less to intellectual imagination than to the needs of government.'[106] Others claim that 'any inclination to define old age as a social problem was not the consequence of any observable changes in the actual numbers of older people in the population or their physical and social condition [but] a response to fluctuations in attitudes ... which in turn reflected changes in political and socio-economic priorities'.[107] Katz pursues a Foucauldian logic, claiming that the 'technologies' of workhouse and old people's homes, the development of pensions and retirement, and social surveys (feeding an 'alarmist demography' which fuelled the demand for control) created 'the elderly' as a problem group and 'the pensioner as a type of person, old, poor, and dependent'.[108] Getting beyond that agenda to the lived experiences of its subjects requires a certain ingenuity with sources that are themselves scattered and sporadic. The methods of social science have enabled

---

[106] P. Johnson, *Economics of Old Age*, p. 1.

[107] M. Hepworth, 'Positive ageing: what is the message?', in R. Brunton, R. Burrows, and S. Nettleton (eds.), *The Sociology of Health Promotion: Critical Analyses of Consumption, Lifestyle and Risk* (London: Routledge, 1995), pp. 176–90 (pp. 184–5). See also S. MacIntyre, 'Old age as a social problem', in R. Dingwall, C. Heath, and M. Stacey (eds.), *Health Care and Health Knowledge* (London: Croom Helm, London, 1976), pp. 41–63.

[108] Katz, *Disciplining Old Age*, p. 75.

novel uses of historical sources to unlock complex issues around work and family relationships as well as broader social values and influences. Thus the crucial connections between public issues and private understandings are becoming less mysterious. As Troyansky observes: 'Informants' testimony falls somewhere between the images and discourses of the cultural historian and the anonymous populations of the social historians and demographers.'[109] In an attempt to clarify further features of that murky middle ground, the present analysis plunders mainly visual sources. First, however, the historical threads need to be drawn into the contemporary social weave.

[109] Troyansky, 'Historical research', p. 58. For a stimulating discussion of potential research, see P. Thane, 'The cultural history of old age', *Australian Cultural History* 14 (1995), 23–39.

# 3    The transformation of retirement

Arber and Ginn have remarked that sociology's founding fathers, writing in the late nineteenth century, may be forgiven for ignoring old age: only 5 per cent of the British population were over sixty-five; with two-thirds of older men still economically active, retirement was not a distinctive life-stage; and two-thirds of older people lived in households containing younger members, compared to today's 15 per cent.[1] Industrial societies were characterised by paid work, and theory reflected the position and interests of the male breadwinner. However, the fact that the state pension was introduced in 1908 reminds us that this profile was beginning to alter, and, as the present century progressed, so the visibility of older people has increased. Today's sociologist has no excuses.

What implications follow from the transformations of age that have occurred? While the secular shift towards an ageing population is undeniable, the cultural effects of this transition remain unclear. Chapters 1 and 2 have suggested that 'old age', 'ageing', and 'the life course' each represent social constructs which connect intellectual formulations, policy, and world views. Academic discourses have tended to apply quasi-scientific categories in marking off old age from adult life and medicalising its definition. These dovetail with an increasingly bureaucratic approach towards the political problems presented by

Parts of this chapter have been presented to an 'Images of Aging' working conference, Bibliothèque Nationale, Luxembourg; the Anglo-Nordic Symposium on Learning, Education and the Lifespan in Mysen, Norway; a residential seminar at Wye College; MSc. seminar groups at Birkbeck and King's Colleges, University of London; and an audience at the King's Fund Institute, London. Joanna Bornat, Mike Hepworth, and John Miles made useful suggestions on earlier drafts; I should also like to thank Chris Phillipson for allowing me to read an unpublished draft paper.

[1] S. Arber and J. Ginn, 'The invisibility of age: gender and class in later life', *Sociological Review* 39 (1991), 260–91. M. Kohli, 'The world we forgot: a historical review of the life course', in V. W. Marshall (ed.), *Later Life: The Social Psychology of Aging* (London: Sage, 1986), pp. 271–303 (p. 281), notes that in Germany between 1881 and 1981 the proportion of those who could possibly benefit from retirement increased from one-fifth to four-fifths, but the male labour force participation rate for those over age sixty-five decreased from 68.3 per cent to 19.1 per cent over the same period.

growing numbers of older people, evident in the institutionalisation of retirement through state pensions. And although the inadequacies of the pension were clear, a subpopulation inured to a Victorian work ethic championing thrift and rewarding 'deservingness' in later life has been perceived as, for the most part, suffering the economic and physical hardships of later life quietly and gracefully.

## From modernity to consumer culture

As we have seen, although their chronologies vary, modernisation theorists contend that traditional values became outmoded as industrial and demographic transition led to a contemporaneous process of population ageing and a devaluing of the status of older people through urbanisation, education, and new technologies which together rendered their skills and knowledge obsolete.[2] As society became increasingly differentiated, the increased classification of life-stages guaranteed that older people were categorised as 'the elderly', a social and economic group delimited by chronological markers that disqualified them from the production process. While the constituents of modernity include industrial capitalism and a social structure differentiated by class, the labour market also requires to be collapsed into stages of socialisation for work (education through childhood), progression through production and reproduction (paid work for adults, many of whom are parents), and retirement. The life course forms a pivot for social engineering. Consequently, political economists see the emergence of retirement as a vehicle used to separate older people from the sphere of production, with evaluations of older people varying according to the perceived 'burden of dependency' of an ageing population and the state of the labour market. As chapter 2 has indicated, marginalisation of older people created reliance by elders on paternalist welfare provision, while recurrent population panics promulgated the view that smaller number of productive workers would be called upon to support increasing numbers of aged.

Such logic helps to explain the stereotyping of old age for much of the twentieth century. Latterly, however, the correspondence between productive rationality and social differentiation has given way to a plurality of positions characterised by consumption patterns. The greater affluence of Western societies creates more disposable income which tends to be spent on leisure products and pursuits whilst commodities are bought to enhance personal styles and lifestyles. Such

[2]  Fennell, Phillipson, and Evers, *Sociology of Old Age*.

items are increasingly 'read' as positional goods, that is, they are used to distinguish members of one social group from another. Thus, rather than status distinctions being dependent on class, as determined by income differentials and 'what one does', or, in the case of a retired person, what one no longer does, social identity increasingly relies upon what one buys, how one dresses, what sports one plays, or where one goes on holiday. What one does with one's leisure time has become highly relevant, and, to the extent that retirement is a form of leisure, we must recognise that it is now a period characterised by rather more than simply being non-productive.

If the first sea change in Western civilisation came with the Agricultural Revolution, and the second with the Industrial Revolution, in the clash of new values and new technologies that characterises post-industrial capitalism, Alvin Toffler discerns a 'Third Wave'. He argues that a new pattern of lifestyles, attitudes, and work roles is emerging to accompany transformations in political, economic, and social structures.[3] The details of these developments need not concern us immediately, but if we accept the overall premiss, then it is clear that fundamental social issues will require rethinking. Once institutionalised through retirement, later life is now being deinstitutionalised. This fracturing suggests that rather than focus on the social construction of the life cycle, as a fixed set of stages occupied by people of particular age bands, we should analyse the ways in which it is being deconstructed by individual elders, or groups of older people, negotiating their own life courses. Perhaps it is no coincidence that as futurologists debate the Third Wave, those of us studying ageing have had cause to speculate about the phenomenon of the Third Age, for arguably, these transitions reflect, first, the impact of modernity and, secondly, its supersession by postmodernity. The institutions, social groupings, and identities that formed the structures and roles necessary to industrial capitalism as a series of age-based production processes culminating in dependency appear to be fracturing in the wake of a shift towards a service economy in which older people are increasingly portrayed as niche markets of self-reliant 'customers'.

The social construction of ageing in twentieth-century Britain reveals three distinct phases. The first half of the century saw the development of retirement as a mass experience, culminating in its institutionalisation via the 1940s Beveridge reforms. There followed a period of consolidation until the late 1960s. However, since then an increasing fragmentation has been evident, both as regards the time at which people leave

---

[3] A. Toffler, *The Third Wave* (London: Collins, 1980).

work and the ways in which they spend their time thereafter – a phase of life that is increasing in length as life expectancy grows. Members of the present generation surviving into deep old age have experienced more changes than any before. Their lives encompass the pre-technological era, the period of high mass consumption, and the revolution in global electronic media. Significant shifts in the imagery of the life course have also occurred during their lifetime.[4] In order to understand the cultural impact of these changes, it is helpful to examine the ways in which those who studied retirement attempted to conceptualise its effects on older people themselves.

## The view from gerontology, 1940–1970

By the 1940s, the emergence of geriatric medicine had ushered in a pattern of surveillance that effectively medicalised the social world of the old while strengthening the myth that all pensioners were suffering from pathological diseases.[5] This was ironic because, paradoxically, the rise of retirement, as a fixed rite of passage dependent upon chronological age, occurred during a period when the link between the point of retirement and onset of poor health was becoming ever more attenuated. The mental and physiological capacities of people reaching sixty or sixty-five were increasingly difficult to differentiate from those of their younger colleagues. However, the development of gerontology as a problem-orientated umbrella for social medicine, societal ageing, and psychology in many ways entrenched the policy position.

Following the imposition of mandatory retirement ages, old age increasingly became regarded by Western governments as a 'social problem'. Among American sociologists this led initially to a function-alist model predicting law-like generalisations about relationships within the social system designed to maintain its stability. Retirement was seen to act as a filter whereby older workers vacated their economic positions to make way for younger employees, 'so that when the inevitable [decline and death] arrive [they do] not disrupt the orderly functioning of society'.[6] Attention focused on the difficulties individuals had in adjusting to non-work roles. Thus, a socially engineered solution to structural problems in the labour market was represented as a 'natural' consequence of population ageing. Such thinking informed the role

[4] Achenbaum and Stearns, 'Old age and modernization'. See also G. Dalley and M. Denniss, *A View of the Century: Centenarians Talking* (London: Centre for Policy on Ageing, 1997).
[5] Armstrong, *Political Anatomy*.
[6] Bond, Briggs, and Coleman, 'The study of ageing', p. 30.

theory of Talcott Parsons who stressed social isolation and the 'roleless role' resulting from loss of workplace contacts and structure. Reincorporation into society was a matter of finding psychologically appealing substitutes for work satisfaction and sociologically effective compensation for organised comradeship.[7]

Disengagement models clung to an assumption – so often evident in the earlier social surveys – that individuals were having to adjust from lives centred around the culture of the workplace to a socially impoverished future where they would be occupied in a losing battle to keep boredom at bay:

Ordinary men and women have relied on cultural scripts throughout their earlier lives, and when these no longer exist they often lack resources and experience to improvise new ones. Instead, many older people just cling to life as they wait to be relieved of a lonely and useless existence.[8]

However, against such pessimism over alienation and withdrawal from mainstream society, activity theorists maintained that 'successful' ageing was a matter of carrying on with the patterns and values of mid-life, thus forestalling the onset of old age, or of discovering fresh and absorbing roles and activities to maintain wellbeing.[9]

By the late 1960s the rejection of the search for a universal gerontological theory brought a new stress upon contextualisation. Both disengagement and activity theorists were heavily criticised, as interest shifted toward 'the meaning of old age and its biographical and sociological content'.[10] Since then, conflict theorists have argued that disengagement provided legitimation for policies of indifference towards the 'inevitability' of retirement or, alternatively, stigmatised those who never had been 'engaged'. Meanwhile, activity theorists were unduly optimistic in expecting elders to flourish when access to crucial resources and activities, specifically those deriving from paid work, were denied. Moreover, there is a problem with generalisation. The meanings attached to roles by individuals are manifold, as are the opportunities and constraints facing each. Whilst a considerable literature subsequently developed in this vein, most discussion of retirement has been

---

[7] T. Parsons, 'Age and sex in the social structure of the United States', *American Sociological Review* 7 (1942), 604–16.

[8] Z. Blau, *Old Age in a Changing Society* (New York: New Viewpoints, 1973), p. 177, cited in Fennell, Phillipson, and Evers, *Sociology of Old Age*, p. 44.

[9] The two approaches are outlined in E. Cumming and W. E. Henry, *Growing Old: The Process of Disengagement* (New York: Basic Books, 1961), and R. J. Havighurst, 'Successful aging', in R. H. Williams, C. Tibbitts, and W. Donahue (eds.), *Processes of Aging*, 2 vols. (New York: Atherton, 1963), vol. I, pp. 299–320.

[10] Fennell, Phillipson, and Evers, *Sociology of Old Age*, p. 49.

framed by the political economy perspective. Here the images attached to retirement are seen as ideological devices.[11]

## Reconstructing and deconstructing retirement

Although the political utility of such polarised ideas was not directly apparent in postwar British policy, disengagement and activity theories mirrored the diametrically opposed justifications offered at different times for retiring or retaining older workers. As we saw in chapter 2, during the interwar depression, high unemployment placed jobs for younger men at a premium and older operatives were retired on the grounds that their physical frailty lessened productive capacity. However, in the postwar era of reconstruction and labour shortage, their experience and reliability were emphasised in order to encourage retention. Such ambiguity allowed policymakers to hold older workers in abeyance as a reserve of labour, using these opposed caricatures as and when they were appropriate.[12] The tactic echoed the way a 'surplus army' of women had been drawn into the workforce during wartime but returned to the domestic hearth during peacetime accompanied by a strong dose of propaganda about their duties as housewives and mothers.

For Harper and Thane, the period from the mid-1940s to the mid-1960s saw a consolidation of the retirement 'tradition' whereby 'the permanent core group of elderly who had always retired for reasons of ill health was greatly swelled'.[13] Since then retirement patterns have become more complex. Rigid age-grading on the basis of state schemes has been modified and lessened by the growth in occupational pensions and the development of varied routes out of employment, including early and partial retirement. What were once regarded as basically male problems of transition into life after work are becoming far less sex-

---

[11] Ibid., pp. 52–4. Motivated by the 'personal involvement research' of Peter Townsend, political economists have politicised the experiences affecting later life. The crisis in public expenditure beginning in the 1970s led to neo-Marxist critiques of a policy agenda that 'welfarised' older people by treating the symptoms of social inequality, rather than examining the causes. While political economists have mounted a sustained assault on both neo-classical economics and functionalist sociology, their influence has been more marked in Europe than in North America, where, it is claimed, the quest for a macro-theory was abandoned and a positivist 'retreat into methodology' came to treat older people 'primarily as scientific objects' (A. Walker, 'Ageing and the social sciences: the North American way', *Ageing and Society* 7 (1982), 235–41 (238)).

[12] E. Mizruchi, 'Abeyance processes, social policy and ageing', in A.-M. Guillemard (ed.), *Old Age and the Welfare State* (London: International Sociological Association/ Sage, 1983), pp. 45–52.

[13] Harper and Thane, 'The consolidation of "old age" '.

specific, as male and female employment trends begin to converge. Moreover, the growth of leisure and lifelong learning have impacted upon notions of the value of paid work.[14] There now exists a greater flexibility around workending, reflected in the use of the term 'decade of retirement'.[15]

Certainly, during the 1950s and 1960s, retirement was characterised as a time of crisis and sickness, worth delaying at all costs. Emphasis on the value of continuing to work promoted a vision of retirement as social death.[16] But, with the mass unemployment of the 1970s and 1980s, retirement was reinterpreted as an active choice.[17] Moreover, staying active no longer meant the need to stay integrated in work; instead, it was for individuals to define their own retirement leisure programme. This reversal, like those before it, and in keeping with shifts elsewhere in Europe,[18] was predicated on the need of employers to 'shake out' older workers in order to make way for the young unemployed.

The spread of both voluntary early retirement and redundancy among men, coincident with a tendency for some women to return to the labour force in mid-life, suggests that the relationship between retirement and dependency is becoming less clear-cut. By 1989, in Great Britain, over half of men aged sixty to sixty-four and one-third aged fifty-five to fifty-nine were no longer in paid employment. Reasons for this decline in labour force participation were fourfold: health, the financial position of the worker, the employer's demand for labour, and the suitability of older workers to fill new vacancies. According to Family Expenditure Survey data analysed by Altmann, during the 1970s 70 per cent of early-retired men were receiving health-related benefits. This led her to conclude that 'most early retirement is not voluntary, but is forced upon people for health reasons'.[19] However, Labour Force Survey data from 1986 suggested that health was no longer the key

[14] F. Laczko and C. Phillipson, *Changing Work and Retirement: Social Policy and the Older Worker* (Buckingham: Open University Press, 1991).

[15] T. Schuller, 'Work-ending: employment and ambiguity in later life', in B. Bytheway, T. Keil, P. Allatt, and A. Bryman (eds.), *Becoming and Being Old: Sociological Approaches to Later Life* (London: Sage, 1989), pp. 41–54.

[16] P. Johnson, *The Structured Dependency of the Elderly: A Critical Note*, CEPR Discussion Paper No. 202 (London: CEPR, 1988), points out that a structured dependency argument attempts, not unproblematically, to explain the construction of 'old age' during these years as a deviant category created by means of social control.

[17] Laczko and Phillipson, *Changing Work*; F. Laczko, 'Between work and retirement: becoming "old" in the 1980s', in Bytheway, Keil, Allatt, and Bryman, *Becoming and Being Old*, pp. 24–40.

[18] A.-M. Guillemard, 'The making of old age policy in France', in Guillemard, *Old Age and the Welfare State*, pp. 75–99.

[19] R. Altmann, 'Incomes of the early retired', *Journal of Social Policy* 11 (1981), 355–64 (358).

variable. Rather, for both men and women – including those with poor health – labour market reasons predominated. In time of recession, older workers were being 'discouraged' from continuing, especially men in heavy industry and manufacturing.[20] Against this there was some encouragement for older women to retrain to fill the skills gap being left by the fall in school-leavers and a tokenistic absorption of older people into unskilled service occupations (supermarket chains, DIY super-stores, and some high street retailers leading this public relations exercise). Health-related factors remained significant, nevertheless, in that one-sixth of women aged fifty-five to fifty-nine left employment to care for a relative in poor health. The transition from paid employment to unpaid caregiving is clearly of considerable import, given that the shrinking age-band from forty-five to sixty-four includes peak numbers of female informal carers.[21]

Whatever the individual reasons for retiring, there would appear to be a popular desire for flexible workending. Of course, income remains a crucial consideration, and as yet there are few occupations that are sufficiently lucrative for people to be able to retire at, say, age forty-five. Many people also enjoy work for its own sake and, while considerable numbers of people leave work, willingly or otherwise, before statutory retirement age, there remains a vocal lobby in favour of the right to work on to whatever age the individual wishes. For example, in the United States the mean age at leaving work has gone down (to sixty-two), but anti-ageist pressure has succeeded in raising the mandatory retirement age to seventy.

Levels of personal satisfaction in retirement will depend on people being able to continue to pursue the types of activities and relationships that matter to them, rather than their being active for the sake of it.[22] It is therefore appropriate that, having described what older people do, sociologists study the motives underlying such action. For role theorists, different individuals will be regarded as retiring more or less successfully depending on their degree of attachment to or disenchantment with work. It has also been claimed that the nature of work can influence one's evaluation of leisure, with heavily absorbed professionals such as medical consultants and physically taxed manual workers both pre-senting relatively limited leisure profiles compared to bored office workers who have more time, energy, and psychological need to develop engaging pastimes. For some, leisure represents an extension of work,

[20] F. Laczko, A. Dale, S. Arber and G. N. Gilbert, 'Early retirement in a period of high unemployment', *Journal of Social Policy* 17 (1988), 313–33.

[21] S. Arber and J. Ginn, *Gender and Later Life* (London: Sage, 1991).

[22] Fennell, Phillipson, and Evers, *Sociology of Old Age*, p. 46.

but for others it functions as a contrast.[23] There may, therefore, be some connection between the nature of one's employment and the smoothness of the transition into retirement. However, the analysis of contemporary lifestyles suggests that increasingly people in all walks of life regard the leisure sphere as their basis for social and psychological identification. The implications of this trend for the meaning of retirement are considerable.

Certainly, the current image of later life would appear to offer more than a series of substitute activities to replace the satisfactions of work. Under modernity, Featherstone and Hepworth claim that the centrality of 'youthful energy in the service of social change' contrasts with an image of retirement as a 'normal' consequence of reaching age sixty, for a woman, and sixty-five, for a man.[24] However, they suggest that such a vision is fragmenting, and that a potential for reconstruction of, even 'customising' one's own retirement is becoming increasingly evident. Such an observation implies a significant shift in the conceptualisation of the relationship between work and society, but to what extent have the subjects of this thinking reflected upon their own predicament?[25]

### Age consciousness

Age consciousness was brought about through the administrative classification of older people which created an enhanced awareness of stigma.[26] It is thus a form of self-consciousness. The critical issue now is what will people do with that awareness. It would be stretching credibility to compare age consciousness directly with class consciousness in the Marxist sense of a group recognising its objective structural position and performing a historic role in the transformation of society. Nevertheless, in the same manner that the proletariat can shift from being class 'in itself' – an aggregate of workers with a shared structural position but no collective identity – to class 'for itself' with a common awareness of its true interests and means of achieving them, so one could hypothesise a situation in which solidarities will develop amongst elders. There are a number of reasons why this has never previously

[23] J. Clarke and C. Critcher, *The Devil Makes Work: Leisure in Capitalist Britain* (London: Macmillan Education, 1985), pp. 18–19.

[24] M. Featherstone and M. Hepworth, 'Images of ageing', in Bond and Coleman, *Ageing in Society*, pp. 250–75 (pp. 266–7).

[25] M. Featherstone and M. Hepworth, 'Ageing and old age: reflections on the postmodern life course', in Bytheway, Keil, Allatt, and Bryman, *Becoming and Being Old*, pp. 143–57 (p. 145), acknowledge that their position is a speculative one: 'It must not be forgotten that such postmodern theorising is as yet far from being an everyday reality. At best these theories draw attention to emergent cultural tendencies.'

[26] Featherstone and Hepworth, 'Images of ageing'.

occurred: several age groups coexist as pensioners, yet each cohort exhibits a different awareness of social change; older people are segregated amongst themselves, especially according to income; retirement itself disperses individuals who might once have benefited from the collective focus of the workplace. Older people have not been powerful, or even particularly influential, in the political arena, not least because retirement tends to entrench lifelong differences and splits the pensioner vote accordingly.[27] Nevertheless, as I will argue in chapter 8, the 'new' politics is one in which the voice of new social movements is increasingly heard. By this I mean that environmental campaigners, feminists, and others have developed a lifestyle politics aimed at change more through altering cultural conventions than via the old political power games based more directly on policy and legislation. In this scenario, age consciousness is about awareness of one's position within a cultural or 'civic' environment, rather than simply as a cipher in the policy process.[28]

As we shall see, there is evidence, albeit limited, that such new consciousness is developing. This is not because seasoned campaigners have suddenly become enlightened and sought to foist new ideas on their peers as they have aged. It is because the material basis for cultural change is shifting in important ways. The meaning and status of work and leisure have altered. Given the ageing of the population, this forces a reconceptualisation of the life course to reflect the emergence of the Third Age at a time when the focus of social interest has shifted decisively from production to consumption. Taken together, these trends have profound implications for the sociology of later life. Nevertheless, the following analysis suggests that news of the death of ageism is premature.

### The future of work and leisure

Kohli has observed the need to challenge some deeply held assumptions about the centrality of paid work: 'Given that social life is structured around work and its organisation, how can we theoretically cope with a situation in which a large (and still growing) part of the population has left the domain of formally organised gainful work?'[29] Retired people are

---

[27]  Blaikie and Macnicol, 'Ageing and social policy', p. 77.

[28]  Political representation on behalf of, rather than by, older people is evident in the campaigns of Age Concern and Help the Aged. The need for advocacy by such 'wise others' is perhaps indicative of a continuing societal rejection of economically or culturally impoverished elders who do not fit the consumerist model.

[29]  M. Kohli, 'Ageing as a challenge for sociological theory', *Ageing and Society* 8 (1988), 367–94 (371).

in no position to overturn the work society, where marginalisation via practices such as schooling and retirement produces forms of isolation which become 'social problems'. Difficulties of adjustment are seen to lie with the agent, not the structure.[30] Alternatively, Gorz argues that those outside work are liberated from it, thus free to oppose it. Yet, since most older people have already worked for most of their lives, any retrospective challenge would be fruitless.[31] They cannot threaten to withdraw their labour, since the employers have done this for them.

However, Handy notes that, as a result of increased mechanisation and the loss of industries to the developing countries, the numbers of jobs in the market economy are shrinking whilst jobs in the state sector have also declined. Hence his prediction of more people working in the 'informal' economy: 'A lot of them will be working at home, doing things for themselves and their neighbours. They will be working in the many different voluntary organisations . . . watching and participating in sport . . . spending less on travel to work . . . they may retain their quality of life on a lower expenditure.'[32]

Through the 1980s Handy argued that mid-lifers would be at the leading edge of this transformation.[33] And bodies such as REACH (Retired Executives Action Clearing House) and the Third Age Network now seek to place retired managers in part-time posts and consultancies: the impulse is largely voluntary, financial gain playing second fiddle to pride of worth. Meanwhile, the Association of Retired Persons demands that not only should retired people provide a pool of potential labour, but it is their right to continue in work – hence the Alliance Against Ageism campaign that lobbies for legislation to prohibit age discrimination in job advertisements.

Against such willingness to work, enforced leisure or unpaid domestic labour remain the lot of the many. The Third Age Network defines the Third Age as beginning 'around fifty, when children have left home, material and career pressures lessen, and there is time to enjoy the fruits of earlier labours'.[34] Ideally, they aver, life should consist of the personalised reallocation of time within the 'three boxes' – education, work, and leisure – which are currently locked in a chronological sequence

[30] See J. Hockey and A. James, *Growing Up and Growing Old: Ageing and Dependency in the Life Course* (London: Sage, 1993), pp. 155–6.
[31] A. Gorz, *Paths To Paradise: On the Liberation from Work* (London: Pluto Press, 1985); Kohli, 'Ageing as a challenge', 377.
[32] C. Handy, *Taking Stock: Being Fifty in the Eighties* (London: BBC Publications, 1983), pp. 21–38.
[33] C. Handy, *The Future of Work* (Oxford: Blackwell, 1984); C. Handy, *The Age of Unreason* (London: Business Books Limited, 1989).
[34] Third Age Network, 'What Is the Third Age?', *Transitions*, 1 (1990), 2.

from childhood through adulthood to retirement.[35] Significantly, however, the tasks of caring falling to many women – and, increasingly, men – in mid-life and after are assumed absent. To adopt Handy's reasoning would also mean putting an optimistic gloss on the willingness of firms to retrain older employees in handling computer technology – but again we hear the refrain of 'obsolete skills' as the Third Wave washes over them. If citizenship is to be the sibling of survivorship, then resources will have to be more evenly spread.

## Rethinking the life course

While most people can now expect to live into their late seventies, many are also leaving full-time paid work at or before age sixty. The implications of this trend are critical for the sociological interpretation of the life course. We have seen that for sociology to regard the sphere of production (and, by extension, reproduction) as its singular focus would be anachronistic, since retirement – the present experience of a fifth of the population and the likely future for a great many more – is defined by the absence of full-time paid work. Secondly, the discussion of the range of inequalities, political, educational, and marketing interventions implies the need to understand cultural shifts in perceptions. Through both pensions and consumption, later life is essentially linked to the economy. Insurance companies, advertisers, and treasury ministers are only too aware of this, yet the social and cultural effects of a changed balance in life-stages remain largely unexplored.

The conceptualisation of society according to life-stages appears to have become progressively more significant. In the same way that childhood was 'invented' in an earlier epoch, the late nineteenth and early twentieth centuries saw the discovery of old age.[36] As part of the Victorian impulse to classify all things, society became a population, statistically monitored and increasingly subdivided into age bands. Since then, via Freud, social work, Dr Spock, Mods, and Rockers, we can trace ever more refined – and redefined – subdivisions of development in early life: from infancy, to childhood, to adolescence and teenage years.[37] Latterly, and especially with the popular recognition that people

---

[35] F. Best, *Flexible Life Scheduling: Breaking the Education–Work–Retirement Lockstep* (New York: Praeger, 1980).

[36] See Ariès, *Centuries of Childhood*. A. J. Benson, *Prime Time: History of Middle Age in Twentieth-Century Britain* (Harlow: Longman, 1997), emphasises the importance of age classifications.

[37] H. Hendrick, 'Constructions and reconstructions of British childhood', in A. James and A. Prout (eds.), *Constructing and Reconstructing Childhood* (Brighton: Falmer Press, 1991), pp. 35–59.

are living longer and staying fit and active for longer, we have begun to talk about the 'young old' and the 'old old', the Third Age of active leisure and a Fourth Age of decrepitude and senility.[38] The extent to which this is merely a semantic reworking of Shakespeare's Seven Ages – what Hazan terms a 'culturally entrenched trope' – or the index of a more profound revision requires exploration.[39]

In a major systematic revaluation Peter Laslett posits a 'New Division of the Life Course': 'First comes an era of dependence, socialisation, immaturity, and education; second an era of independence, maturity, and responsibility, of earning and of saving; third an era of personal fulfilment; and fourth an era of final dependence, decrepitude, and death.'[40] As we saw in chapter 1, the advent of the Third Age presents a distinctive demographic phenomenon. Laslett suggests that a society where over half of all men and women aged twenty-five can expect to reach seventy may be characterised as a Third Age society. This mark was reached in the UK for the first time in around 1950.[41] If one plots a graph of the total population over pensionable age (a curve which rises from 2.7 million in 1901 to 9.7 million in 1981) and superimposes over this the trend-line indicating the proportion of the male population over sixty-five years old who were occupied in paid work (a curve which falls from around 60 per cent in 1911 to 11 per cent in 1981), the point of intersection again falls very near to 1950. In other words, the advent of the Third Age coincides with a point where Britain switched decisively into being an ageing society characterised by high numbers of men in retirement (the figures for women are difficult to compute, and not strictly comparable, because of the prevalence of interrupted (paid) work schedules and consequent statistical distortion).

The messages attending such a major social trend have been remarkably muted. Here we have, for the first time in history, the emergence of a large (and potentially vast) social group whose daily experience does not consist of work or schooling – at least, not in the traditional sense of socialisation for work– and who, crucially, can expect to live for up to a third of their lives in this state. It might, of course, be advanced that population panic over the 'burden' of an ageing population does represent a response to an imminent high demand on the Treasury for pensions and on the National Health Service for medical resources. But

---

[38] B. Neugarten, 'Age groups in American society and the rise of the young old', *Annals of the American Academy of Political and Social Science* 415 (1974), 187–98; P. Laslett, 'The emergence of the Third Age', *Ageing and Society* 7 (1987), 113–60.
[39] H. Hazan, *From First Principles: An Experiment in Ageing* (Westport, CT, and London: Bergin and Garvey, 1996), p. 11.
[40] Laslett, *A Fresh Map*, p. 4.      [41] Laslett, 'The emergence', 145.

this is to miss the point that most of these people are and will be relatively healthy adults whose social and cultural needs over many years stretch far beyond what can be delivered by the state. It is not simply that, blinkered by an adherence to a view of society driven by work, we – both intellectual commentators and the general public – have difficulty in conceiving of a world orientated towards the consumption of leisure. Rather, the legacy of the Enlightenment teaches us that that world must also be one motivated by positive moral imperatives, and we have difficulty in seeing leisure as anything but self-indulgence – that is, time spent not endeavouring to work for the betterment of society. A profound contradiction exists when we cannot conceive a useful role – either as producers, reproducers, or wise elders – for a social group that will shortly be larger than any other. The once abrupt transition from work and adulthood to old age decline no longer applies. A space has opened up which the term 'retirement' does not wholly elucidate. Sealey thus appeals: 'It seems to me that [here] the true meaning of retirement is to be found: not at the beginning of old age but at the very end; that is, where relinquishment, the release of our hold on what has become too burdensome, is truly appropriate ... [H]elp me find a word to replace "retirement" which would affirm the potentially joyous new freedoms and opportunities of life after sixty.'[42]

'Potentially' is the keyword in the above quotation. In defining the Third Age as the 'era of personal fulfilment', and 'the crown of life', Laslett adds an important proviso to what might be mistakenly regarded as a simply numerical argument.[43] Personal fulfilment can be achieved only when society at large adjusts to the cultural requirements of a Third Age group, themselves perceived as a cultural vanguard or as the 'trustees of the future'. Whilst it is manifestly evident that such a situation does not currently exist, the conditions of existence for such a changed societal disposition are not entirely clear. They must include the provision of routes through the 'fresh map' that Laslett has drawn, as well as resources, educational and otherwise. But the underlying will to imagine a different future lies with younger age groups and there is as yet little evidence of a changed world view amongst SecondAgers.

---

[42] J. Sealey, 'Whither the aged?', *Listener*, 14 June 1990, 6–8 (8).

[43] By the same token, the Third Age need not be age-based: for instance, Mozart lived his Third Age simultaneously with the First and a great athlete may be said to be enjoying shared Second and Third Ages. The implication, in both these cases (though perhaps not always), is that the Fourth Age comes too soon, hence the observation that Olympic swimmers, for instance, are 'past it' at twenty-five (while, generally, sports-persons still competing beyond forty are considered 'extraordinary') (Stearns, *Old Age*, p. 156, discussing Mark Spitz). Nevertheless, such an early peak remains the preserve of the chosen few.

Nevertheless, it is reasonable to predict a shift in thinking among succeeding generations, for:

The time when, at the age of twenty-five, an English woman has longer to live in the Third Age than the Second Age, cannot be far distant, and English men will no doubt be in the same position a decade or two later. The Third Age has come to stay, and covers a considerable and increasing part of everyone's experience. It is becoming more and more realistic to make plans for the Third Age at the outset of the Second.[44]

## Avenues of empowerment?

The devaluing of the state pension in real terms has created mass insecurity. As a result there is no shortage of banks, building societies, and life insurance companies clamouring to give financial advice on savings and investments, including pension plans, and all are eager to catch their customers sooner rather than later. The demand for such services reflects a degree of expectation that a lengthy retirement will be the norm and that all should calculate accordingly. However, there is little evidence among 25-year-olds that a cultural vision of 'our future selves' accompanies such directed financial foresight. It would perhaps be foolish to expect those committed to the future of the work society to provide a lead here. Indeed, despite the fact that a quarter of the UK population is now looking ahead to between two and three decades of post-work experience, in the 1980s less than 10 per cent of retirees underwent systematic preparation.[45] However, this inadequacy has been seized upon by the pre-retirement movement, and latterly mid-life planning consultants, whose mission has been to provide survival kits. Nevertheless, practical manuals about 'taking stock' and 'coping with change' necessarily stress individual adjustment, rarely commenting on the structural upheavals that form the backdrop.[46] To the extent that retirement culture is portrayed at all, it is presented as a set of personal projects.

Certain of these will coalesce around collective programmes, notably in the local community, where a discernible demand exists for adult education courses that, in Cooper and Bornat's memorable phrase, are 'combating the woolly bunny' by replacing special needs strictures with an equal opportunities philosophy.[47] Peer health counselling and, indeed, the Universities of the Third Age are forms of mutual aid that

---

[44] Laslett, *A Fresh Map*, p. 90.
[45] A. Coleman, *Preparation for Retirement in England and Wales* (Leicester: NIACE, 1990).
[46] Handy, *Taking Stock*; A. Coleman and Chiva, *Coping With Change*.
[47] M. Cooper and J. Bornat, 'Equal opportunity or special need: combating the woolly bunny', *Journal of Educational Gerontology* 3, 1 (1988), 28–41.

testify to self-selected challenges. 'Education for leisure' becomes a priority as retirees find they have to 'relearn some of the arts of living lost in the Industrial Revolution'.[48]

Against this, we have seen that the work ethic dies hard. However, different cohort effects may become apparent in the coming decades. Older people tend to continue to vote as they did when they first entered paid work. Thus, rather than becoming more politically conservative as they have aged, a sizeable minority of today's pensioners have preserved socialist convictions.[49] Likewise, the National Pensioners Convention, a coalition of groups peopled by those whose formative experiences included the Second World War and the creation of the welfare state, and whose working lives saw both the rise and fall of manufacturing, purports to have 1.5 million members, many of whom were voluble in their dissent against the dismantling of the welfare state by government in the early 1990s.[50] By 2025 the over-50s will represent 51 per cent of the electorate, but these children of the 1960s may well see things differently. As Martin points out, 'newer, more hedonistic imperatives are essentially individualistic'.[51] The ways in which such ideology informs the Me Generation as it ages will be critical to future age consciousness, particularly if this generation manages to shift the balance of power in society towards later life.

Allied to the rejection of deficit models some writers have displayed commitment to the empowerment of elders by stressing their potential as a social resource – for instance, as educators, Justices of the Peace, voluntary workers, community activists, and spiritual guides.[52] For Midwinter the route to recognition lies less in material redistribution than through an enhancement of citizenship. Clearly, this requires a sufficient 'social wage' to enable truly egalitarian access to full social participation. Yet, he states, 'the seachange would and must be cultural rather than economic. It must amount to an acknowledgement that disappearing work, properly appreciated, is a liberation, not a frightening disbenefit. It requires that we believe that the old man on Sinbad's shoulders has been stultifying labour, not, in fact, "the burden of pensions".'[53]

[48]  E. P. Thompson, 'Time, work discipline and industrial capitalism', *Past and Present* 39 (1967), 56–97 (91).
[49]  R. Jowell and C. Airey (eds.), *British Social Attitudes: The 1984 Report* (London: Gower, 1984).
[50]  M. Whitfield, 'Pensioners poised for a pivotal role', *Independent*, 21 March 1994, 8.
[51]  B. Martin, 'The cultural construction', p. 76.
[52]  S. Jones, 'The elders; a new generation', *Ageing and Society* 6 (1986), 313–31; Laslett, 'The emergence'; Laslett, *A Fresh Map.*
[53]  E. Midwinter, 'Workers versus pensioners?', *Social Policy and Administration* 23 (1989), 205–10 (210). See E. Midwinter, Review of P. Johnson, Conrad, and Thomson, *Workers Versus Pensioners, Ageing and Society* 9, 4 (1989), 449–50 (p. 450):

Yet it may be argued that citizenship too has changed, from a rights-based philosophy to a consumer-based ethos, where pensioners are another client group in the mixed economy of welfare or, rather, several differentiated sets of customers. While a market-driven approach to needs may better fulfil specialised requirements, it may also weaken the clout of 'pensioners' as a unified political entity.[54] One might also speculate as to a theoretical schism in which consumer culture 'explains' the Third Age, while structured dependency continues to capture the plight of those in the Fourth.

## The impact of consumer culture

The current imagery of a retirement lifestyle evokes a transition to a new life, rather than a continuation of the old. The picture of later life, promoted especially in magazines such as Choice (the very title is indicative), has shifted from sickness and decline to health, liberation, and 'refurbishment'. The later phases of life are now less fixed, the order less definite. The 'chronological bonds' which once bound people in to age-appropriate behaviours – marriage at twenty-five, children at thirty, retirement at sixty or sixty-five, and so on – are being manipulated. As the boundaries of adult life get increasingly hazy, as grandmothers start to dress as their daughters do and grandfathers jog with their sons, so the routemaps for retirement become less distinct. Popular perceptions of ageing have shifted, from the dark days when the 'aged poor' sat in motionless rows in the workhouse to a paternalistic pause when 'the elderly' were expected to don the retirement uniform to modern times, when older citizens are encouraged not just to dress 'young' and look

> Of course, there is a grave challenge to be faced, but it is about culture as well as arithmetic. We require a more universal acceptance of the character of old age now as something new and positive: a goodish last phase of life beyond the age-old chores of work and child-raising with human beings, thus freed, realizing other talents and finding other identities. With that general acceptance of a decent balance of work and leisure over the lifespan, older people may come to be regarded as citizens rather than pensioners.

[54] P. Higgs, 'Citizenship theory and old age: from social rights to surveillance', in Jamieson, Harper, and Victor, Critical Approaches, pp. 118–31 (p. 128), remarks: 'Citizens, through "technologies of the self" . . . are encouraged to take greater personal responsibility for their health and for extending the period of their third age; however, as those who move into a fourth age of needing health and welfare services discover, at this point they are transformed from consumers into objects of consumption [by the "medical gaze"]'. See also C. Gilleard and P. Higgs, 'Cultures of ageing: self, citizen and the body', in V. Minichiello, N. Chappell, and H. Kendig (eds.), Sociology of Aging: International Perspectives (Melbourne: International Sociological Association, 1997), pp. 82–92, and L. Martin, H. Gutman, and P. Hutton (eds.), Technologies of the Self: A Seminar with Michel Foucault (London: Tavistock, 1988).

youthful, but to exercise, have sex, diet, take holidays, and socialise in ways indistinguishable from those of their children's generation. A cursory glance at any one of the range of magazines now targeted at ThirdAgers (see chapter 4) will provide a flavour of the new morality. Take, for example, this list of features from the cover of a recent issue of *Good Times*: 'Do dads make good mums? Role swapping in later life'; 'Super cruise offers to Europe and the Caribbean'; 'Take a jump! You can parachute at any age'; 'Working from home: how to set up in style'.[55]

The reasons behind such shifts in imagery lie with the emergence of consumer culture.[56] The character of that culture owes much to its focus in the 1960s and after on younger adults but, as the Western world ages, so businesses have become sensitive to a potential 'mature market'. The continuing financial disadvantage of many pensioners has not held back the drive to 'capture the Grey Panther' by tapping supposedly vast reserves of disposable income: 'a market currently worth a conservative £10 billion'.[57] Characteristically, *Choice* was voted General Consumer Magazine of the Year for three years running between 1994 and 1996 in the Bradford and Bingley Personal Finance Media Awards 'for excellence in personal finance journalism'.[58] Market researchers sometimes appear to know more about what goes on in the minds of today's elders and mid-lifers than social scientists. Yet for all the sophistication of psychographic segmentation, lifestyle analysis, and other forms of detailed niche marketing, the bottom line in selling to the old seems to be age itself. Paradoxically, the more producers recognise and respond to the diversity of the mature market, the more chronology comes into play. Thus, while targeting reflects a sensitivity to demographic, socio-economic, and health variables within the 50+ population, all appear to be closely correlated with specific age cohorts or generational clusters with a supposedly common experience of historical events. As a result, under-65s ('primelifers') are distinguished from people over sixty-five ('seniors'), the 'young old' from the 'old old' from the 'oldest old', the 1900–10 cohort segregated from the 1910–20

---

[55] *Good Times*, February/March 1996.

[56] M. Featherstone and M. Hepworth, 'Changing images of retirement: an analysis of representations of ageing in the popular magazine *Retirement Choice*', in Bromley, *Gerontology*, pp. 219–24; Featherstone and Hepworth, 'Images of ageing'.

[57] BEST Limited, *The Grey Market: A Golden Opportunity* (conference mailing, 1989). Beck notes that 'by 2030, when the oldest [baby]boomers are eighty-four and the youngest have turned sixty-five, there will be an estimated 65 million Americans sixty-five and older – more than twice as many as today' (M. Beck, 'The new middle age', 56).

[58] *Choice*, December 1996, 3.

cohort on the basis of mindsets attaching to the key 'time signatures' of each decade. The market is not just trailing the babyboomers or the thirtysomethings or the Synthesizers, it is also exploring the psychology and 'value-programming' of the Traditionalists (aged ten at any point between 1919 and 1949), In-betweeners (postwar, pre-pill), and so on. Whereas the implication remains that the impact of an era on upbringing was uniform, clearly not all people who grew up during, say, the Depression will have a respect for authority, a preference for stability, and an emphasis on group work as the Traditionalist categorisation predicts.[59] Too many other variables – class, education, ethnicity, gender, geography, media exposure, social network – have to be taken into account. There is clearly a world of difference between a 'go/go' and a 'no/go' (based on health status), or a 'Glam' and a 'Neo-puritan' (based on income differential). Such images and expectations do not rest comfortably with either the desire to abandon myths and stereotypes leading to ageism or the fact that consumer lifestyles cannot be attained without sufficient occupational pensions, cultural capital, or requisite vitality.

More insidious is the taboo on deep old age fostered by the continued obsession with youthfulness. In contemporary consumer culture, the body is a legitimate site for all manner of rejuvenatory discourses and cosmetic practices. But, if, through these, mid- and later life stages become increasingly difficult to differentiate, so deep old age suffers from yet greater distancing, stigmatisation, and denial. The 'positive' ageing discourse effectively eclipses consideration of illness and decline, yet final decay and death take on a heightened hideousness since these will happen, regardless of whatever cultural, economic, or body capital one might possess: Rita Hayworth suffered long and hard from Alzheimer's disease; Marlene Dietrich died 'lonely and confused . . . a little old lady, crippled and bed-ridden . . . in constant pain'.[60]

Signs of ageing have been equated with bodily betrayals, stigmata of actual or incipient frailty or dependency, of barrenness and loss of self-control. As the visual mass media become increasingly invasive, such outwardly visible 'aversive' properties can only strengthen desires to age gracefully, maintain mid-life postures, and retard the inevitable via an array of distancing techniques. In *The Loneliness of the Dying*, Elias imagines the alienation felt by those who have crossed the Rubicon

---

[59] J. Ostroff, *Successful Marketing to the 50+ Consumer: How to Capture One of the Biggest and Fastest Growing Markets in America* (Englewood Cliffs, NJ: Prentice Hall, 1989).

[60] J. Dalrymple, 'Dietrich: the last take', *The Sunday Times*, 10 May 1992, Focus section, 11.

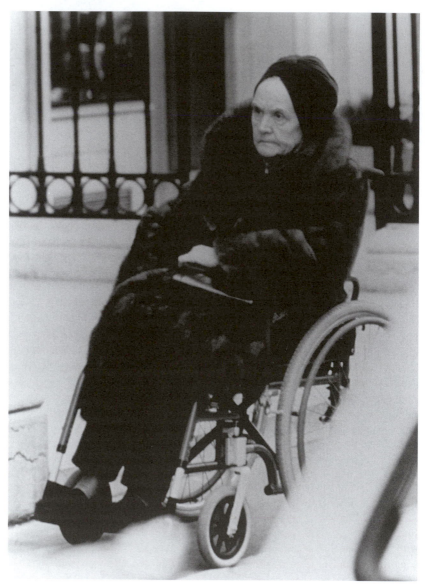

2    Marlene Dietrich as few will remember her. Glamour has its sell-by date.
© People in Pictures Ltd, photograph by Peter Sylent.

into 'senility' and implicates medicalisation.[61] Dying tends to occur in twilight institutions, screened from the everyday world of the non-aged, socially, temporally, and spatially marginalised. Hockey and James analyse the implications of metaphorically picturing life as a cycle, with infantilisation – the return to 'second childhood, mere oblivion' – the logical terminus.[62]

'Old age' has been supplanted by two, sequential categories, the Third Age and the Fourth. There is tragic irony in this reworking of life stages, for while the Third Age suggests an emancipatory view of retirement as adult life without the responsibilities of career and children, this has been achieved only by a socially suppressing the darker side of retirement as death's ante-chamber. Shakespeare's seventh age 'sans teeth, sans eyes, sans taste, sans everything' – has simply been renamed the Fourth Age.[63]

## Gender, race, and ethnicity: difference and diversity

This is not the only tear rending the Panglossian veil of the 'liberation of the elders'.[64] Divisions among our elders are considerable: retirement for many continues to be an economically dependent phase, characterised by poverty, material deprivation, and a dwindling quality of life while, for a minority, later life means endless holidays in the sun, busy volunteering, and 'lifestyle' – Woopies (well-off older persons), Glams (grey, leisured and moneyed), and the like. The emergence of such acronymic social identities may be 'consistent with an individualistic ethos, describing faceless individuals who serve as representatives of lifestyles', but it does reflect a degree of cultural segmentation among real people.[65] Meanwhile, as the discussion above intimates, better health statuses and higher life expectancy allow a sharper gradient to emerge between the fit and active ('use it or lose it') majority and a minority group suffering from chronic and acute illnesses. A general judgement might be that most older people are neither affluent nor infirm, but both poor and relatively fit and well. Most older people have incomes not far above subsistence and most certainly not on a par with Yuppies.[66] Yet, it would be a mistake to assume that this

---

[61] N. Elias, *The Loneliness of the Dying* (Oxford: Basil Blackwell, 1985).

[62] Hockey and James, *Growing Up and Growing Old*.

[63] W. Shakespeare, *As You Like It*, Act II, Scene VII, lines 164–6, in Shakespeare: Complete Works, ed. W. J. Craig (Oxford University Press, 1906), p. 227.

[64] See S. Jones (ed.), *The Liberation of the Elders* (Stoke-on-Trent: Beth Johnson Foundation, 1976).

[65] Hockey and James, *Growing Up and Growing Old*, p. 137.

[66] J. Falkingham and C. Victor, *The Myth of the Woopie: Incomes, the Elderly, and Targeting*

commonality confers homogeneity in lifestyle. Whilst differences exists according to class, health status, age, and cohort, it is also necessary to account for the fragmentation of later life experience by gender, race, and ethnicity.

The sharp discontinuity affected by the end of paid work was not a common experience for many of today's retired women, whose domestic labours have remained continuous, and often increased as their partners and parents have aged. Moreover, as life expectancies continue to increase, growing numbers will also have to tend ageing parents.[67] Indeed, the discourse around the feminisation of later life, where not only more women live longer but their disadvantaged lifetime pensions position carries through into an impoverished standard of living relative to men, produces a new and disturbing inflection to old arguments: domestic labour, continuing into retirement, becomes community care on the cheap.[68]

Arber and Ginn indicate the extraordinary invisibility of women from sociological accounts of ageing. Given the disproportionate numbers of women compared to men in later life – one-fifth of women are over sixty-five against 13 per cent of men; in the seventy-five to eighty-four age range women outnumber men by 75 per cent – research is lacking in three key areas: the distribution of household resources and domestic division of labour; family relationships, including divorce, grandparent-hood, and widowhood (an experience affecting half of all women over sixty-five, but only one-sixth of men); and class. The bases of gender differentiation in later life can be addressed only using a processual approach that considers lifetime shifts in circumstances. Taking, for example, husband's last occupation as an indicator of an older woman's social class is problematic since less than 40 per cent of women over sixty-five are currently married and half live alone. On the other hand, to classify according to a woman's last occupation would be equally perverse since many have not engaged in paid labour since they married forty years ago.[69]

A similar opacity concerns issues of race and ethnicity. Alongside the disadvantages faced by many older people, discrimination based on non-white status, perceived absences in access to services, and being

---

*Welfare*, STICERD/LSE Welfare State Programme, Discussion Paper No. 55 (London: LSE, 1991).

[67] A situation mirrored elsewhere in the West: by the mid-1980s, for the first time the average American couple had more parents than children.

[68] J. Finch, *Family Obligations and Social Change* (Oxford: Polity Press, 1989).

[69] Arber and Ginn, 'The invisibility of age'.

non-English-speaking have exercised applied researchers.[70] Although discrimination and disadvantage strongly imply victim status, Blakemore and Boneham suggest two further ideal types, both of which reflect the significance of the past life courses in ongoing culture contact. The 'self-reliant pioneer' notion suggests that 'older people in minority ethnic groups will be more influenced by their roles and position in their own communities than by majority norms and expectations', while the 'gradually adjusting migrant' image implies integration.[71] If such markers of difference are integral to the experience of retirement, then serious questions have to be asked of the suppositions underlying its conceptualisation, not least those ideas concerning the changed role of the family and status of older persons within it. The modernisation thesis contends that nuclear family living has supplanted extended kinship connections. Consequently, older people's once vital household roles have been devalued. Popular myth holds that older black and Asian people in Britain inhabit, or wish to inhabit, more extended networks which preserve their statuses intact. However, research indicates varying forms of accommodation to conflicting pressures: 'Some minority ethnic communities demonstrate a surprising degree of resilience, adapting traditions, and family structures but retaining core values and making care of older people a priority; in others, there is inter-generational conflict and a loss of community identity.'[72] Accordingly, any unilinear historical understanding of changing family and community structures in retirement is found wanting. The persistent material effects of discrimination, be they on grounds of gender, race, or ethnicity, are reflected in unequal access to resources. Such inequality is connected to failures to perceive variations in retirement experience that are often grounded in lifetime differences.

### Research agendas

How, then, are we to grasp what the sociology of later life looks like? What meanings, what social processes fill the lacuna to which we have attached the label? What is the 'ordinary' popular culture of retirement? What are the qualities of 'ordinariness' and under what conditions could they be regarded as acceptable and normative or unacceptable and deviant? What might constitute an effective, sympathetic analysis of

---

[70] L. Donaldson and M. Johnson, 'The health of older Asians', in J. Johnson and R. Slater (eds.), *Ageing and Later Life* (London: Sage, 1993), pp. 76–83.

[71] K. Blakemore and M. Boneham, *Age, Race and Ethnicity: A Comparative Approach* (Buckingham: Open University Press, 1994); K. Blakemore, 'Ageing and ethnicity' in J. Johnson and Slater, *Ageing and Later Life*, pp. 68–75 (p. 72).

[72] Blakemore and Boneham, *Age, Race and Ethnicity*, p. 37.

popular consciousness? Although good investigative research into such issues does exist, some major shifts in the languages of later life have yet to be understood. The cultural lag identifiable in the use of ageist stereotypes and myths which not only assume all older people to be the same, but which also elide the experiences of Third- and FourthAgers, percolates to the higher ground of academic endeavour such that books and articles about 'ageing' are, in fact, not about ageing generally, but at best concern processes of normal ageing beyond the guillotine point of pensionable age or, at worst, are misnomers for treatises on old age. Either way, they fail to confront the continuing relationship between earlier and later life episodes and social and psychological processes. Nevertheless, it is possible to identify ways in which ageing and old age are currently being rethought.

The empirical test of a life course approach is multifaceted: it involves the adoption of a holistic approach to adult life that embraces issues of health, finance, relationships, employment, leisure, and education. It also entails a fusion of psychological and sociological approaches to both personal development and social change – ideally, but not uncritically, a blending of lifespan developmental psychology and life course analysis.

Aside from the sheer complexity of this task, there are several methodological drawbacks. First, although damaging generalisations may be reduced, such an intensively biographical project encounters the danger of producing studies of individual experiences without broader applicability. Secondly, longitudinal research is always difficult because it demands that resources are provided over the very long term and, perhaps more significantly, that teams of researchers remain consolidated over an equally long period. Investigations into later life are hampered by the fact that social scientific interest in longitudinal data began only during the 1940s. Wadsworth's MRC National Survey of Health and Development embraces individuals born since 1946: by 2000 they will be just fifty-four.[73] The National Child Development Survey follows all children born in the week 3 to 9 March 1958, while the British Births Survey (now Child Education and Health) includes all children born in one week in 1970. The OPCS Longitudinal Study has much the largest sample size – approximately 500,000 compared with 16,500 in the National Births Survey – but did not begin to record information until the 1971 census. It will be a long time before such programmes come to consider the retirement phase of their samples. However, the current ESRC Health Variations Programme places an

[73] M. Wadsworth, *The Imprint of Time: Childhood, History, and Adult Life* (Oxford: Clarendon Press, 1991).

emphasis on life course perspectives, and one project by David Blane and colleagues is currently using information from survivors of a 1930s survey into child health and nutrition: 'The participants, now well into their sixties and seventies, are being questioned about their lifetime occupational history, residential history, smoking, and health related behaviours ... Data from the original survey ... are being combined with information about the rest of their lives to investigate how experiences of childhood and adulthood act together to produce socio-economic gradients in health in early old age.'[74]

Other studies, including those discussed in chapter 8, have attempted to assess attitudes and behaviour in later life by reference to survival strategies learned throughout the life course.[75] It is plausible to assume that coping with crises throughout life is a cumulative learning process that can aid in managing the experiences of ageing, but we can only infer such a hypothesis from an understanding of the testimonies of the survivors. However, this will not tell us why others among their cohort did not make it to a ripe old age. Furthermore, research into the lived experience of deep old age (the Fourth Age) is frequently rendered difficult by the social construction of 'confusion' via a medical model which systematically distorts communication. And whilst acknowledgement of the need to rework one's identity provides the therapeutic rationale behind many a reminiscence group, the recognition of the increased number of developmental tasks to be accommodated in later life is far from the minds of most marketers and will not be evident from the imagery of the Third Age alone.

In coming to terms with the challenges to explain and redirect our social philosophies, a literal history of retirement policy is unlikely to provide suitable cues. What is required is an analysis of the cultural ingredients of both past and present policy.[76] Despite the fact that the proportional rise in persons aged over sixty-five – 160 per cent between 1911 and 1951 – was considerably greater than it has been since, the visibility of this earlier phenomenon appears to have been subdued by comparison with shock statistics informing us that the numbers of pensioners will increase by anywhere between 25 and 50 per cent by

[74] C. Power, 'Life course influences', *Health Variations* 1 (1998), 14–15 (D. Blane, 'Social variations in health in early old age: an investigation of precursors in a sixty-year follow-up study'). Other ongoing projects in the Programme include C. Power, 'Social settings at home and work: early and later life influences on health variations', and G. Watt, 'The role of perceptions of family history in persisting inequalities in health and lifestyle'.

[75] P. G. Coleman, *Ageing and Reminiscence Processes: Social and Clinical Implications* (Chichester: Wiley, 1986).

[76] G. B. King and P. Stearns, 'The retirement experience as a policy factor: an applied history approach', *Journal of Social History* 14 (1981), 589–625.

2025. The fears voiced by successive governments over 'alarming rises' in the numbers of older people testify to a recurrent political fear about state support for the less well-off. Such sufferers are frequently cast as victims, whereas, unlike the media amplification of youth revolt, the discourse surrounding population ageing reads like a moral panic without its attendant folk devils.

Towards the end of the nineteenth century youth became 'the most potent metaphor for social change'.[77] A hundred years later, old age does not yet seem set to capture the mantle. However, the postwar rise of consumer culture has opened up new territory. In 1959 Mark Abrams published *The Teenage Consumer* and set in train discussions about youth culture that began to appear quaint by the 1980s as unemployment soared and new fears of delinquency arose. 'Resistance through rituals' became the clarion cry of subcultural theorists, while Abrams had moved on to exploring old age.[78] Social rebellion casts young men as protagonists, but other marginal groups are now mounting challenges to conventional expectations. Indeed, striking parallels between feminism and anti-ageism are being revealed not just in scholarship – some from vanguard women academics themselves now ageing – that fuses the two approaches,[79] but also in reflexive, radical primers like the Hen Co-op's *Growing Old Disgracefully*, which was voted 'Best Book of the Year' by *Choice* magazine in 1993.[80] Meanwhile, applied gerontologists, noting the traditional 'association of race and ethnic relations with "youth" problems such as unemployment and job discrimination', have pointed to the growing needs and claims of ethnic elders and the requirement for multicultural understandings of age.[81] To the broader political discourse framed by advocacy, consciousness-raising, and self-help groups, we should add the impetus of a cultural emphasis on health and lifestyle issues, empowering to ThirdAgers, but often disabling to the image and experience of those inhabiting the Fourth.

Previous experience clearly impacts upon attitudes, behaviour, and circumstances in old age. Thus life course perspectives may be styled 'vertical', in that they aim to trace individual and cohort lifelines through time. The necessary complement, along the 'horizontal' axis, is

[77] D. Hebdige, 'Youth culture', lecture to Birkbeck College Centre for Extra-Mural Studies Summer School, London School of Hygiene, 12 July 1989.

[78] M. Abrams, *The Teenage Consumer* (London: Routledge and Kegan Paul, 1959); M. Abrams, *Beyond Three Score and Ten: A First Report on a Survey of the Elderly* (Mitcham: Age Concern, 1978).

[79] B. Friedan, *The Fountain of Age* (London: Jonathan Cape, 1993); G. Greer, *The Change: Women, Ageing and the Menopause* (London: Hamish Hamilton, 1991).

[80] Hen Co-op, *Growing Old Disgracefully* (London: Judy Piatkus Publishers, 1993).

[81] Blakemore and Boneham, *Age, Race and Ethnicity*, p. 1.

an acknowledgement of the dimensions that fragment the contemporary ageing experience – gender, race and ethnicity, class, and age variations. And whilst inequalities consistently characterised the retirement experience under modernity, in line with postmodernity the life course has become more fragmented. All this requires a shift in emphasis from macro-level studies of relations of power to micro-studies of integration and segregation, and from a political economy perspective to more evidently cultural considerations. However, it is important to retain a materialist focus: the dependency of older people upon the state and its fiscal machinations continues to ensure that standards of living, lifestyles, and quality of life are determined to a degree by socio-structural factors outside the control of individuals. Overlying this are the double jeopardies suffered by older women (ageism plus sexism) and the ethnic elders (ageism plus racism). Meanwhile, although health statuses are vastly improved, death remains certain, chronic disability possible, and decline probable. Thus, whilst positive ageing stresses agency, self-reliance, and empowerment, the ageing experience is characterised by widening inequalities. Social transition can be both enabling and disabling: the revolution in technology has made some older workers redundant while other ThirdAgers are riding the 'Third Wave' and turning the electronic media to their advantage, not just as a form of communication, but, for some, as a means of temporarily escaping immediate constraints by creating virtual bodies.[82] Similarly, modern medicine and design solutions might enhance and prolong life, but ultimately we all run up against a biological limit.

Rather than simply state that everyone fears ageing, it may be more useful to conceive a spectrum of anxieties.[83] Some, such as fear of losing one's earning power and social status, will accompany thoughts about retirement; others – like dysmorphophobia, or the intense fear of looking ugly – signal a desperate wish to cling to youth which appears affected in the face of the deep-seated dread of Alzheimer's disease, incontinence, and death. In between lie apprehensions of reduced mobility, falling capacities, isolation, and dependency. Arguably, people worry more about income and status while still SecondAgers, but, as the ThirdAge progresses, threats of physical and mental decline advance ever closer. Whatever the case, against the economic and social odds, a great deal of personal effort is put into managing the ageing process. It is

[82] M. Featherstone, 'Virtual reality, cyberspace and the ageing body', in C. Hummel and C. J. Lalive D'Epinay (eds.), *Images of Aging in Western Societies* (Geneva: Centre for Interdisciplinary Gerontology, 1995), pp. 246–86.

[83] See, for example, the 'fourteen nameable fears' discussed in Laslett, *A Fresh Map*, pp. 14–15.

this tension between desires to maintain or refashion identities in later life, the unevenly spread resources with which to do this, and the deep inevitability of mortality that will exercise the sociological imagination of the future.

# 4    Altered images

'If politics is the present tense of history, media is the present tense of politics.'[1] Thus speaks a feminist analyst of the 1970s. In so far as it is an acknowledgement of how the more powerful judge significant events or determine the ways in which minorities are portrayed, the remark bears as much relevance to ageism as it does to sexism. Historical analyses help us to interpret the social construction of the life course as we know it today; equally, visual representations of ageing indicate the immediacy of popular understandings. Much has been written and said on the negative stereotyping of older adults in the various media. Indeed, codes of practice to combat visual ageism are now evident, for example in such models as the Gray Panthers' 'media watch' checklist and the publisher Cornet's guidelines.[2] However, relatively little is known of the cultural history of changing images of age in modern Britain.[3]

I have attempted to draw some generalisations from an overview which is admittedly far from comprehensive: some significant sources – for example, television – are mentioned only in passing; others, like photographs, are considered methodologically in depth in the following chapters, but are again far from being a representative cross-section. My aim here has been to suggest possible interpretations rather than to present conclusive content analyses.[4] In particular the goodness-of-fit, or not, between images and lived realities is questioned from a number of angles, each of which indicates the pliability of perceptions. Many of

---

[1] A. V. Mander, 'Her story of history', in A. V. Mander and A. K. Rush (eds.), *Feminism as Therapy* (New York: Random House, 1974), pp. 63–88 (p. 68).

[2] E. Midwinter, *Out of Focus: Old Age, the Press and Broadcasting* (London: Centre for Policy on Ageing in association with Help the Aged, 1991), pp. 54–5.

[3] The first attempt to develop a sociological analysis pertinent to the concerns of social gerontology was that of Featherstone and Hepworth, to whose pioneering endeavours any serious study henceforth must be indebted. See Featherstone and Hepworth, 'Images of ageing', for a synopsis.

[4] There appears to be a fashion, particularly in US research, to quantify images and produce percentage counts of, say, the occurrence of older characters in weekly cartoon strips. Whilst this can produce indicators of general social trends, I prefer to consider the nature of individual representations rather than their volume or incidence.

the same caveats apply to literary sources or auditory sources, neither of which is discussed here, although both are now subjects of increasing gerontological attention.[5]

## Introduction

The emergence of consumer culture entails a shift from the purchase of goods according to need to the inculcation of desire for the aesthetics of particular lifestyles. Advertising becomes increasingly sophisticated, its representations ever more imaginative. For the consumer, individuality is heightened, each of us self-consciously perceiving ourselves as different from the masses; the clothed body becomes the symbol of competitive self-expression. Objects are purchased as aids to self-development.[6] Thus the culture we inhabit is increasingly obsessed with visual presentation. We are constantly on display. In this climate, outward bodily signs become mirrors of morality: if you don't work at keeping your body in shape, then it is implied that you don't care about it.[7] Arguably, in comparison with earlier times when a certain disengaged resignation applied, it has become a duty to resist the onset of signs of decline. So too, our bodies are mirrors of mortality. Each of us is engaged in a losing battle against the ravages of time, ravages that inscribe themselves upon our faces, our hands, our sense of self. Consequently, ageing has become an increasingly sensitive social and personal issue. In focusing attention on the power of images, this chapter aims, first, to locate some of the more salient cultural trends as they affect older people. Secondly, since concepts and experiences of age are scarcely static either, I consider the impact of more people living longer, healthier lives upon the priorities of a society hitherto obsessed with youth.

I am often puzzled when I hear people discussing 'normal' ageing or the 'natural' ageing process. We are all biological creatures, but does age hold much meaning beyond the cultural gloss we paint it with? And, if it does, has not science enabled us to manipulate our destinies? A few years ago the *London Evening Standard* emblazoned the words: 'Test-tube granny has triplets' across its front page. Similarly, 'generation-hopping' was in the news again as two Italian women in their sixties

---

[5] See, for example, M. Sohngen, 'The experience of old age as depicted in contemporary novels', *Gerontologist* 17, 1 (1977), 70–8; J. Traynor, 'Musings on the place of pop records in our lives', *Generations Review* 5, 4 (1995), 7–8.

[6] M. Hepworth, 'Consumer culture and social gerontology', *Education and Ageing* 11, 1 (1996), 19–30.

[7] M. Featherstone, 'The body in consumer culture', in Featherstone, Hepworth, and Turner, *The Body*, pp. 170–96.

became pregnant thanks to advanced reproductive technology.[8] And, in the wake of revelations concerning a sixty-year-old new mother who had apparently told doctors at the London Fertility Centre she was forty-nine, the Human Fertilisation and Embryology Authority was urged to apply closer scrutiny to potential clients and impose an upper age limit of fifty or fifty-five.[9] Rejuvenation has come a long way since the days of dubious treatments offered to actresses in Swiss clinics. We need only look at the increasing popularity of hormone replacement therapy among women in mid-life. In a more gradual, but dramatic way, medical and social interventions have helped us to prolong life expectancy in an unprecedented manner. What does this mean in terms of images and beliefs that have circulated about the ageing process and in what ways have they been changing? Clearly, ageing cannot be reduced to biological processes of decline for, although these affect us all, they occur within a social framework which superimposes a series of cultural codes, symbols, and expectations that vary with the chronological time of the individual life course, historical period, and particular societal setting. Is it more 'normal', therefore, to grow old naturally, or, conversely, to conform to convention and attempt to defy or disguise such a process? The ensuing discussion aims to establish some of the changing backdrop against which older people are enjoined to construct their performances, their 'strategies of masquerade'.[10]

### Images of the past

It is helpful to begin by considering what might constitute past stereotypes of ageing. If we think of the early years of this century, then the images are broadly negative. I have a sepia postcard – retailed today as 'people's heritage' – of 'H' block in Hackney workhouse, 1902.[11] There's a particular striped serge uniform being worn, literally the uniform of the aged poor. Old age was also about segregation; all the old ladies were inmates in the same room, the women's ward. The image is of a certain formality, and most certainly about a rigidity or fixedness being attached to the notion of later life. In 1910 Corra May Harris made the gloomy claim that 'a woman would rather visit her own grave than the place where she has been young and beautiful after she is old

[8] 'Test-tube granny has triplets', *London Evening Standard*, 5 May 1992.
[9] *PM*, BBC Radio 4, 21 January 1998.
[10] S. Biggs, *Understanding Ageing: Images, Attitudes and Professional Practice* (Buckingham: Open University Press, 1993).
[11] Q5, 'Hackney Workhouse, "H" Block, the women's ward, 1902' (London Borough of Hackney Library Services, Archives Department, 1984).

and ugly'.[12] This dark vision of poverty, loss, and humiliation has lineages going back to Victorian philanthropists and forward to some campaigns today.[13] In the period of social and economic renewal after the Second World War it was still routine to present 'the elderly' as a problem category. Welfarist academic treatises abounded with pleas for more humane treatment for 'our future selves'. Peter Townsend's *The Last Refuge* (1962) provided an exposé of the rather desperate state of older people 'warehoused' in institutions, depicting a twilight world of old workhouses with whitewashed brick walls and long corridors peopled by the halt and lame.[14] Much has been written since about the design of old people's homes, geriatric wards, and nursing homes. However, the point that I wish to stress is that perceptions of *later* life did not change all that radically over the first three-quarters of the present century. If there was an increased popular awareness of old age as a stage in life, then it was a rather narrow, segregationist perception that tended to parallel directives enshrined in successive retirement policies. The attendant imagery remains steadfastly monochrome, two-dimensional, predictable. One thinks of Bert Hardy's photograph of the husband and wife, dressed in black, wandering off into the twilight, or of old men in flat caps, a working-class vision of beer drinking, bowls, and blether. But to what extent do the archives emphasise this retrospective, received memory of gentle, gumsucking grannies in pinnies, jovial grandads, or, more occasionally, lascivious dirty old men?[15]

### Popular perceptions: cartoons as unwitting testimony?

In *Aspects of the Novel*, E. M. Forster considers characterisation in terms of 'roundness' versus 'flatness'. 'Round' characters are distinguishable by their uniqueness as artistic elaborations. On the other hand, 'flat' characters serve a purpose in so far as 'they are easily recognized whenever they come in ... they never need reintroducing'.[16] They are important not just to tell the story but as psychological reinforcement of the status quo. Marwick has referred to such tacit, colloquial taken-for-

---

[12] C. M. Harris, *Eve's Second Husband* (1910), cited in K. Stoddard, *Saints and Shrews: Women and Aging in American Popular Film* (Westport, CT, and London: Greenwood Press, 1983), p. 3.

[13] Blaikie, 'Emerging political power'.

[14] Townsend, *The Last Refuge*.

[15] For a comparison with Victorian imagery, particularly in paintings, see M. Hepworth, 'Where do grannies come from?': representations of grandmothers in Victorian paintings', *Generations Review* 5, 1 (1995), 2–4.

[16] E. M. Forster, *Aspects of the Novel* (London: Edward Arnold, 1927), p. 105.

grantedness as 'unwitting testimony'.[17] The present discussion does not consider older people in literature in any depth. Nevertheless, in the vocabulary of human social characters drawn upon by both political commentators and fictional observers, old people were broadly reduced to this lesser – because not multifaceted or mutable – category of personhood.

During the interwar years, the tabloids represented old age as phase characterised by infirmity, forgetfulness, and semi-idiocy. A scan over Joe Lee's work for the London *Evening News* illustrates how cartoonists codified the fears and resentments of the non-aged. For example, a 1934 sketch has a stooped old man with inordinately long beard and a stick, peering over his spectacles at an ape behind bars. The caption reads: 'Excuse me, Sir, can you direct me to the chimpanzee's cage?'[18] Another shows an octogenarian in a bathchair being wheeled past Waite's statue *Physical Energy* in Kensington Gardens. Wartime images, meanwhile, pillory Dad's Army and geriatric postmen on penny-farthing bicycles. One has a vision of the artist's bottom drawer, labelled 'Old Fogeys' and filled with a series of (cut-out) stencils for rapid reference. Such caricatures do not exactly suggest a sublime gerontocracy. However, there were more sympathetic penmen, such as the *Daily Mirror*'s Vicky, who parodied the minister of state in the likeness of Marie Antoinette, saying 'If they can't afford bread, why don't they eat statistics?' – a reference to the Radio Doctor's claim that the elderly were eating increasing amounts of food. In another cartoon, a bedraggled elderly couple huddle before a backdrop of slum tenements. The caption reads: 'We've got one consolation, dear, our plight's *always* on the mind of the Chancellor (Parliament will debate old-age pensions on Wednesday).' Vicky's messages come from the early 1950s and reflect a dawning concern. Nevertheless, old people were still presented as in the main ravaged, shabbily clad, and rather undignified.

Such imagery was also invoked by pensioners' groups in support of political campaigns. When the National Federation of Old Age Pensioners' Associations portrayed old people as raggedly impoverished in its *Pensioner* cartoons, the visual shorthand operated in a context which used biting invective and political reasoning to explain them. In one sketch, from 1943, an emaciated old lady stands barefoot before the plump Means Test Man, who smokes a cigar and carries a briefcase monogrammed 'Snooper Esq.' She holds a pair of heavily patched

---

[17] A. Marwick, 'Visual sources in twentieth-century British history', seminar at Institute of Historical Research, London, 20 November 1985.

[18] Cartoons from *London Evening News* and *Daily Mirror* are housed in the Centre for the Study of Cartoon and Caricature, University of Kent at Canterbury.

bloomers whilst he retorts 'Rot woman! You don't want new ones – they won't show underneath – it's extravagance.' In another, a tousled old man is picking a cigarette butt from a gutter – the caption, 'Can the Brains Trust explain?' Graphic statements like this were designed to mock the assumption that poverty was the fault of the elderly, that they had been in any sense dissolute.

If older people maintain lifelong divergences and social distances amongst themselves, such fragmentation is counterbalanced by solidarities that endeavour to abolish rather than sharpen the boundaries of stigma. However, marginalised status may itself provide a rallying point for negotiation. In terms of the claim for adequate aid pensions campaigners had to legitimise their case. The distinction between mass circulation press cartoons and pressure group propaganda lay in attitudes: the former presented a social stereotype, or visual myth, whilst the latter reworked this negative symbolism to make a political point. Nevertheless, it remains the case that pensioners' campaigns – like many later ones – reproduced conventionally negative images, rather than new versions of later life that challenged the assumptions behind them. They drew on popular perceptions held by the non-aged. Neither these nor press cartoons can be said to have conveyed historical reality by means of line drawings. Rather, cartoonists operated with a kind of visual ready-reckoner, a shorthand vocabulary consisting of disaggregated parodies of physical features. Age symbolism was represented by lines and wrinkles to be added to the template 'face'.[19]

Perhaps the most popular aged cartoon figure in the UK since the Second World War has been the Grandma figure appearing in Giles's topical cartoons in the *Daily Express* and *Sunday Express*. Still in the 1990s dressed in heavy black coat, gloves, gaudily decorated hat, and fox-fur stole, out of doors she brandishes her umbrella defiantly against the onslaughts of children, bureaucrats, or anyone else who might dare to cross her path. 'Nobody's granny could be as awful as Grandma Giles', writes Magnus Magnusson, 'and yet there is something about her that is every indomitable granny who ever lived.'[20] Indoors, she is likely to be besieged by naughty children, who frequently attempt to exploit her relative inertia as occupant of the living room armchair. Woe betide them, however, should she notice them out of the corner of her eye as she studies her newspaper for racing tips. Indeed, more often than not, it is she who terrorises the home. Her spectacles appear opaque,

---

[19] I am grateful to Bill Bytheway for this observation.
[20] M. Magnusson, 'Foreword', in *Giles: Sunday Express & Daily Express Cartoons*, Forty-fourth Series (London: Express Newspapers, 1990).

disguising any sense of fear or other emotion; her chin forever juts out stoically.

Frequently she appears as one amongst several figures in a domestic *mis en scène*, always part of the action. Giles's humour pivots around the family – 'They are so *family* ... everybody's family'[21]– and Grandma's omnipresence renders her at once matriarch, accessory, and perpetrator of chaos. One caption reads: 'I only said if the Germans take over, Grandma would make a first-class head Gauleiter.'[22] This said, she is also legendary for her readiness to gamble at cards or have a flutter on the horses, nor is she averse to a spot of skiing. When she takes up wallpapering the result is predictable: she papers over the door, a sheet peels off, landing on Dad, but up her ladder she blasts on, sustained by a battery of her own curses. The vicar enters, remarking: 'As a matter of fact I read that a doctor's journal said that swearing is good for you – but not that good.'[23] The stereotype itself is invested with instant recognition: Grandma never changes, her character is fixed. She looks identical in the 1990s to Grandma Giles of the 1940s. As one of the children suggested when the prime minister announced her intention to remain in office: 'If Mrs Thatcher is staying on until she's 70, Grandma will be over 200.'[24] Her image clearly contradicts the frail, warm gentility of the Victorian grandmother, yet it is as the enduring archetype of true patriotism, learned in another era, that she adorns the cover of the 1992 Giles Annual in the guise of Britannia.[25] The self-conscious familiarity with her male counterpart, Alf Garnett of television notoriety, is evident from a cartoon which appeared when the Garnett series was dropped by the BBC: Granny stands on the steps of the local politician's house, Alf lurking behind a wall. She points her brolly at the maid and declaims: 'Please tell my MP I've got another candidate for him to vote for.'[26] Frequent allusions are similarly made to 'the War', and, in one instance, the children chain her up in the garden 'to celebrate the Suffragettes' anniversary'.[27]

Another tabloid character noticeable by his resistance to change through time is Granpaw Broon. Today every Scots (and many an English) newsagent sells the *Sunday Post*, in which this cartoon figure represents a central source of mirth in the children's Fun Section. His white beard and huge Kaiser Wilhelm moustache, the black suit and waistcoat, braces, tackety-boots, and bunnet (flat cap) render him more

[21] Ibid.        [22] *Giles*, Forty-fourth Series.
[23] *Sunday Express*, 14 April 1974.        [24] *Giles*, Forty-fourth Series.
[25] *Giles, Sunday Express & Daily Express Cartoons*, Forty-sixth Series (Risborough: Annual Concepts Limited, 1992).
[26] *Sunday Express*, 18 November 1990.        [27] *Sunday Express*, 2 July 1978.

a throwback to the 1930s than a contemporary grandfather. The cover of the 1985 *Broons* annual depicts him nodding off under a sign saying 'Ancient Monument'. Arguably, he has become part of the popular cultural heritage to whom present-day readers' grandparents can relate as being identified with *their* memories of older men.[28] Like Granny Giles, his presence is central to the family – and the Broons, like the Gileses, are a family *par excellence*, with their slogan 'Scotland's happy family that makes every family happy'. Both Grandma Giles and Granpaw Broon inhabit idealised homes befitting the working-class conservatism of their parent newspapers and, of course, their ideal readers.

As in their television equivalents Victor Meldrew (whose exasperated cry of 'I don't believe it!' became a *leitmotiv* in the television situation comedy *One Foot in the Grave*) and the aforementioned Alf Garnett, or his transatlantic cousin Archie Bunker, these *enfants terribles* are always running up against bureaucracy, and new-fangled ways of working. Nevertheless, the most significant similarity found among these older characters lies in their playful collusion in children's games and pranks. This childlike, winning idiosyncrasy finds resonance in popular children's fiction. For example, Hepworth's analysis of the relationships between young and old characters in Richmal Crompton's 'William' stories elaborates what he calls 'positive infantilisation'. Whereas treating older people like dependent children (infantilisation) is 'usually defined as an unwelcome imposition', Crompton's plots illustrate 'occasions when infantilisation may be regarded as a voluntary or chosen mode of resistance on the part of older people to the decrements and impositions of later life . . . involving processes of mutual identification of the old with the young; in certain instances even as a form of conspiracy between these two age groups against the wider society'.[29] Betty Friedan, on the other hand, catalogues numerous examples of images in the mass media that reduce older people to childlike status. One instance she cites is Dr Seuss's *You're Only Old Once!* for 'obsolete children'.[30]

---

[28] *The Broons* (London: D. C. Thomson & Co. Ltd., 1985). When the famous children's story cartoonist 'Dr Seuss' produced an American bestseller for old people in the 1980s, *You're Only Old Once!* (London: Fontana, 1986), the book was equally popular with young children and their grandparents alike (see B. Martin, 'The cultural construction', p. 65).

[29] M. Hepworth, '"William" and the old folks: notes on infantilisation', *Ageing and Society* 16 (1996), 423–41 (423).

[30] Friedan, *The Fountain of Age*, pp. 56–8.

## Whatever happened to Baby Jane?

Against the apparently unchanging drawn image, notwithstanding its many uses, the rise of visual culture stemming from the great motion picture industry appears to have been particularly significant for the revaluation of mid-life and its subsequent expansion at the expense of old age. Douglas Fairbanks, 'the first international cinema superstar', athlete and stud, did much to popularise outdoor adventure, and with it the suntan, thereby 'going against the established wisdom which held that the fashionable body must avoid the effects of the sun, lest it be associated with the tanned labouring body'. By the late 1920s, sunbathing – previously touted only as a tuberculosis treatment – became widely fashionable with the beach transformed into a site for mass exposure: 'For the first time sunbathing on the beach brought together large numbers of people in varying degrees of undress, legitimating the public display of the body.'[31] This was to have a marked effect on the development of ageist humour, as chapter 7 points out. Such exhibition upset codes of buttoned-up Edwardian respectability, audaciously challenging a status hierarchy based on respect for elders. The early Hollywood role models extolled the virtues of youth: to be young and slim was to be beautiful; signs of ageing, such as flabbiness and wrinkles, were emblems of ugliness. This shift towards a new morality of self-presentation and -preservation through diligent regimes of diet, exercise, and grooming was complemented by the insurance companies who began to tutor the middle classes in body maintenance techniques as weight gain and poor posture came to signify 'bad risks'.[32] Such notions of active refurbishment suggest a subterranean stream of 'lifestyle' promotion that was to become the deluge we see today. Yet *old* age, as against middle age, long remained a less pliable construct.

It is now conventional to cite Sontag's 'double jeopardy' claim that older women are victims of both sexism and ageism: whilst men's experience qualifies them for wisdom and grey hair and lined faces lend distinction, women are judged on appearance alone, such that signs of bodily ageing can signify only deterioration.[33] Thus, as Stoddard points out, 'it is difficult to find masculine counterparts to terms such as *crone*, *witch*, and *hag*, each of which has the ability to call forth strong visual

---

[31] Featherstone, 'The body', 180–1.
[32] Hepworth and Featherstone, *Surviving Middle Age*.
[33] S. Sontag, 'The double standard of aging', *Saturday Review*, 23 September 1972, 29–38.

images of maliciousness and degeneracy'.[34] In film, an icon who immediately heaves into view here is the Wicked Witch of the West from *The Wizard of Oz*. In the cinema's heyday, successful ageing was rare, and although Mae West, whom age did not wither nor desexualise, was forty when she made her first film, Angela Carter makes the telling point that by then she was 'the middle-aged woman, whose literary prototype is the nurse in *Romeo and Juliet*, [who] may say what she pleases, wink at and nudge whomever she desires but we know it is all a joke upon her, for she is licensed to be free because she is so old and ugly that nobody will have her'.[35]

In similar vein, Marie Dressler had been a huge box-office attraction, the talkies' 'first major superannuated star' having 'upstaged Garbo as a bibulous crony'. Clearly not the 'cliché of doddering frailty', this Ugly Duckling, as she called herself, used her 'dreadnought shape' and 'India-rubber animation of that bulldog face' to great farcical effect. Her popularity alone 'forced MGM to come up with scripts about un-glamorous old ladies'. Nevertheless, very few older people who broke through into silver screen success also broke the mould of stereotypical identification. If in silent movies elderly actors had 'functioned as peripheral parents to their flapper offspring in the center of the frame – stern WASP fathers wagging disapproving fingers at madcap Gloria Swanson', or been identified with 'mawkishness ... associating white hair with martyrdom',[36] little was to change thereafter:

Hollywood's legions of elderly statespersons were usually called on only for local color. If you wanted guttural imperiousness, there was Maria Ouspenskaya; for crustiness with a soft center, there was May Robson. That icon of dour sagacity, Lewis Stone, and that irascible old sweetie, Lionel Barrymore, were maintained on MGM's roster for decades ...

The forties and fifties presented essentially the same old set of charming elderly archetypes, incarnated by a new group of old faces – cantankerous codgers either adder tongued (Monty Woolley) or randy eyed (Charles Coburn); serenely omniscient matriarchs with quavery voices and firm, no-nonsense voices (Ethel Barrymore's speciality) ... In the fifties and sixties, the rule was that if you had a role for a black man and Sidney Poitier was unavailable, the project was doomed. Nowadays [1981], if you substitute lovable old ladies and Katharine Hepburn, the equation still seems to apply. *On Golden Pond* ... adroitly burnishes the comfortingly familiar images of the old which the screen has been offering up for decades.[37]

[34] Stoddard, *Saints and Shrews*, p. 3.
[35] A. Carter, *The Sadeian Woman: An Exercise in Cultural History* (London: Virago, 1979), p. 61.
[36] S. Harvey, 'Coming of age in film', *American Film* 7, 3 (1981), 52–3 (52); M. Dressler, *The Life Story of an Ugly Duckling* (New York: Robert McBride & Co., 1924).
[37] Harvey, 'Coming of age', 52–3.

In postwar films the focus was firmly on youth, older people being mostly fools, figures of fun, or paragons of virtue. In 1945, 65 per cent of cinema tickets were sold to people under thirty, and with the latter-day concentration by Hollywood on commercial success through targeting teenagers using high-tech action – Superman, Mad Max, Rambo, Indiana Jones, the Terminator – older figures have stayed marginal.[38]

Films featuring older people in leading roles have been designed to draw older audiences, and some – *Driving Miss Daisy*, *Trip to Bountiful*, *On Golden Pond*, *Cocoon* – have enjoyed commercial good fortune, partly because of their upbeat messages of self-actualisation and rejuvenation. Nevertheless, the negatives abound. The unprecedented phenomenon of three actresses of sixty or older winning Academy awards for Best Actress during the 1980s is compromised by the observation that the women they portrayed were stereotyped: 'argumentative, incompetent, suspicious, and stubborn [Jessica Tandy] as in *Driving Miss Daisy*, powerless and ill [Geraldine Page] as in *Trip to Bountiful*, or all-accepting and self-sacrificing [Katharine Hepburn] as in *On Golden Pond*'. And, as Markson and Taylor ruefully conclude, 'the "women's pictures" we see, with rare exceptions, do not seem to ring true'.[39] In line with Sontag's classic 'double jeopardy' of ageism plus sexism, film portrayals of older women in film offer few positive role models, although older actresses (see pp. 104–6 below) now present a happier picture.

On the stage, *pace* John Gielgud's extraordinary endurance, a great many 'elderly' parts have been played by made-up younger actors, King Lear being no exception. Hilary Sesta, who has made a career from playing 'old', in television commercials and serials as well as repertory theatre, claims that 'casting directors need me because they think I'm not as easily daunted as a really old person'.[40]

British films have focused on deviancy and subversion in their portrayals (incendiarism and homosexual desire against the deadening conformity of institutionalisation in *Past Caring*), lonely, frail, and forgetful parents (Mum in *High Hopes*), or broadly sympathetic portrayals of the idiosyncrasies of old age (Alan Bennett's *Talking Heads*

---

[38] By 1987, 81 per cent of cinema-goers were aged between sixteen and thirty (United Kingdom, Central Statistical Office, *Social Trends No. 20* (London: HMSO, 1990)).

[39] E. W. Markson and C. A. Taylor, 'Real world versus reel world: older women and the Academy Awards', in N. D. Davis, E. Cole, and E. D. Rothblum (eds.), *Faces of Women and Aging* (New York: Haworth Press, 1993), pp. 157–72 (pp. 161, 170, 171). Between 1927 and 1991, fewer than a third of female nominees for Best Actress were over thirty-nine (27 per cent), as against 67 per cent of men nominated for Best Actor. Katharine Hepburn (winning aged sixty in 1968) and Marie Dressler (winning aged sixty-two in 1930–1) were the only women over sixty to win as Best Actress between 1927 and 1968 (ibid., p. 160).

[40] H. Sesta, 'Down the old, bent road . . .', *Guardian*, 12 September 1996, 6–7 (7).

series). The personal and social problems associated with ageing are being addressed more closely, but what is most striking is the way in which these films highlight the absence of solutions. In the final scene of *Past Caring* the protagonists have sprung themselves from the nursing home and are sitting on a train. Now they are free, yet neither has a clue where they will alight. *High Hopes* ends with an awestruck Grandma on top of a London tower block, clearly the first time she has ever been higher than the top deck of a bus. 'The top of the world', she says, as she surveys the panorama, at once feeling above it but knowing she has to return. Ultimately there is no way out.[41]

## Small-screen portrayals

In 1988 Malcolm Johnson asked:

Why is it that in a society where nearly one person in five is over retirement age, older people are virtually absent from our television screens? Except in stereotype roles, older people are very rarely included in adverts and, when presented on the small screen, all too often they are misrepresented as poor, decrepit, sick, stupid, and asexual. Yet audience research shows that old people form the most loyal and attentive section of the viewing public.

His answer was ageism: either current affairs programmes stuck to a policy of using younger presenters or sitcom producers found it convenient to 'roll out the stereotypes for a laugh'.[42]

As with cinema, fewer older people appear than is justified by their proportion in the overall population. Meanwhile, very little serious research has been conducted into the design and impact of television images of age, despite the fact that people aged sixty-five and over watch an average of 50 per cent more television per week than the rest of the viewing public.[43] When the Cambridge University of the Third Age monitored a fortnight's British viewing (terrestrial channels) in winter 1983, they discovered that the over-60s appeared in 62 per cent of BBC

---

[41] There has been no attempt to produce anything like a comprehensive survey of 'ageing' films. Although I aim to identify general trends, of course there are interesting exceptions, *Fried Green Tomatoes* and *Harold and Maude* to name just two from recent decades. The realist portrait of poverty and family abandonment in *Over the Hill* (1921), where the toilworn mother ends up scrubbing poorhouse floors, and the more stereotypical *Make Way for Tomorrow* (1937), where a couple are forced to separate, thereafter becoming burdens on their offspring, both shocked large audiences in their day.

[42] M. Johnson, 'Never say die', *Listener*, 23 June 1988, 21–2 (21).

[43] A. Cave, 'The portrayal of the family relationships of older people in films of the 1980s as compared with films of the 1920s, 1930s and 1940s', Diploma in Gerontology dissertation, Centre for Extra-Mural Studies, Birkbeck College, University of London, 1991, Appendix 1, p. 40.

1 programmes, 51 per cent on BBC 2, 57 per cent on ITV, and 63 per cent on Channel 4. However, the apparent high profile was largely accounted for by the inclusion of world leaders on the news. By contrast, older people rarely played leads in plays, serials, soaps, adventures, comedies, or children's programmes: older men were central to the action in 23.5 per cent, compared with older women at only 3.8 per cent. The 'young old' were depicted as fit and healthy, whereas the 'old old' were dependent and in poor health. Sexual elements were minimised whilst the exaggeration of income levels served to underplay financial hardships. Like Johnson, they concluded that producers judged older people as 'boring, marginal, and of little account'.[44]

A later content analysis of the twenty-seven television programmes 'watched by the largest numbers of elderly people during one week' found that 'old people at work occupy a relatively wide variety of roles within a broad range of programmes. These range from politicians appearing as central figures in news reports, through hosts of religious affairs programmes, to detectives in fictional series. Images of retired old people seem to occupy a far narrower ground, appearing mainly in "soaps" and situation comedy.' The latter differed in that, according to interviews with older people, 'elderly characters in soaps tended to be viewed from a realistic standpoint', but those in sitcoms were simply caricatures to which they could not easily orientate themselves. They highlighted a propensity to 'play down the connections between old age, disability, ill health, and death', with the possible consequence of reinforcing 'a background assumption that such matters should not be exposed to public view ... but should be looked after discreetly and privately'. In the most popular soap operas, *Coronation Street* and *East-Enders*, older characters played significant roles as community watchdogs, but were often crotchety, interfering nuisances, the negative implication for real elders being that 'those old people who do complain run the risk of invalidation'.[45] This despite the fact that 41 per cent of *Coronation Street*'s audience is over age fifty-five.[46] During the 1990s the popularity of US imports, such as *The Golden Girls*, may have alleviated the negativity of British humour (and struck a blow for active sexuality in later life). However, the degree to which British women identify with their North American sisters remains unresearched.

In line with the tenor of the above generalisations Palmore

---

[44] J. Lambert, P. Laslett, and H. Clay, *The Image of the Elderly on TV* (Cambridge: University of the Third Age in Cambridge, 1984), pp. 3–12 (p. 8).

[45] G. Rodwell, S. Davis, T. Dennison, C. Goldsmith, and L. Whitehead, 'Images of old age on British television', *Generations Review* 2, 3 (1992), 6–8.

[46] 'Free radicals', *Generations Review* 7, 2 (1997), 24–5 (24).

summarised a variety of studies over two decades which used content analysis of jokes, cartoons, and birthday cards, concluding that negative images outweighed the positive. Longevity, physical and mental debility, unattractiveness, and sexual disability predominated, while jokes about elderly women were more negative than those about men. By contrast, only 3 per cent of jokes told by older people were about loss of attractiveness. Three-quarters of 'old maid' jokes were negative, satirising older single women as 'an evaporated peach', 'a lemon that has never been squeezed', or 'a woman always looking under the bed in the hope of finding a burglar'. Significantly, he found no 'old bachelor' jokes.[47] At first sight it appears that a brand of visual ageism instantly recognisable by a limited range of signifiers has taken root and remained pervasive in all significant realms of popular culture. However, the print media suggest otherwise. A recent study of American comic strips indicates two trends: first, an increasing number of portrayals of older women in positive roles, with fewer images portraying men negatively; secondly, a decline overall in comic strip drawings of older people. The authors speculate that this may be because 'ageing is less frequently seen as a life occurrence or transition to be feared or avoided', or because editorial decisions are taken 'not to offend a growing proportion of the readership, older readers ... to avoid the humorous treatment of "sensitive" subjects in the popular media'.[48] Meanwhile, magazines developed specifically for the ageing market have forged challenging fresh possibilities. While these do not necessarily limit the scope for age discrimination, they do mark significant departures from the weary script of monolithic negative labelling.

### On the news stands

As long ago as 1984, Featherstone and Hepworth published a study of changing images of ageing in the magazine *Choice*.[49] The main points they noted are worth reiterating. Tellingly, the periodical starts out as a vehicle for the Pre-Retirement Association, in October 1972, with the title *Retirement Choice*. The visual emphasis is on the masthead RETIREMENT, in block capitals, superseding 'Choice' in lower-case.

---

[47] E. B. Palmore, 'Attitudes toward aging shown by humor', in L. Nahemow, K. A. McCluskey-Fawcett, and P. E. McGhee (eds.), *Humor and Aging* (Orlando, FL: Academic Press, 1986), pp. 101–19 (pp. 118, 113, 104).

[48] H. Hanlon, J. Farnsworth, and J. Murray, 'Ageing in American comic strips: 1972–1992', *Ageing and Society* 17, 3 (1997), 293–304 (303).

[49] Featherstone and Hepworth, 'Changing images of retirement'; developed more fully in M. Featherstone and M. Hepworth, 'Images of positive aging: a case study of *Retirement Choice* magazine', in Featherstone and Wernick, *Images of Aging*, pp. 29–48.

The cover shows a black-and-white shot of a large crowd of men, with speech-bubbles pasted on, rather in the vein of *Private Eye*, only this is serious.[50] The message is not vigorous or glamorous but worthy and rather drab, reflecting the concerns of male retirees as a mass, along the lines of 'What about our rights?' Yet, even this first issue carries a section on women's fashions, lambasting the 'dull uniform' of retirement and praising modern grandmothers for their modish outlook. By the next year, a fresh, individualised focus becomes evident. Instead of the great mass of undifferentiated 'pensioners', the cover image is of the married couple – further acknowledgement of the importance of older women as the numerical majority, if not the majority voice. In late 1974, the magazine was taken over by a commercial organisation and the format became more bookstall-friendly, filled with colour photographs. There are the beginnings of a discourse on what people might do with their leisure time. There are articles about how to fill two and a half thousand hours, and about travel and DIY. Shifts in the magazine's title reflect this transformation: first the emphasis switches from 'RETIREMENT Choice' to 'Pre-retirement CHOICE'; then the wording becomes 'CHOICE – the only magazine for retirement planning' and another magazine, *Life Begins at 50*, gets incorporated. Eventually, the subtitle becomes '*leisure* and retirement planning'. We see a move from what might be considered a retirement broadsheet for those immediately contemplating their pension, to agenda-setting about self-help and change management (note the word 'planning' in the subtitle) for the over-50s. The glossy visual appeal is altogether more bright-eyed and bushy-tailed.

As the 1970s run into the 1980s, *Choice* comes to reflect a broader cultural reorientation. All the resonances are there: financial awareness, 'heritage' holidays, Prime Minister Thatcher on the cover, a role model of careful grooming, juxtaposed with an inset shot of her from the 'milk snatcher' years, looking older, staider, out-of-fashion, when in fact she was decades younger. (Ironically enough the same cover advertises the lure of a free redundancy booklet within.)[51] A 1984 issue carries a feature by Miriam Stoppard inviting readers to 'put the sparkle back into your sex life'. By now, the publisher's house style makes it difficult,

---

[50] A sign of the times was the launch of the satirical *The Oldie* magazine, edited by Richard Ingrams of *Private Eye* fame, in February 1992.

[51] *Vanity Fair* later revealed that Mrs Thatcher was 'undergoing the ancient Hindu therapy of Ayurveda ... she lives basically on vitamin C, coffee, and royal jelly ... she has also called in the "tooth capper, the hair dyer, eyelid lifter, and varicose vein remover"' (J. Passmore, 'How Maggie stays in charge', *London Evening Standard*, 18 May 1989, 3).

3   *Choice* – the Third Age is here.
    Cover picture by Marc Schwartz/*Notre Temps*.

in places, to distinguish *Choice* from *Cosmopolitan*.[52] Sexuality would never have been openly discussed in a retirement magazine twenty, or even ten, years previously. The perceived 'naturalness' of sex in later life renders clichés like 'dirty old man' and 'mutton dressed as lamb' increasingly obsolete. 'Sexagenarian ... it comes after sex in the dictionary' noted a cover story by famous popular writer Jilly Cooper in the summer 1997 issue of *World of Retirement*.[53]

A number of magazines from the 1980s and 1990s very much echo this reworking. The titles themselves are indicative of pro-active Third Age awareness. Take, for example, *Retirement Planning and Living*, whose message lies in getting readers to ask of themselves a series of questions about time management: what are we going to do with these twenty, twenty-five, thirty years? We cannot go on that cruise of a lifetime forever, so what happens when we get home? Finance, fitness, fashion, travel – the remit is beginning to widen – and it is very much about self-help, planning one's own lifestyle. The Association of Retired Persons' *O50* magazine promotes consumerism through attractive discounts but also considers second careers and educational opportunities. *Saga* is renowned for its golf-buggies and high-living style of package-travel selling. Meanwhile, in the United States, *Grandparents Today* illustrates the increased youthfulness of the modern grandparent and *Lear's* filled an important lacuna in the women's magazine market as 'the magazine for the woman who wasn't born yesterday'. Along with the fresh *Choice* subtitle – 'Britain's magazine for successful retirement' – comes *Good Times* – 'changing attitudes to age', later 'for those old enough to know better' – *Yours* – 'for the young at heart' – *Active Life* – 'the lively magazine for the years ahead', and *World of Retirement* – 'for people who enjoy life'. Research is only beginning to map the field of older people's magazines in ways similar to that done for, say, those directed at teenage girls.[54] Parallels are none the less obvious in the broadening of the range of titles and themes on offer to both audiences, in the foregrounding of topics such as sex, and – *People's Friend* excepted – a shift from romance narratives dependent on heroic others to 'a new, more confident, focus on the self'.[55]

---

[52] This 'modernisation' of retirement imagery is also evident elsewhere in Europe, for example in *Notre Temps*, the French counterpart of *Choice*.

[53] J. Cooper, 'If life begins at 40, let it rip at 60', *World of Retirement* (Summer 1997), 5–7.

[54] McRobbie, *Feminism and Youth Culture*, pp. 81–188. Doctoral research by Lesley Tidmarsh, Department of Sociology, University of Aberdeen, is the sole known example of current British work on older people's magazines.

[55] McRobbie, *Feminism and Youth Culture*, p. 183. Nevertheless, in the continuance of regular features like 'Way we were news' in *Yours*, replete with many a monochrome

Undoubtedly, the leading edge has come from the United States, where the American Association of Retired Persons makes great play on its 30 million plus and growing membership.[56] In the UK, although the political culture of Thatcherism – certainly the emphasis on consumerism – helped to break the mould, numerous contradictory messages can also be found: neither sexual sparkle, nor older postwomen, for instance, rest comfortably with Victorian values. But the point is that nowadays much of what is marketed at mid-lifers is indistinguishable from the interests of younger adults. The inculcation of 'lifestyle' covers a vast domain that embraces all ages.

## Mid-lifestyle – and after?

Mid-lifestyle suggests the forging of a positive, extendible phase of life through the active development of appropriate symbols. Style is very much the key word: it means refashioning the body to maintain a certain posture and panache. Mid-lifestyle is transgenerational – in the words of a *Mirabella* article, it heralds the arrival of 'the new age, no age woman' (and man). We have entered an era where, 'the standard Ages of Woman – from Madonna to Matriarch – have never been less relevant. You can run an empire at twenty-two, be a mother at forty, start a new career ten years after that – and look better as the years go by . . . the old palliative of being as young as you feel is becoming a quaint irrelevance. Forget it. With today's array of nips, tucks, serums and syringes, you are as young as you look.'[57] In a postmodern age, where adults are becoming more playful and less formal, children have more access to 'adult' information through television. As adults become childlike and children adultlike, 'uni-age' styles come into their own. Fashions are blending across the generations.[58] For older women, the message is that, no matter what your years, you can be one of the girls. Thus features on dress design depict mid-life mothers and thirtysomething daughters in the same outfits, while an advertisement for Jockey underwear captures

snapshot, a strong element of nostalgia persists, and, as chapter 7 illustrates, we would be foolish to ignore the importance of this past-minded cultural strand.

[56] The scale of the American ARP should not be taken as indicative of mass political activism. It is, in effect, a vast marketing operation offering a wide range of discounted products and services. Having trawled 'any place an unsuspecting consumer might have listed his birth date somewhere along the line', the AARP takes pride in the fact that 'on or about their birthdays, roughly 75 percent of the 2.7 million Americans who turned 50 this year received an offer to partake – for just $8! – in all the benefits of membership' (M. Beck, 'The new middle age', 50).

[57] L. White, 'The new age no age woman', *Mirabella*, 'Private View' (1991), 4–7 (4–5).

[58] J. Meyrowitz, 'The adultlike child and the childlike adult: socialization in an electronic age', *Daedalus* 113, 3 (1984), 19–48.

grandmother (a banker) and granddaughters in the same frame, thereby making it clear 'that both grandmothers and their grandchildren can wear Jockey underwear' (intriguingly, the generation in between is not included).

For the menopausal male there used to be those Levi's Action Slacks, with their 'unique hidden Action waistband'.[59] But nowadays, Levi's have become much more challenging in their advertising campaigns: eight midwest veterans, aged between sixty and eighty-six, were recently featured as models, while a television commercial begins with a topless rear view of a woman in denim jeans, with flowing hair and looking every bit the teenage sylph, who surprises the viewer when she turns around to reveal herself as a woman in her sixties. This is not simply a shock tactic: a recent Mintel research report found that over 50 per cent of men aged between forty-five and fifty-four had bought a pair of jeans in the past year.[60] Needless to say, many other advertisers and designers are already gearing up for major shifts in market orientation as inter-generational marketing appeal comes into its own. The American Association for Retired Persons' *Modern Maturity* has overtaken *Reader's Digest* as the US magazine with the largest circulation.[61]

If the earlier twentieth century was about consolidating the idea of retirement, where before there had been none, its closing decades reveal a growing fragmentation, both as regards the point at which people leave work and what they do with the time thereafter. The later phases of life are now less fixed, the order less definite. In 1972 *Retirement Choice* pleaded for men and women to free themselves from the 'chronological bonds' which once bound them to behaviours appropriate to specific ages and stages – marriage and childbearing between twenty and thirty-five, retirement at sixty or sixty-five, and so on.[62] As the boundaries of adult life get increasingly hazy, so the routemaps for retirement become less distinct. Now, as women return to work from the 'empty nest' while their partners opt for, or confront, an early exit, grandmothers are dressing like their daughters and grandfathers jogging with their sons. As Lurie relates, the transition from maturity to later life is no longer

[59] Ostroff, *Successful Marketing*, p. 217.
[60] T. Blanchard, 'Not fade away', *Independent Magazine*, 19 October 1996, 30–3. Another view of the Levi's campaign of 1996 holds that the company used models who were neither young nor conventionally beautiful, the idea being that all the models were original wearers of 'Original' jeans. Cowboys, for instance, wore them as working trousers rather than for the sake of fashion. However, rather than valuing the age of the wearers, the advertising text stressed the originality of the clothes (European Resource Unit, *Older People in Europe Oct. '96 Report* (London: Age Concern England, 1997).
[61] J. J. Pirkl, 'Transgenerational design: a design strategy whose time has arrived', *Design Management Journal* (Fall 1991), 55–60 (56).
[62] 'Then and now', *Retirement Choice* (November 1972), 8.

marked by a change of costume.[63] Indeed, popular perceptions of ageing have shifted, from the dark days when the 'aged poor' sat in motionless rows in the workhouse, to a modernising interwar phase when 'the elderly' were expected to don the retirement uniform, to postmodern times when older citizens are encouraged not just to dress 'young' and look youthful, but to exercise, have sex, diet, take holidays, socialise in ways indistinguishable from those of their children's generation. There are no rules now, only choices.

Of course, none of this has been achieved without effort. At the heart of the new age are body maintenance, fitness routines, exercise diets, and grooming. How else can we disguise the passage of time? It is all about presentation: looking good, feeling great. Positive ageing involves shedding both the retirement uniform and the work uniform, formal suit for track suit or shell suit, escaping the straitjacket of old age as our parents or grandparents knew it. It is more about cycling back to your youth and fitness than about shuffling off this mortal coil into the dusk. Added to this is a moral injunction – the work ethic displaced on to exercise – summarised neatly by one of our heroines of ageing, Joan Collins: 'After a certain age, you get the face you deserve. The women of my age who look good are the ones with the right attitude ... But for all this positive thinking, you don't look sensational at sixty simply because you want to. You have to work at it.'[64]

Kohli has noted the tendency among sociologists to interpret all forms of activity as work, and 'relationship work', 'emotional labour', and 'body work' have certainly become familiar terms. Thus the notion of 'working out' is more than just metaphorical, whilst it becomes appropriate 'to view some forms of highly institutionalised leisure activities as structurally analogous to formal work by calling them "consumption work"'. Moreover, there is evidence that retirement is partly legitimated by a 'busy ethic', emphasising leisure that is earnest, active, and occupied. In this way, claims Ekerdt, retirement is brought into line with mainstream societal values.[65]

Alternatively, and increasingly, people are resorting to body alteration – plastic surgery, facelifts, liposuction, hormone treatments. Popular photo magazines like *Hello!* and the American *People Weekly* are replete with glamorous shots, accompanied by titillating copy such as: 'Do they or don't they? Here's an inside report on the miracles, mishaps, and real

[63] A. Lurie, *The Language of Clothes* (London: Heinemann, 1981).

[64] R. Barber, 'I love being Joan Collins', *Sunday Post Magazine*, 9 January 1994, 20–1 (20). See also J. Kercher, 'Joan Collins: my old-fashioned values', *Yours*, April 1997, 10–12.

[65] M. Kohli, 'Ageing as a challenge', 382; D. J. Ekerdt, 'The busy ethic: moral continuity between work and retirement', *Gerontologist* 26 (1986), 239–44.

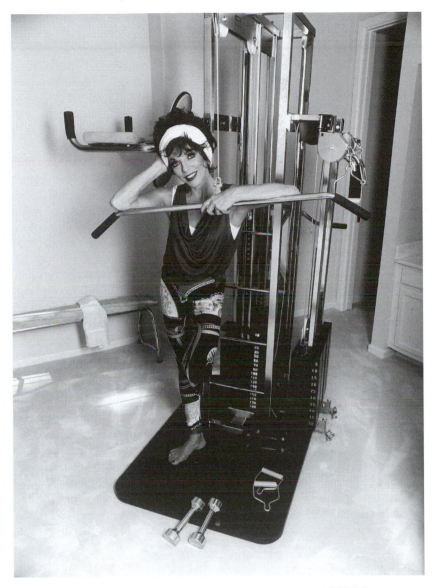

4   Joan Collins at sixty. Picture by Eddie Sanderson, © SCOPE Features.

risks of looking forever young.'[66] Postmodernists assert that 'the matter-of-fact acceptance of one's "natural" looks and one's "natural" personality is being replaced by a growing sense that it is normal to reinvent oneself' and 'the new construction of self is conceptual rather than natural ... Plastic surgery is not only accepted and encouraged by many of our social role models but is enthusiastically shown off. For the generation that has watched and perhaps tried to imitate the self-transformation of Jane Fonda, there is already a strong sense of one's freedom to control and alter one's body.'[67] Arguably, what was once the preserve of the rich and famous is becoming routine. However, this newly prevalent orthodoxy has its detractors. First, it has been argued that reconstructive medicine is pursuing a 'hidden aesthetic' by which ideals of youthful perfection drive the effort to obliterate the growing complexities and asymmetries of the face and body that ageing involves and which can be construed as the traces of an alternative 'aesthetic of imperfection'. Wrinkles, for example, constitute the inscriptions of experience.[68] Secondly, decrying the need to prolong youth by tampering with nature, Germaine Greer, in her disavowal of hormone replacement therapy, has codified a feminist strand which seeks to rehabilitate the crone. Being and appearing post-reproductive can free women from the biological tyrannies of fecundity and the social – not least imagined – expectations of an ageist, gendered game.[69]

To reiterate: the reasons behind such shifts in imagery lie with the emergence of consumer culture. And as the Western world ages, so businesses have become sensitive to a potential 'mature market'. As we saw in chapter 3, the continuing financial disadvantage of many pensioners has not held back the drive to 'capture the Grey Panther' by tapping supposedly vast reserves of disposable income: 'a market currently worth a conservative £10 billion'.[70] This is no idle or insular boast: already over half of discretionary income in the USA is in the hands of people over fifty, as will be a third of Canada's by 2006.[71] Nevertheless, despite the recent rhetoric about Woopies and Grumpies (growing numbers of mature professionals), most older British people

---

[66] Front cover, *People Weekly*, 27 January 1992. The American Society of Plastic and Reconstitutive Surgeons reported the following figures for 1990 (US totals): facelifts – 48,743 (91 per cent women), percentage aged 35–50: 27, percentage 51–64: 58; tummy tucks – 20, 213 (93 per cent women), percentage aged 35–50: 64, percentage 51–64: 15 (M. Beck, 'The new middle age', 56).

[67] Deitch, *Post Human*, pp. 27, 33, 39.

[68] B. M. Stafford, J. La Puma, and D. L. Schiedermayer, 'One face of beauty, one picture of health: the hidden aesthetic of medical practice', *Journal of Medicine and Philosophy* 14 (1989), 213–30, cited in Hepworth, 'Consumer culture', 26.

[69] Greer, *The Change*.       [70] BEST Limited, *The Grey Market*.

[71] Featherstone and Wernick, 'Introduction', p. 9.

are neither particularly affluent nor desperately infirm; they are relatively poor, but also fit and active, with partial, remediable disabilities and dependencies as they grow older.[72]

Whatever our own socio-cultural position, expectations have changed. We no longer draw in our breath as we read about marathon-running grannies, as if they were bizarre exceptions. Indeed, many of us would consider such portrayals to be ageist. If Raquel Welch could be portrayed in the *Sun* as 'fit, fantastic, and fifty' in 1980, since then we have seen the normalisation of extendible youth via Joan Collins, Jane Fonda, and other 'heroes and heroines of ageing', as one by one not just the movie stars, but also the pop icons pass the magic half-century in style – Cliff Richard, Bob Dylan, Mick Jagger, Paul McCartney, David Bowie, Cilla Black . . . Perhaps glamour no longer has its sell-by date. Or has it simply been extended, reprieved? Certainly the cultural burden laid on stars is considerable: ' "People have this obsession", Jagger once said . . . "They want you to be like you were in 1969. They want you to, because otherwise their youth goes with you, you know." '[73]

Research requires consideration of several features of the contemporary cultural landscape. First, two historical trends are important: one is the rise of consumer culture; the other is the emergence of the Third Age of 'personal fulfilment'.[74] The two combine to create an ageing population that expands the market for leisure and lifestyle. Secondly, however, since by no means all our elders are affluent (indeed a third still live on or below subsistence level) or in good health, design strategies – if such things exist – must be sufficiently flexible to capture a growing diversity of needs if we are not to run the risk of marginalising those who do not inhabit the Floridian landscape of the glossy magazines, but instead measure out their days in urban squalor, rural deprivation, or institutional oblivion. Thirdly, whilst the cultural denial of death, dying, and – increasingly – deep old age might provide a shaky base on which to build a sense of youthful immortality, such extenuation requires diligent attention to self-presentation: 'If you just work at it hard enough, you can keep your looks and sex drive and never grow old. In a sense, it is a displacement of the work ethic from work on to leisure; work becomes the prerequisite of pleasure.'[75] But, as Martin points out, 'what we do not need . . . is a rigid cultural formula for functionally extended "youthfulness" which gives a privileged and definitive place,

[72] Falkingham and Victor, *The Myth of the Woopie*.
[73] G. Burn, 'Jagger pushing 50', *Observer Magazine*, 10 January 1993, 17–23 (23).
[74] Laslett, 'The emergence'.
[75] B. Martin, 'The cultural construction', p. 63; Hepworth and Featherstone, *Surviving Middle Age*.

either to glamour or to active sexuality . . . After all, there cannot be very many people who *really* want old age to become a caricature of youth culture.'[76]

The increasing refinement of visual communication suggests that the ways in which the body is clothed, and the significance of posture (or body language) will create a climate of high sensitivity towards masking the visible signs of age. By contrast, such signs may act to disguise the cognitive and emotional youthfulness of the selves within.[77] Thus, at the end of the day, we can only realise so much. Yes, there can be a Third Age of busy volunteering, endless holidaying, and 'lifestyle', especially if you possess the resources. But, even if you do so in abundance, there comes an end to the journey that nobody can deny. And, for some, it will be a longer and more harrowing end than for others. As chapter 3 noted, the stars are no exception (Rita Hayworth and Marlene Dietrich). It is very easy to push the idea of infinite youth, especially if you are in the business of selling goods and services, but the image sometimes comes face to face with the stark features beneath the mask, the negatives that are exposed only after the legend has passed on.

A positive imagery is winning the day, one that emphasises the maintenance of youth, fitness, and discernment through leisure until well past the point of retirement. This represents, above all, an ideal of perpetual autonomy. Even funeral insurance companies are now offering free personal organisers to aid with the instalments.[78] Thus girded, one can plan one's death dynamically, in the style of thrusting youth, while safely overlooking the incipient reality of the ageing process. The following letter to the *Guardian* from the Rev. Bernard E. Jones is indicative of the surreality of our present cultural condition:

The ancients buried useful articles with the corpse but the Norwich Union offers three useful gifts in advance if you join their funeral expenses plan and reduce the financial burden on your loved ones.

I can 'travel in first class with a smart luggage set'; I can 'wake up to the sound of music (harps?) with a sleek radio alarm clock'; then there's a camera which will enable me to 'take great photos anywhere'.

There's even a built-in flash, useful if I get somewhere where it's dark.

Morituri Norwich Union Salutamus.

The accompanying cartoon has an insurance salesman trying to convince a client with the words: ' . . . or we have a fast maturing policy so that you can enjoy the funeral while you're still young'.[79] Two

---

[76] B. Martin, 'The cultural construction', p. 76.
[77] Featherstone and Hepworth, 'The mask of ageing'.
[78] B. Thompson, 'Dying by numbers', *New Statesman and Society*, 9 March 1990, 24–5.
[79] 'Showering gifts over my dead body', *Guardian* (letters page), 14 May 1991. A. Wernick, 'The dying of the American way of death', in Hummel and Lalive

observations occur: first, with the decline of state support and the rise of private personal pensions, personal equity plans, and other financial arrangements, individuals are being encouraged to have a greater say in the management of their own affairs, even unto death; secondly, one has to ask: has not the denial of decrepitude and dying – so important as a 'functional engine of consumer culture'[80] – gone too far? Of course, in Goffman's terms, fending off old age is an act of defiance against an incipient spoiled identity.[81] But in the slippage from individual strategy to societal vision whole social groups and areas of life become marginalised. If sex was the taboo subject of the nineteenth century, and death that of the twentieth, perhaps deep old age will be the great prohibition of the twenty-first? Dying – or, rather, killing – happens all the time on our television and cinema screens, but fantastically, violently, and dramatically, therefore quickly and without dwelling on pain or grief. We remain detached from its realities.

The constant quest for youth, in stigmatising the old and sick, casts off these people as human failures. Although the period of decrepitude (the Fourth Age) may be mercifully brief for some, increased longevity also means more incontinence, more dementias, more bodily betrayals and breakdowns in communication. (The slow drip of permissive attitudes since the 1960s means that eventually later life may no longer be regarded by the non-aged as a sexual desert, but the popular image of intercourse between doubly incontinent, arthritic partners – however fulfilling the reality for those partners – remains a strongly negative one.)[82] It may be true that less than 5 per cent of the retired population lives in institutions or hospitals nowadays, but that small percentage of people still represents considerable and increasing absolute numbers.[83]

D'Epinay, *Images of Aging*, pp. 69–90, suggests that whereas dying has been medicalised, the disposal of the dead has been commodified. The nature of funeral marketing today encourages individuals to have a greater say in their own arrangements.

[80] B. Martin, 'The cultural construction', p. 63.

[81] E. Goffman, *Stigma: Notes on the Management of Spoiled Identity* (Harmondsworth: Penguin, 1984).

[82] The drip may be slow indeed. In January 1998 artist Melanie Manchot presented five huge billboard posters of her 66-year-old mother outside South Kensington underground station in London. With 'acres of bare flesh, underwear, and a challenging smile on each', these images deliberately emphasised sexual attraction. However, a sample of young men interviewed strongly disapproved, the editor of men's magazine *FHM* claiming that 'it's like your parents having sex when you're little – you don't really want to think about it' (*PM*, BBC Radio 4, 15 January 1998).

[83] While the creeping sense of unease about being left financially stranded when in medical need has been seized upon by private health care companies, advertisers appear wise to the costly implications of insuring older people. See, for example, this 1989 advertisement: 'Now anyone up to seventy-four can afford to join BUPA. If you think you can't afford private hospital care, think again.' Presumably if one is seventy-five or over, then one need not think again.

Our improved health status and life expectancy, the much vaunted compression of morbidity, help to elongate the active 'mid-life phase' or plateau. But in building up the illusion of immortality, are we not blotting out from social consciousness – and conscience – the darker side of dying? In hiding away deep old age behind the screens of nursing homes and geriatric wards we make it a very lonely, desolate experience. As Young and Schuller point out, 'elevating the third [age] ... is only done by treading down the fourth. The labelling problem is wished on to even older and more defenceless people.'[84] Such is the 'pornography of death'.[85] Although the Fourth Age aggregates mental and physical decline, the brutal inhumanity of the 'disgust function' is reflected in the power of relatively superficial corporeal decrements to invite revulsion regardless of spiritual accomplishments. Where such mind/body dualisms persist, they are often dealt with by questionably sardonic black humour. For instance, the caption on a greetings card with the image of an old man in a rocking chair reading the paper states: 'Though grown-up now, the kids still loved their Father ... a wise and noble man, versed in the ways of the world, knowing and understanding. But they still decided to put him in a home anyway because he smelt funny.'[86] Alternatively, in Alan Bleasdale's film *No Surrender*:

a party of grossly impaired elderly patients is taken into a Liverpool nightclub to participate in a New Year's Eve celebration. The impact of this visit is such that several of the younger (though not much younger) visitors are provoked to aggressive or tearful resentment of the slovenly and repulsive behaviour of the patients: 'Is this the future?' asks one active and still physically combative man in late middle life; whilst an elderly woman in a state of near collapse moans 'I don't want to end up like that', demanding that the patients be taken away and hidden from sight.[87]

The near-medieval grotesqueness of this encounter shockingly accentuates the disjunction between Third and Fourth Ages by juxtaposing two social groups who would normally be held apart through the socially and spatially marginalising effects of institutionalisation. For a moment here the boundaries have collapsed and the reality of deep old age stands revealed.

---

[84]  M. Young and Schuller, *Life After Work*, p. 181.
[85]  G. Gorer, 'The pornography of death', *Encounter* 5, 4 (1955), 49–52.
[86]  M. Stennett, *On-the-Ceiling*, C171 Smelt Funny (Cheltenham: Emotional Rescue Ltd. [1997]).
[87]  Featherstone and Hepworth, 'Images of ageing', pp. 259–60.

# 5    Exploring visual memory

The previous chapter has considered the stereotyping of older people through different versions of visual shorthand – cartoons, political propaganda, film, television, and popular magazines. While surprisingly little has been written on the sociological interpretation of age in paintings,[1] still less is known about the essentially modern medium of photography. My study suggests that, during the earlier twentieth century, modernity produced an enhanced awareness of stigma via the growing administrative classification of older people as a chronologically determined social group with a fixed identity – hence a gallery of figures such as the decrepit pensioner and the gentle granny. Latterly, however, the growth of consumer culture has led to the emergence of a post-modern life course accentuating a range of possible lifestyle choices. Advertising both reflects and creates social trends, with 'positive' ageing images increasingly to the fore.

In the following three chapters, I will focus on photography as a form of popular culture, as art, and as the source for the imaginative recreation of appropriate 'pastness'. Chapter 5 raises a number of methodological issues – several of which apply to qualitative sources generally – that force us to resist the unqualified acceptance of images as facts, but also to appreciate their value as sources. Chapter 6 develops these themes further by exploring some of the different photographic contexts in which age and the image have coincided. Finally, in chapter 7, the connections between ageing, heritage, and visual imagery are

Parts of this chapter, originally published in *Ageing and Society* 14, 4 (1994), 479–97, were presented to an international seminar on Images of Aging held in Sierre, Switzerland, in July 1993. I should like to record my thanks to Tamara Hareven and Mike Hepworth for their comments. An earlier conference, unrelated but with the same title, was held in Luxembourg in June 1991. I am especially indebted to Andrew Achenbaum for his remarks on that occasion, and subsequently on an earlier draft of the current paper. I am also grateful to an anonymous referee for further critical insights. Chris Waters's presentations on collective memory (at the Thomas Reid Institute for Cultural Studies in Aberdeen) lent further inspiration.
[1]  Although see Cole, *Journey of Life*, pp. 244–51.

explored in an examination of British coastal communities. These chapters should be read as complementary essays, with a number of interlocking themes, which in their different ways are attempting to research possible avenues of investigation into a particularly rich but unexamined cultural source. They are, if you will, forays into a new field, entered each time by the same gate, but traversed by varying routes.

## Introduction

Although photographs are frequently used to illustrate discussions about ageing, they have not been assessed critically as gerontological sources. This chapter argues that the pictorial record since the 1840s contains many problems and possibilities. A case study of Victorian Scotland indicates the methodological pitfalls of acknowledging images at face value. Uncritical acceptance of the assumptions of modernisation theory has underlain much of the received wisdom on ageing in former times. More generally, both academics and advocates in postwar Britain have reworked stereotypes of old age to suit their own aims. Against this, the convergence of reminiscence and a willingness to develop more interactive approaches to understanding the life course allows photographs to provide a resource for interpreting the ageing self. Nevertheless, as the examples show, difficulties again arise as the ambiguity and malleability of images all too easily enable generalised fictions to shroud the diversity of individual experience.

In its evocation of 'the power of sensation rather than intellectual memory to recover "the past"', as well as its 'objective presentation of a wonderful gallery of portraits', Marcel Proust's remarkable fiction captures a contradiction common to any enterprise that tries to interpret history as time remembered.[2] And, in the nature of things, this tension between felt experience and faithful rendition is particularly poignant when we come to study human ageing. While literature, art, and photography have often been used to provide interesting leaven in more strictly scientific discourses – apposite quotations adding a flavour-of-life experience to a statistical passage, the monochrome close-ups adorning the foyer at the annual conference, displays of popular ageism in birthday cards, an Old Master's self-portrait as striking copy for a dustjacket – recent studies have attempted to contextualise these cultural productions. Some areas are reasonably served: ageing in literature

[2] P. Harvey (ed.), *The Oxford Companion to English Literature*, 3rd edn (Oxford University Press, 1946), p. 641, discussing M. Proust, *À la recherche du temps perdu* (Paris: Gallimard, 1919–27).

has been discussed in considerable detail by Woodward and others,[3] and popular magazines have been subjected to careful sociological monitoring.[4] But other fields, such as television, film, and photographic coverage of older persons or ageing, are less well-documented.[5] This is especially true in the United Kingdom, where analysis is conspicuous by its absence.[6] As one attempt to remedy the situation, this chapter addresses some of the possibilities and drawbacks for potential studies in one of these areas, namely photography.

In Ridley Scott's oft-cited film *Bladerunner* genetically manufactured 'replicants' simulate their life histories by stealing snapshots and inventing anecdotes about themselves to fit the images. The moral of the tale is that 'history for everyone has become reduced to the evidence of the photograph'.[7] Although the year is 2019, like Orwell's *Nineteen Eighty-Four*, the text is a parable of our own time. Pictures are never naive, yet too often we treat them as self-explanatory texts, without regard for the circumstances of their production, presentation, and consumption. How much detail do we require before an image becomes meaningful? What makes a photograph photogenic, gives it salience in the here-and-now? What status do images have; what relationships do they bear to the life they purport to represent?

Reviewing the relationship between medical history and visual imagery, Ludmilla Jordanova has remarked that: 'The Reformation made images theologically contentious, now they are epistemologically

[3] K. Woodward, *Aging and Its Discontents: Freud and Other Fictions* (Bloomington: Indiana University Press, 1991), begins with a discussion of the responses of academic conference-goers to an exhibition shot of an elderly man; M. Sohngen and R. J. Smith, 'Images of old age in poetry', *Gerontologist* 18 (1978), 181–6; C. E. Kelley, 'Ageism in popular song: a rhetorical analysis of American popular song lyrics, 1964–1973', Ph.D thesis, University of Oregon, 1982.

[4] Featherstone and Hepworth, 'Changing images of retirement'; W. Gantz, H. M. Gartenber, and C. K. Rainbow, 'Approaching invisibility: the portrayal of the elderly in magazine advertisements', *Journal of Communication* 30 (1980), 56–60; J. Range and M. A. Vinovskis, 'Images of the elderly in popular magazines: a content analysis of *Littell's Living Age*, 1945–1982', *Social Science History* 5 (1981), 123–70; H. Wass, L. V. Hawkins, E. B. Kelly, C. R. Magners, and A. M. McMorrow, 'The elderly in Sunday papers, 1963–1983', *Educational Gerontology* 11 (1985), 29–39; K. M. Dillon and B. S. Jones, 'Attitudes toward aging portrayed in birthday cards', *International Journal of Aging and Human Development* 13, 1 (1981), 79–84.

[5] P. W. Dail, 'Prime-time television portrayals of older adults in the context of family life', *Gerontologist* 28 (1988), 700–6; R. H. Davis and J. A. Davis, *TV's Image of the Elderly: A Practical Guide for Change* (Lexington, MA: Lexington Books, 1985); J. C. Elliott, 'The daytime television portrayal of older adults', *Gerontologist* 24 (1984), 628–33; M. Petersen, 'The visibility and image of older people on television', *Journalism Quarterly* 50 (1973), 569–73; Stoddard, *Saints and Shrews*.

[6] Although see Rodwell, S. Davis, T. Dennison, C. Goldsmith, and L. Whitehead, 'Images of old age'.

[7] D. Harvey, *The Condition of Postmodernity* (Oxford: Basil Blackwell, 1989), pp. 312–13.

contentious.'[8] By 'epistemologically contentious', I take her to mean that images force us to debate the procedures by which we acquire social knowledge. Here I will argue that photographs about ageing are anachronistic thrice over: first, because of the values that we attribute to old photographs; secondly, because of the way we have constructed our understanding of the social history of old age; thirdly, because our sense of ourselves requires the elaboration of historical fictions about the life course and family cycle. The discussion takes the form of three case studies: images of ageing in old photographs in Victorian Scotland; how images have been deployed in twentieth-century Britain; and the uses of photography to interpret our own ageing.

### Refashioning the past: Scotland in sepia

Questions of provenance are critical, a prior requirement being to understand the means and motives of the very photographers on whom we rely for evidence. Most of the early images I will discuss by way of example were produced and circulated in Scotland in the age of Victoria, a period when, as Alastair Durie shows, photographers would 'manipulate the scene in order to maximise commercial advantage'. Whether such doctoring is always detected – or detectable – is another matter, although in the age of digitised airbrush techniques we ought at least to have learned to be sceptical.[9] I discuss Scotland because it was here that much of the pioneering work in portrait photography was done, while this country also saw some of the more successful business ventures, particularly in postcards.[10] When the nascent tourist market set the agenda, as it did for the big firms like Valentine's of Dundee, we can hardly expect to see shots of slums and disease, even if, inadvertently, the details of, say, street scenes in Edinburgh lend illuminating social commentary – the children playing barefoot in the gutter, the old woman sewing in the doorway. If photographs were the only source

---

[8] L. Jordanova, 'Medicine and visual culture', *Social History of Medicine* 3, 1 (1990), 88–99.

[9] A. Durie, 'Tourism and commercial photography in Victorian Scotland: the rise and fall of G. W. Wilson & Co., 1852–1908', *Northern Scotland* 12 (1992), 89–104 (99); R. Smart, ' "Famous throughout the world": Valentine & Sons Ltd, Dundee', *Review of Scottish Culture* 4 (1988), 75–87. On the manipulation of politically sensitive photographs, see G. Dyer, 'Accentuating the negative', *Observer Review*, 17 August 1997, 4.

[10] S. Stevenson, 'Photography', in P. H. Scott (ed.), *Scotland: A Concise Cultural History* (Edinburgh and London: Mainstream, 1993), pp. 253–66, notes that 'both scientifically and artistically Scotland made an outstanding contribution to the development of this new medium' (p. 253). Annan, Valentine, and Washington Wilson all established their businesses during the 1850s.

available for reconstructing nineteenth-century Scotland, 'it would be a land of history, scenery, and architecture, with an economy that was largely pastoral ... There would have been, apparently, almost no heavy industry and the main support of the population would have been fishing and the provision of leisure services.'[11] Old people provided charming period detail, but, among several major collections, I have discovered just one portrait taken as an illustration of illness (a woman with seriously developed goitre).[12] Death, except in the theatre, is similarly absent: although I have found a singularly macabre *carte de visite* showing a dead baby, I have yet to see one that portrays a laid-out adult. High rates of infant mortality were reflected in funeral cards carrying portraits as well as poems, but older people do not seem to have been remembered in such ways.[13] Neither, by contrast, are they pictured as fitness fanatics.

The selectivity exercised by purchasers, among them specialist collectors, was considerable. Similarly, the significance with which we invest the celluloid image, still more daguerreotype and calotype, cannot be dubbed 'nostalgic' in any simple sense.[14] Collective memory is a fickle friend, discovered, lost, and found again in fashions. When in the 1960s 'new wave' social history inaugurated a search for 'human documents', photographs satisfied an appetite for immediacy and authenticity, 'unwitting testimony' giving names and faces to 'the masses'. According to Raphael Samuel the *annus mirabilis* of the revival was 1972, the year when the Arts Council appointed its first photographic officer (ushering in picture research as new profession); it was the year also when the fate of the collection of Scots pioneers David Octavius Hill and Robert Adamson was debated in the public press. Such intellectual enterprise coincided with the growth of the 'national village cult', the importation of Scandinavian stripped pine, Laura Ashley, and the 'country kitchen' syndrome. Sepia became 'an all-purpose signifier'.[15]

---

11  Durie, 'Tourism', 100. Of the major professional photographers in Scotland, only Thomas Annan, who captured the dereliction and filth of old Glasgow closes immediately before the Corporation demolished and rebuilt them, could be said to have been spurred by an impulse for social realism.

12  S. Stevenson, *David Octavius Hill and Robert Adamson: Catalogue of Their Calotypes Taken Between 1843 and 1847 in the Collection of the Scottish National Portrait Gallery* (Edinburgh: National Galleries of Scotland, 1981), p. 150.

13  J. Hannavy, *A Moment in Time: Scottish Contributions to Photography, 1840–1920* (Glasgow: Third Eye/Interbook Media Services, 1983), p. 6; M. Anderson and D. Morse, 'The people', in W. H. Fraser and R. J. Morris (eds.), *People and Society in Scotland*, 3 vols., vol. II, *1830–1914* (Edinburgh: John Donald, 1990), pp. 8–45 (p. 16).

14  S. Kinnes, 'Private collection. Photography: Edinburgh International Festival Study Guide', *Scotland on Sunday*, 27 June 1993, 13.

15  R. Samuel, 'The "eye" of history', *New Statesman and Society*, 18 December 1992–1 January 1993, 38–41.

For our purposes, we should note that 1972 also saw the publication of Cowgill and Holmes's *Aging and Modernization*, one of the more significant conceptual markers in the history of social gerontology. Their argument codified a series of Parsonian assumptions about how 'in the past, people looked after their own', whereas today they do not. Modernisation was accompanied by demographic transition and population ageing, but the forces of new technology, urbanisation, and education 'set up a chain reaction which undermined the status of older people': new technology devalued their skills, migration and the city disrupted family life, especially the extended family network, and the development of mass education put paid to the traditional role of elders as the fount of wisdom, skills, and knowledge.[16] For Cowgill and Holmes, and a generation of scholars after them, the shift from the pre-industrial Golden Age, 'the classical family of Western nostalgia',[17] to the marginalised 'aged poor' reliant on institutional support was a powerful myth. Taken together, the historicist turn in the appreciation of photography and the yoking of the modernisation thesis to the history of ageing by gerontologists produced a Kondratieff-like moment in the appreciation of images of ageing. And, despite the fact that more recent gerontologic theory-builders have been at pains to discredit such notions, its ideological effects remain profound.

When British historians first seriously considered photographs in the 1960s it was 'in a modernising spirit, as a way of bridging the gap between past and present . . . a way of seeing the nineteenth century with twentieth-century eyes'. But after the 1970s, 'Images came to be chosen . . . for their aura of pastness', as an alternative to the present rather than a prelude to it. Likewise, gerontology still then embraced the before-and-after models beloved of modernisation theory. The cumulative effect was the creation of a fresh iconography of the national past and of the role of older people on that stage:

a whole new gallery of national characters. Fishermen, who figure not at all in mainstream economic and social history, here take pride of place with their sou'westers, their seaboots and their guernseys, the most photographed (and the most painted) class of working men in nineteenth-century Britain, and the subjects of one of photography's founding texts, the Hill/Adamson Newhaven pictures of 1843. The world of rank and fashion – or those whom the Victorians called the Upper Ten Thousand – also acquires a new visibility.[18]

---

[16] Fennell, Phillipson, and Evers, *Sociology of Old Age*, p. 28.

[17] W. Goode, *World Revolution and Family Patterns* (New York: Free Press of Glencoe, 1963), p. 6.

[18] Samuel, 'The "eye" of history', 40.

This retroactive process represented a second distillation of archives that had already been selected with an individual aesthetic sensibility and a particular public in mind, via the ideologies of both the photographer and the collector. Samuel goes on to argue that industrial photography was enthusiastically welcomed by Victorian employers who produced edifying images spreading the gospel of work. Backbreaking labour appears heroic while there exists a certain sturdiness among those now at rest from toil: 'In place of the coffin-ships we have wizened old sea-dogs [Washington Wilson's 'An Old Salt' being the most famous], seated on the harbour wall, pulling pensively at their pipes.' Women workers appear still more robust: 'Scotch herring girls standing proudly by their baskets'. Photography thus 'gave Victorianism a human face' and 'Victorian Values' appeared in an altogether more benevolent light when seen through the camera's eye.[19] At once Victorian businessmen were happy while conservative interests a hundred years on had a voluminous archive on which to draw. Inadequate technology ensured that illustrated history books carried only engravings of people in dark places – down the mines, in the sweatshops – and nobody took the time to set up their tripod outside such places, for who would have paused to pose after a gruelling shift? Interestingly, when older people appear it tends to be as practitioners of dying trades, the last of the breed. Handloom weavers, for instance, were photographed in Angus as late as 1908, by which time octogenarians must have been the only such craftspeople remaining. Like Kailyard literature, such images were wistfully nostalgic (J. M. Barrie's *Auld Licht Idylls* (1889) focuses on the struggles of 'a group of former labour aristocrats, the handloom weavers, caught in the inexorable pressure of growing factory production' in the fictional community of 'Thrums' (meaning literally the ends of thread left on a loom after the woven cloth has been taken off)).[20] When older people do not figure as bearers of near-vanished skills, they crop up as eccentrics – Coconut Tam, a midget with a bowler hat and a High Street fixture in Edinburgh, or Tom Kent's Annie Harper, the bearded fortune-teller.

Such characters of a bygone era pepper many a newsagent's postcard racks: as examples of deviant ageing, legends immortalised on glass plates because of their idiosyncrasies. But they certainly cannot be held to be representative. Like Mayhew's street-sellers (themselves, incidentally, illustrated by engraved copies of photographs), they become Dickensian archetypes, selected to exemplify the cultural richness (and

---

[19] Ibid.
[20] I. Carter, 'Kailyard: the literature of decline in nineteenth-century Scotland', *Scottish Journal of Sociology* 1, 1(1976), 1–13 (5).

material poverty) of another world, rather than for their typicality of the everyday.

Some figures, such as Hill and Adamson's Newhaven fishwives, acquired an emblematic appeal. As Durie remarks, they 'must have spent nearly as much time in front of the camera as selling their fish!'[21] These women from one of Edinburgh's outports were photographed again in the 1880s by the Aberdeen photographer George Washington Wilson. One picture, captioned 'Three Generations of Newhaven Fishwives', indicates the vital importance of all family members in performing the various tasks necessary to maintain a boat, catch and process fish, and sustain trade. The continued presence down the years of particular dynasties within the one community is borne out by Paul Thompson in his oral history of Scottish fishing communities.[22] However, other images are more ambiguous. Although Frank Meadow Sutcliffe's portrait 'Morning and Evening', showing an old man cuddling his nephew, has been interpreted as conveying a sense of the shared social marginality of youth and age,[23] it might be more appropriate to argue that, since both children and older people performed indispensable roles such as baiting lines, the picture reinforces the centrality of the extended family in coastal communities.[24]

Often these posed portraits, 'Bound and stiff in bible-black', could suggest little more than the discomfort undergone in sitting or standing still and doing nothing with one's hands for half an hour.[25] Arguably, the slow shutter speeds of the time allowed subjects to adjust their poses premeditatively, compared to today's sneaky snapshots that catch them in more realistic mode. Alternatively, this demanded a certain formality that often means we lose any sense of 'natural' gesture or posture.

Overlaying this enforced formality was a predisposition to anthropological caricature. It is no accident, for example, that the obsession with

---

[21] Durie, 'Tourism', 100. (Unlike today's 'heritage experiences' where redundant miners dress up to guide the public around mining museums, these women were still working in fishing.)

[22] P. Thompson with T. Wailey and T. Lummis, *Living the Fishing* (London: Routledge and Kegan Paul, 1983). Around 1900, Valentine's published a photograph captioned '*Four* Generations of Newhaven Fishwives'.

[23] Hockey and James, *Growing Up and Growing Old*, pp. 18–21.

[24] In several occupations, each generation had a different role in the production process. For example, domestic yarn making involved, in each household, young girls in carding, mothers in spinning, and grandmothers in winding the wool. See F. Thompson, *Victorian and Edwardian Scotland from Old Photographs* (Edinburgh: Tantallon Books, 1976), illus. no. 164.

[25] Much may be read into the picture, nevertheless. Ken Morrice's poem 'Old photograph: fisherman and wife', opens with the line 'These salt-hard hands gave few caresses' (A. Scott (ed.), *Voices of Our Kind*, 3rd edn (Edinburgh: Chambers, 1987), pp. 108–9).

fisherfolk coincided with a Darwinian impulse to classify the Gael and the Pict, that engravings of 'fish-people' can be arrayed beside eugenicist tracts distinguishing small, dark, inter-bred coastal villagers from slow-speaking, big-boned country folk.[26] Griselda Pollock and Fred Orton remind us of the 'naturalist' imagery the European peasantry acquired in the later nineteenth century via the brush of Van Gogh: in paintings such as *The Potato Eaters* those closest to the earth were rendered animal-like in their appearance.[27] If this artistic trend is mapped on to the gerontological narrative, the potential for old age as disgusting (in the sense intended by Norbert Elias) is high – a throwback to Goya's grotesques. Equally, the Impressionist tradition of *la veillée*, the old couple at prayer or weaving around the cottage hearth, reflecting Burns's *The Cotter's Saturday Night*, suggests an altogether more romantic impulse.

Photographic imitations of this are rare (although the amateur James Cox's bleak images of Fife fisherfolk, said to derive from the French realist paintings of Jean Bastien-Lepage, present a harsh contrast to the Hill–Adamson genre).[28] Victorian technology determined that only wealthy families could afford the indoor studio backdrop. Several portraits of 'Great Men' nevertheless suggest the ravages of time. While Thomas Chalmers, the famous church leader, is shown, in his mid-sixties, preaching in a commanding pose, an off-guard sitting portrait depicts him slumped in a large armchair. Sculptor John Henning, in his seventies, stands upright by a Parthenon frieze but, again, the sitting pose exposes his frailty (not only his torso and arms, but also his cheeks display a sagged resignation). This begs the question: how many customers refused to be photographed sitting down? Equally, given the length of time one had to stand still while posing, it is surprising that more old people are not pictured using walking sticks as supports.

By contrast, the peasant couple and the farm labour crew could be posed relatively inexpensively outdoors by itinerant photographers. The formality, if often rendered humorous by the teams of sitters, is seldom dropped, although when on occasion it is we see a rather different state of dress and body language: the rod-up-the-back and say-cheese posture gives way to a submissive slouch. More interesting are the 'documentary' images of older people outside their homes. As the travelling camera roves between relatively prosperous small farmers in

[26] J. Gray and J. F. Tocher, 'The ethnology of Buchan, part III: the physical characteristics of adults and school children in East Aberdeenshire', *Transactions of the Buchan Field Club* 6 (1901), 37–68.

[27] G. Pollock and F. Orton, *Vincent Van Gogh: Artist of His Time* (Oxford: Phaidon, 1978).

[28] S. Stevenson, 'Photography', p. 262.

Aberdeenshire to impoverished crofters in the Hebrides, the age and state of the buildings begins to mirror the age and state of its occupants: decrepitude and disrepair replace upright family respectability.

Relationships between family members are often difficult to assess and the connections between age-norms and family obligations rarely clear from formal portraits. The simple presence of grandparents and grandchildren in the same frame reflects enhanced longevity, but the meanings attached to their putative relationships are largely conjectural. Often we are told the date when the picture was taken, but the ages of the subjects are less frequently given and inferences can be misleading. In other portraits, intergenerational relationships are clear, but the ages of the parties are not given. Moreover, there are dangers of inferring that the picture represents a whole family, when often members are missing. I have a postcard of a crofting family that carries the caption: 'Mary Macleod and her husband John, a shoemaker, with their children, Donald not yet 2, Angus 3 and Mary Ann 6, and a neighbour'. The mother is heavily pregnant with child number 4, but it is difficult to guess either her age or her husband's.

### Understanding ageing in the twentieth century: a question of method

Of course, these considerations apply more generally. Dorothea Lange's itinerant pea-picker ('Migrant Mother'), Nipomo, California, 1936, holds three children, but she was in fact the mother of seven even though she was only thirty-two.[29] Such photographs of poor Okies on the move – the static record of Steinbeck's *Grapes of Wrath* – signify for Samuel another *locus classicus*, the Depression years of the 1930s.[30] While Agee and Evans took to field observation in the Dustbowl, British historians charted the progress of modernisation, seen in the rise of new industries, advances in public health and the welfare idea, planning, and the spread of leisure culture. Class distinctions were secondary to such consensus. Yet, simultaneously, photography 'fixes obsessively on the insignia of class, sticks to the backstreets while ignoring the out-county estates and the suburbs ... worried faces of Humphrey Spender's Worktowners ... Bill Brandt's down and out – head bowed, cap down,

---

[29] In what appears to be an attempt to suggest that this image was a single example of a mass experience, Lange did not identify this woman in a labour camp by name.

[30] Between the 1800s and 1920s both technological innovations and fresh professional conventions came to dominate 'realistic' and 'surrealistic' imagery, not least in France where the work of Atget is particularly significant. Although space precludes consideration of such major developments, they necessarily obtrude upon any agenda for detailed historical research.

setting out on road to nowhere'.[31] The monumental photographic record of the US Farm Security Administration sees Van Gogh mimicked in image after image. To a degree, one might argue that shots of gnarled farmworkers' hands, bent thin bodies, and worried, lined faces were accurate enough representations of human suffering – the camera did not lie.[32] In postwar Britain one has reason to be more sceptical as images of ageing – and I stress images as perceptual constructs, rather than realist renditions – sank to a new nadir.

In 1948, the Liberal Party recycled one of Van Gogh's more profoundly depressing drawings (a sketch entitled 'Despair', showing an old man holding his bowed head between his hands) as a cover for their pamphlet *The Aged and the Nation*,[33] and Peter Townsend's study of warehoused elderly in old workhouses (*The Last Refuge*, 1962) continued the trend begun by prewar pensions campaigners of representing age as dire impoverishment.[34] The image, once an experiment in symbolism, becomes a political vehicle, regardless of what most older people might have looked like. *The Last Refuge* includes thirty-eight consecutive monochrome plates which act as an essay in photographs. Many of these illustrations must have been deeply distressing, if not shocking, both because of the desperate apathy and decrepitude of the figures and faces and the prison-like architecture and decor. This contrasts sharply with the happy couple who smile from the front cover of Townsend's previous book *The Family Life of Old People* (1957), the message being that institutions are bad, lonely places but 'the community', and especially the extended working-class family, provide a haven of care.[35] Similarly, the cover picture of Young and Willmott's sociological classic, *Family and Kinship in East London* (1962)[36] depicts a happy grandfather smiling wildly to catch the eye of a baby cradled by his daughter (or a friend) – clearly a source of intergenerational cheer – while his wife chats animatedly with the younger women. By the mid-1970s a contrast had emerged between 'the imagery of age as desolation

---

[31] Samuel, 'The "eye" of history', 41.

[32] J. Agee and W. Evans, *Let Us Now Praise Famous Men* (Boston, MA: Houghton Mifflin, 1939; republished, 1980); Photo-Poche, *Amérique. Les Années noires: Farm Security Administration, 1935–1942* (Paris: Centre National de la Photographie, 1983).

[33] Liberal Party, *The Aged and the Nation* (London: Liberal Party, 1948).

[34] See A. Blaikie and J. Macnicol, 'Towards an anatomy of ageism: society, social policy and the elderly between the wars', in Phillipson, Bernard, and Strang, *Dependency and Interdependency in Old Age*, pp. 95–104.

[35] Richard Crossman, in a *New Statesman* review, claimed that '*The Last Refuge* combines the impact of the Dickensian novel with the detachment of social science' (quoted on back cover of abridged edition, Routledge and Kegan Paul, 1964). Townsend also took photographs in Bethnal Green at the time he was conducting interviews there. These are deposited in the Qualidata Archive, University of Essex.

[36] Harmondsworth: Pelican.

... found graphically in the cover photograph for Marris's *Loss and Change* (1974): an elderly person is depicted as an urban waif, lost in a concrete jungle she never made and far more positive portrayals emerging in holiday brochures and Third Age magazines such as *Choice* (see chapter 4).[37] Photographs have performed signal service in the cause of changing policy attitudes.

It would be cynical to regard such advocacy as in any way inappropriate or disbeneficial to real older people in real poverty, economic or spiritual, but the historian must always subject sources to careful scrutiny, and the photographic essay surely presents no exception. As one commentator says of the use of the photo essay in *Life* magazine: '*No* essay is truly singular ... More than one intellect, more than one set of prejudices and aesthetic standards are involved in its creation. I can think of no other visual form in which this plurality of influences prevails.'[38] Thus social constructionists have argued that, whereas a 'welfarist imagery, with its pathological overtones and emphasis on needs' prevailed until the 1970s, a 'rival imagery ... of old age as opportunity'[39] has recently developed. Ultimately, both engender specious stereotypes designed for effect. Photographic historians of postwar Britain cannot therefore rely on the attendant imagery as being in any wise 'faithful' to the times.

Aside from images such as Townsend's, collections of photographs of older people deliberately chosen or commissioned to illustrate facets of policy are rare. Usually the analyst is confronted with the task of unearthing illustrations lurking in the margins of general archives and then creating a story about ageing from the range of copies so gleaned. This, of course, builds the effects of observer bias into the exercise: the researcher decides what is representative and what is not, depending upon what is being sought. Relatedly, to what extent are subjects able to control how they are depicted, both at the time of the photograph being taken and in terms of how it is subsequently used?[40] In chapter 4 we saw how, for declining movie actresses, the camera lens could cruelly reveal (or impose) the loss of beauty. It is only on the rare occasions when photographer and subject actively collaborate – as in photography as art

[37] Fennell, Phillipson, and Evers, *Sociology of Old Age*, p. 8; P. Marris, *Loss and Change* (London: Routledge and Kegan Paul, 1974).

[38] M. Edey, *Great Photographic Essays from LIFE* (Boston, MA: New York Graphic Society, 1978), p. 4. Presumably the Magnum agency's Generation X project, through which Capa, Bischof, and other photojournalistic luminaries attempted to capture images from the lives of postwar youth in different countries, falls into this category.

[39] Fennell, Phillipson, and Evers, *Sociology of Old Age*, p. 8.

[40] On the repeated use of the same individuals to portray different images, see J. Johnson and B. Bytheway, 'Illustrating care: images of care relationships with older people', in Jamieson, Harper, and Victor, *Critical Approaches*, pp. 132–42.

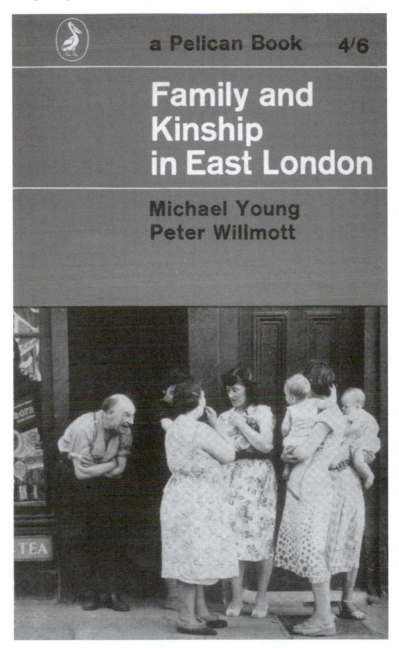

5   Young and Willmott: intergenerational harmony, early 1960s.
Photograph by Don Hunstein.

(see chapter 6) – that the otherwise powerless victim may be granted a right to some say.[41]

Critics of Philippe Ariès's *Centuries of Childhood* (1962) have pointed to the 'documentary fallacy' – accepting images as if they were direct translations of social reality, where images themselves offer a unifying concept. On the one hand, picturesquely grouped genre scenes, 'painterly in origin and intention even if . . . documentary in form',[42] display a poetics of ageing and the family. On the other, stark images of lonely old folk are often ideological by design, displaying a philanthropic pathos. Thus, in comparing images from different epochs we need to question whether it was the attitudes of people at large that changed, the types of invective used politically, or simply the fashions, forms, and features of art. Moreover, pictorial lacunae do not simply testify to the absence of, say, negative emotions or older factory workers; rather they might indicate either the principles of convention at the time or a kind of archival selective amnesia since. Ariès's present-mindedness means he records the absence of modern sentiment, but this does not tell us how children *were* perceived. Past society lacked our awareness, but this does not mean it had no awareness.[43] The same can be said for his work on perceptions of death and dying, or, indeed, attempts such as that of Georges Minois to construct a history of ageing in the West.[44] On the basis of compositional shifts in family portraits, David Hackett Fischer supposed there to have been a 'revolution in age relations' in North America between 1770 and 1820. Using alternative evidences Lawrence Stone debunked the argument, while Andrew Achenbaum argued that the transformation in generational attitudes came about much later.[45]

Modernisation assumes a linear shift from the veneration of the aged to their degradation. As we have seen in chapter 2, much recent scholarship has questioned this. However, it is difficult to see how photographs can contribute to the revaluation of status. If we assume physical and emotional security, respect, and playing a useful part to be universal goals to which older people strive, how can we demonstrate the presence or absence of each in snapshot images? Secondly, it is always possible

---

[41] See J. Spence and T. Dennett, *Metamorphosis; or Do We Have the Right to Determine Our Own Images of Ourselves After Death? A Pre- and Post-Death Collaboration* (1991), series of photographic prints, Glasgow Gallery of Modern Art.

[42] Samuel, 'The "eye" of history', p. 9.

[43] A. Wilson, 'The infancy of the history of childhood: an appraisal of Philippe Ariès', *History and Theory* 19, 2 (1980), 133–53.

[44] P. Ariès, *Western Attitudes Toward Death: From the Middle Ages to the Present* (Baltimore: Johns Hopkins University Press, 1974); T. Walter, 'Modern death: taboo or not taboo', *Sociology* 25, 2 (1991), 293–310; Minois, *History of Old Age*.

[45] Fischer, *Growing Old*; Stone, 'Walking over grandma'; Achenbaum, *Old Age in the New Land*.

that one indicator of high status may be satisfied while another is not –
peasant farmers could guarantee physical security by dint of their
control over inheritance, but this did not automatically ensure respect
from their sons and daughters; others may have had the material security
of a pension, but as advocates of structured dependency have demonstrated, this did anything but guarantee them a useful role within the
family or community.[46] Similarly, increased political power as a function
of age does not guarantee being adored by younger generations.[47]
Relationships between image and status are, indeed, complex, with the
accommodation of age-norms to family obligations rarely clear from
token prints of family groups.

Other sources have provided rich pickings. For instance, Susan
Tamke's study of old age in Victorian children's literature, songs, and
games reveals three predominant stereotypes: passive, passionless,
white-haired grannies; mutton-dressed-as-lamb characters who present
pathetic caricatures of their former selves; and the 'simply old' – the
dependent and senile.[48] None of these models is proactively positive, yet
neither is it in the nature of the sources to yield or take account of the
multiplicity of roles assumed by non-fictional elders. In his book *King
Twist*, Jeff Nuttall juxtaposes two action shots of the interwar stage
comic of the Northern music hall Frank Randle, one sitting in an
armchair, wearing slippers and reading a story to his grandchildren (the
Grandpa figure), the other his infamous Old Hiker, tousled hair, gap-
toothed, ragged, lascivious, and drunk.[49] The one actor, with a quick
change of props and masks, can convey two stereotypes of ageing
masculinity. But does Randle's latter caricature (which prefigures the
likes of Steptoe and Alf Garnett of British television comedy fame in the
1960s) typify a closely observed reality or – remembering that most
humour articulates prejudice – is it simply a culturally convenient peg
on which to hang a joke?[50]

All these qualifications should act as a warning to anybody intending
to mount an exhibition about aspects of ageing that relies upon photographs (or, indeed, any visual images). In the mid-1970s, gerontologist
Andrew Achenbaum and art librarian Peggy Ann Kusnerz collaborated
to produce an annotated travelling exhibition for the Smithsonian

[46] Quadagno, *Aging*, pp. 202–4.     [47] Fischer, *Growing Old*.
[48] S. S. Tamke, 'Human values and aging: the perspective of the Victorian nursery', in
S. F. Spicker, K. M. Woodward, and D. Van Tassel (eds.), *Aging and the Elderly:
Humanistic Perspectives in Gerontology* (Atlantic Highlands, NJ: Humanities Press,
1978), pp. 60–94 (p. 64).
[49] J. Nuttall, *King Twist* (London: Routledge and Kegan Paul, 1978).
[50] See Nahemow, McCluskey, and McGhee, *Humor and Aging*, and Blaikie and Macnicol,
'Towards an anatomy', for analyses of the vocabulary of cartoons.

Institution.[51] The tale of how certain images were selected while thousands of others were rejected indicates an acknowledged selectivity on the part of two advocates against ageism attempting to educate the public. Intriguingly, too, Achenbaum's re-evaluation of the exercise argues that, if, with hindsight, he were to conduct the process again, he would search for examples to illustrate themes which have only become salient, or significant, since – political correctness, feminist theory, and postmodern criticism would demand more positive exemplars of people of race, women, and gays as well as, in a pluralistic epoch, 'more images inviting multiple interpretations'.[52] The point to bear in mind is not whether such pictures actually exist, but what objectives inform and motivate the searcher. On this we are not always open or sufficiently self-critical. Social knowledge is produced from a variety of perspectives and social and intellectual locations that ought to be acknowledged: the unexamined 'view from nowhere' is no longer tenable.

### Biscuit tin memories: snapshots and family lives

Thus far, I have concentrated on sources available in the public domain, but, of course, modern technology allows most Westerners to own cameras and keep their own private record. At the same time, we inhabit bureaucracies that can function only by issuing identification cards, passports, bus passes, each presenting ourselves to others in the form of individuated, if not individualised mugshots. The photograph is thus doubly democratic: on the one hand, it becomes a precondition of citizenship (no passport photo, no travel abroad, no half-price fare, no entry); on the other, compared to the business of purchasing prints made by photographers in the past, nowadays we can all take our own pictures and have them developed at relatively little expense.

The impact of visual and televisual culture upon lifestyles should not be underestimated. In the 1970s Susan Sontag presented us with not just a classic set of essays about photography but also a pathbreaking analysis of differing gender expectations of ageing. A glance at almost any women's magazine will indicate that, in the generation since she wrote 'The double standard of aging', advertising has refashioned the 'acceptable' imagery quite markedly.[53] Not least we have seen profound

---

[51] W. A. Achenbaum and P. A. Kusnerz, *Images of Old Age in America: 1790 to the Present* (Ann Arbor, MI: Institute of Gerontology, 1978).

[52] Achenbaum, W. A., 'Images of old age in America, 1790 to the present: after a second look', paper prepared for working conference on Images of Aging, Luxembourg, June 1991.

[53] S. Sontag, *On Photography* (Harmondsworth: Penguin, 1979); Sontag, 'The double standard of aging'.

shifts in expectations concerning women's roles across the adult life-span. In parallel with these transformations, gerontologists have adopted a dual role as analysts and enablers. The image can be interpreted as the emblem of a changing trend, or it can be utilised as a vehicle for change. As we have seen with pensioners' campaigns, negative stereotypes of older people may be heavily criticised, and more positive icons projected in their place; alternatively, 'old and poor' can act as a *cri de coeur* around which to mobilise public opinion.[54] Help the Aged's posters from the 1980s are a recent case in point.

There are other, more directly interactive ways in which the photo-graph may be used. For instance, gerontologists and social workers have joined psychoanalysts in the quest for reconstruction of the self via reminiscence.[55] Here the catalytic role of the image is becoming increas-ingly evident, as a 'trigger' to alert people to various past phases or incidents in their lives and thence as an aid to oral recall. Although such pictures are rarely considered problematic in their own right, recent thinking suggests that visual sources are fundamental to our sense of self as we move through time. There exists a point of convergence between the life course as remembered time and the sequencing of our memories through the medium of the photograph, and, to the extent that we collect photographs of ourselves and construct a plausible story around them, we are all essayists.

Rosalind Coward considers women's fascination with the family snap-shot and its record of people's likenesses.[56] Mothers, she says, frequently become guardians of the unwritten history of the family. Collections of snaps in old chocolate boxes or biscuit tins get used as evidence, tangible proof of our genealogies. Indeed, 'for those with humble origins, the birth of photography quite literally founds the family ... With the birth of photography, history becomes real, but above all the family becomes tangible.' Again, of course, selectivity plays a major part, with certain moments considered more significant than others, particularly those where women see themselves in roles and actions affirming family solidarity – fiancée, bride, mother. Such poses are heavily underlain by contemporary cultural scripts:

Looking at her own family album. Jo [Spence] found herself posing, at the age of five, as Shirley Temple. All through her life, the snapshots echoed previous ways in which women had been represented. The kind of poses and the styles are influenced directly by religious, ideological, and artistic conventions. Behind

[54] Blaikie, 'Emerging political power'.
[55] P. G. Coleman, *Ageing and Reminiscence Processes*.
[56] R. Coward, *Female Desire: Women's Sexuality Today* (London: Paladin, 1984), pp. 47–54, essay entitled 'The mirror with a memory'.

every new mother sits a Renaissance Madonna, and behind every young woman the contemporary 'glamorous' image. Doubtless there are not many weddings in the 1980s that are not haunted by the spectre of the Royal Wedding. Women being much observed and defined cannot escape those coercive definitions even in their own homes.[57]

In a detailed examination of his own parents' pasts, Ignatieff notes that 'from its beginnings, photography was recognised as a new source of consciousness about the family past'.[58] However, family albums offer us no signs of hardship, labour, grief, sibling rivalry, painful adolescence, or death. They are about growing up rather than growing old: 'there is no attempt to deal with the deep underground streams of family emotions ... we have happiness and solidarity in the family (snapshots) and we have "social problems" [like ageing alone in poverty] which are not supposed to happen in the family and are recorded by "professional" photographers'.[59] Photographs are supposed to represent how we see ourselves and others see us. They might appear to present a true reflection, but they in fact trick us into self-delusion:

Instead of objective record, we encounter absence ... images of something which is no longer happening, is no longer there. It recalls the possibility of our own absence, and death, and fails to yield up a view of a full world and our existence in it.

And to cover this absence, we deny it and find a way round to restore our love for our images and the full world which accompanied our early narcissism. We abolish the images which don't correspond to our mirror faces and fall back in love with ourselves as if there were no cultural super-ego and no absences or separations. And we set about collecting likenesses of our antecedents and children which feed our narcissism and re-create an undamaged world. We view new-born babies with all the narcissistic gratification which we first invested in our own likenesses. Surrounded by photographs we attempt to re-create an infantile world, a world where there is no critical super-ego and where we have not encountered the pain of separation and loss.[60]

Coward's analysis suggests an intriguing methodology for looking backwards over our lives, not least because it helps to explain the ways in which emplotment (the weaving of events into a coherent narrative) and the tendency to order in all our self-realisations are articulated.[61] There is therapeutic as well as socio-analytic value in trying to 'picture the silences' in conventional images of family life. Indeed, photo therapy

[57] Ibid., pp. 49–50, 51.
[58] M. Ignatieff, *The Russian Album* (Harmondsworth: Penguin, 1988), p. 3.
[59] Coward, *Female Desire*, p. 51.    [60] Ibid., pp. 53–4.
[61] J.-E. Ruth and P. Öberg, 'Ways of life: old age in a life history perspective', in J. Birren, G. Kenyon, J.-E. Ruth, J. J. F. Schroots, and T. Svensson (eds.), *Aging and Biography: Explorations in Adult Development* (New York: Springer, 1996), pp. 167–86. I am grateful to Hans-Dieter Schneider for the suggestion that the psychological need for a harmonious 'good *Gestalt*' in later life might underlie the glorification of one's past.

seeks to recapture emotions and conflicts lurking below the surface of the smiling snapshot and thus prompt a reappraisal of memories and, in turn, identities.[62] Subjective experience of ageing may be far adrift from the ways in which it becomes objectified by outsiders. Thus, Freud, in his case study of the Wolf Man, implied that 'narrative truth, order, and sequence does not much signify in the eliciting of a life history'.[63] Accounting for how we got to be the way we are is a transactional process that has to transcend personal memory: for my past to become a coherent story requires the articulation of significant symbols; I must connect in some way with my hearers. Visual culture operates in similar ways.

Walter Benjamin brilliantly foretells that the passage of photography into everyday currency would entail the acquisition of a means of expression closely articulated with how we remember.[64] Appearances constitute a 'half-language' of the life course. In *Another Way of Telling* John Berger and Jean Mohr go beyond the family album to explore the multiple meanings inscribed in the visual. The book's centrepiece is an essay told in 150 photographs, about which Berger notes:

memory, based upon the visual, is freer than reason.

There is no single 'correct' interpretation of this sequence of images. It attempts to follow an [imaginary] old woman's reflections on her life. If she were suddenly asked: what are you thinking about?, she would invent a simple answer, because the question, when taken seriously, becomes unanswerable. Her reflections cannot be defined by an answer to a question beginning with *What?* And yet she was thinking, reflecting, remembering, recalling, and doing so in a consecutive manner. She was making sense of herself to herself.

By considering her own life, she reflects, like everyone who grows old, on life in general: on being born, on childhood, on work, love, emigration, work, being a woman, death, the village, work . . .

The photographs of this sequence are not intended to be documentary . . . There are photographs included of moments and scenes which she could never have witnessed . . . We have tried here to speak this [visual] language so as not only to illustrate, but also to articulate a lived experience.[65]

Here the creative artist uses images to invent rather than describe. Yet, as Hareven's work suggests, the historian's craft is not dissimilar.[66] Specific social groups, be they families, friends, communities, cohorts, or generations, will provide frameworks for the memories of their

[62] M. Benjamin, 'Picturing the silences', *New Statesman and Society*, 25 June 1993, 32–3.
[63] C. Steedman, *Landscape for a Good Woman: A Story of Two Lives* (London: Virago, 1986), p. 132.
[64] W. Benjamin, *Illuminations* (London: Fontana, 1973).
[65] J. Berger and J. Mohr, 'If each time . . .', in Berger and Mohr, *Another Way of Telling* (London: Readers and Writers, 1982), pp. 131–275 (pp. 133–4).
[66] Hareven, 'Family time and historical time'.

members.[67] Are we then to classify photos in the register of 'remembered time' and then listen for secret harmonies with other temporalities? What cultural effectivity, what resonance do such imagined psychic imprints have? At the personal level, we will never really know. But we can observe that the salience a picture acquires *retrospectively* in the course of its subsequent career involves our active participation in its transformation: a process of reconfiguration in which posed genre tableaux become 'Nostalgic Images' postcards, whilst, in turn, these are re-presented as simulations of real lives.

But, then, far from wishing to debunk myths by positing a crude dichotomy between image and reality, I am concerned with the malleability of the visual. 'Images are both local and general. They can pass between times and cultures with a facility that often blinds us to their local qualities, to the centrality of their circumstances of production and consumption.'[68] In *Local Knowledge* Clifford Geertz reminds us of the importance of acknowledging how visual skills are learned, developed, and deployed.[69] Our globally visual culture contrasts with the 'period eye', the specificity of visual cultures in the past. While the photographic enterprise constructs coherence, the gerontological tradition emphasises the radical schism in putative attitudes to ageing before and after modernisation. What we must do is explain how 'transforming a more or less chance residue of the past into a precious icon' does violence to the fragmentation, difference, and diversity that clearly existed.[70]

[67] See M. Halbwachs, *On Collective Memory*, edited, translated, and with an introduction by L. A. Coser (University of Chicago Press, 1992).
[68] Jordanova, 'Medicine and visual culture', 89.
[69] C. Geertz, *Local Knowledge: Further Essays in Interpretive Anthropology* (London: Fontana, 1993).
[70] Samuel, 'The "eye" of history', 41.

# 6  Pictures at an exhibition: representations of age and generation

In the climate of a growing awareness of the sociological relevance of visual imagery, this chapter reflects on how ageing has been portrayed in photographic exhibitions and collections. As the previous chapter indicates, in the recent past age has been conveyed via readily recognisable devices. The fact that disguises can easily be created either to emphasise or to hide signs of age suggests that, contrary to the supposition that 'the camera never lies', pictures are often deliberate fictions. Similarly, the context in which images are presented can be critical in how we interpret them: ageing may be equated with nostalgia, but it can also be presented as a diverse range of contemporary experiences. Intergenerational relations are often evident, but, as Jo Spence's work shows, conventional imagery is highly selective, promoting happy moments while rendering problems invisible.[1] The advent of the cheap portable camera means that nowadays most people include snapshots among their biographical and family archives. While such material requires to be subjected to the same careful scrutiny as publicly accessible sources, it also presents us with a valuable basis for reminiscence work. In the ensuing analysis, two particular aspects are considered: first, the perceived role of images of age within the broader frame of the general photographic exhibition; secondly, the creative uses of photography, as art, to convey messages about ageing.

## Introduction

John Berger has noted that: 'In the age of pictorial reproduction the meaning of paintings is no longer attached to them; their meaning becomes transmittable: that is to say it becomes information of a sort, and, like all information, is either put to use or ignored.'[2] Not only this, but the advent of photography has produced new sorts of information,

[1] J. Spence and P. Holland (eds.), *Family Snaps: The Meanings of Domestic Photography* (London: Virago, 1991).
[2] J. Berger, *Ways of Seeing* (Harmondsworth: BBC/Penguin, 1972), p. 24.

images capable of manipulation in an infinite variety of ways. Bolton adds: 'the photograph is polysemic ... it has no single independent meaning, but many possible meanings depending upon context and use ... [but] just as a social context makes certain readings possible, it can make other readings impossible. Institutions authorize certain meanings and dismiss, even silence, others. Thus there is a politics of interpretation that one contends with immediately, whether one knows it or not. To interpret a photograph, or any cultural object, is to negotiate a sea of choices already made.'[3] The implications for the understanding of ageing are clear, yet surprisingly little cognisance has been taken of such observations: images of old age tend to be accepted as true likenesses.

Against this, cultural theorists have observed that one feature of postmodernity is the aestheticisation of everyday life.[4] This operates in two directions: while artists turn people's commonplace reality into objects of curiosity, people themselves draw on objects such as clothes to develop lifestyle projects. Photographic artists, like writers, have elaborated metaphoric understandings by, for example, comparing the texture of worn skin to that of frayed fabric in an endeavour to capture the 'look of age'. Equally, photographs are a reflexive resource in everyday life. Snapshots, often collated as family albums, facilitate comparisons between past and present, both across generations (for instance, changing dress styles and pastimes) and within one's own biography ('Was I really that slim?', 'Did I really wear those shoes?' ... ).

Images are both sources (of meaning or evidence) and resources, in the sense that they may be deployed to convey particular impressions. Experiments in 'photo therapy', photo journalism and documentary photography, and photography as art, advertising, and illustration use images in different ways, each needing critical attention. Alternatively, we might also use photographs 'to answer questions the photographer did not have in mind and that are not obviously suggested by the picture ... We can thus avoid interminable, unresolvable, and irrelevant questions about the photographer's intent.'[5]

Although the development of visual culture has had a fundamental impact on both the representation and interpretation of ageing, all images are manufactured and are ultimately contestable as forms of

---

[3] R. Bolton, 'In the American east: Richard Avedon Incorporated', in R. Bolton (ed.), *The Contest of Meaning: Critical Histories of Photography* (London: MIT Press, 1992), pp. 261–82 (p. 281).

[4] M. Featherstone, *Consumer Culture and Postmodernism* (London: Sage, 1991), pp. 24–5, 66–72.

[5] H. S. Becker, 'Do photographs tell the truth?', in H. S. Becker, *Doing Things Together: Selected Papers* (Evanston, IL: Northwestern University Press, 1986), pp. 273–92 (p. 277).

evidence. I begin with the premiss that the current gerontological interest in visual images of age too readily accepts pictures as unmediated reflections of social reality whereas the uses of the photograph suggest the ambiguity of ageing, both in terms of the range of identities exposed and of the experiences and relationships hinted at. Such a contradiction provides many possibilities for reflection, discussion, and collaborative interpretation for those working with photographs as teaching or learning resources. While it is first necessary to subject sources to methodological scrutiny, our rich familiarity with images of ourselves and others allows for personal and biographical engagement and interaction as well as more straightforwardly intellectual appreciation.

## The construction of 'tradition'

The media have substituted themselves for the older world. Even if we should wish to discover that older world we can only do it only by an intensive study of the ways in which the media have swallowed it.[6]

The advent of the camera, the possibility of mass reproduction of images, including paintings, and the scale of these phenomena have utterly transformed visual culture. Thus, in the words of John Berger: 'The uniqueness of every painting was once part of the uniqueness of the place where it resided. Sometimes the painting was transportable. But it could never be seen in two places at the same time. When the camera reproduces a painting [or, by extension, a photograph is reproduced], it destroys the uniqueness of its image. As a result its meaning changes. Or, more exactly, its meaning multiplies and fragments into many meanings.'[7] While, therefore, the circulation of images was relatively ill developed in the earlier nineteenth century, the progression of photographic technique since has enabled an increasingly dispersed mass of images to emerge.

In the first half of the present century, the uses of different versions of a range of media – cartoons, postcards, family portraits – depicting older people variously as always dressed in black, frail, poor, humorously obese, or, like grannies, sublimely benign, suggest an iconography reflecting the ways in which different social groups could use particular images as vehicles for achieving their own particular ends: as we saw in chapter 5, the pensioners' movement, representing its constituents in cartoon form as impoverished and raggedly dressed in order to press

[6] Marshall McLuhan, cited in Sontag, *On Photography*, p. 102.
[7] J. Berger, *Ways of Seeing*, p. 19.

home claims about low living standards, was certainly implicated. Likewise, in everyday popular culture the repertoire was amenable to playful combination and recombination, as in the music hall where, for instance, Britain's highest-earning comedian and entertainer Harry Gordon posed famously in drag as Whistler's Mother. In several Victorian and Edwardian paintings the fact that the subject was an imitation of an earlier work of art was indicated by positioning the original on a wall in the background and in the photograph of Harry Gordon, the humour is heightened by doing just this, since the subject in the foreground, while feigning mimicry in terms of dress and positioning, deliberately fails to be a true likeness by dint of a broad, moronic grin and skirts coyly hitched up to reveal woolly slippers.[8] Similarly, we saw in chapter 5 how, with one quick change of props, Lancastrian comedian Frank Randle switched from an alcoholic tramp figure to being the 'gentler patriarch' Grandpa sitting by the fire and telling stories to his grandchildren.[9] Privately, too, family snapshots may use everyday stereotypes to achieve humorous effects: my mother has a snapshot of herself, aged twenty, dressed in her father's postman's uniform; she is deliberately slumped in an armchair, wearing thick spectacles and pulling on a pipe, the intention being to poke fun at his ageing masculinity. This ability to suggest age by means of readily recognisable disguises is complemented in the later twentieth century by cosmetics. Indeed, the potential expansion of social roles in later life has not been overlooked by advertisers whose degree of commercial success serves to remind us that the of art of disguise is not just the preserve of professional actors and is not simply humorous. Nevertheless, although we are all conscious of the ways in which all manner of props can be used to 'combat the signs of ageing', we sometimes fail to appreciate the subtler ways in which our visual culture may be manipulated.

### In the gallery

In 1994, the Barbican staged a major exhibition of photographs from the massive Hulton Deutsch Collection, entitled *All Human Life*. Although older people were not especially predominant among the range of images on show, both the leaflet and accompanying catalogue featured them. The front cover of the latter presented a close-up shot, taken in 1939, of a couple celebrating their golden wedding with a

[8] I. Watson, *Harry Gordon 'The Laird of Inversnecky'* (Aberdeen: Aberdeen District Council, 1993), pp. 66–7.
[9] Nuttall, *King Twist*, pp. 46–7.

kiss.[10] Meanwhile, the free leaflet portrayed 'Old Tom' Owen having his head shaved. The justification for selecting these two images – from a total of no less than fifteen million in the collection – is provided in the text which introduces the catalogue: 'Amongst my own personal favourites are pictures of some of the old characters who you might still, if you are fortunate enough, stumble across every now and again ... people like old Tom Owen, the hedge-laying specialist, loving every moment of his haircut.'[11] Whether or not Tom was enjoying being barbered is a moot point: what constitutes his appeal is the fact that he is considered a 'character' and that his type is considered a rarity, only 'stumbled across' by the fortunate 'every now and again', like antique stoves still in use, or classic cars. Old Tom is a figure of yesteryear, valuable precisely because, although we shall not look on his like again, the camera has immortalised his memory. The picture has become a motif synthesising times gone by and old age in the same frame. The barber is one Handel Lewis, a man whose other jobs, according to *Picture Post*, were 'farmer's help, chimney sweep, special constable, electric lighting engineer, and mender of the village shoes' whilst his day job was village postman.[12] This is rural England in 1944, another time and place, before specialisation, when people could turn their hands to many crafts, where everyone knew everybody else and Lewis's shed sufficed as a styling parlour.

If such an image represents a rarity, it is none the less typical of the wistfully nostalgic world of curio cards, sepia prints, and heritage centre kitsch, in which older people symbolise the last of the old order, either as bearers of vanished skills (white-bearded handloom weavers), and disappearing communities (aged tenants outside condemned houses in postwar photo essays), one-off eccentrics (octogenarians riding penny-farthing bicycles), or simply 'old characters' like Tom. They have, of course, been selected for their strangeness to us today, rather than because they represent ordinary ageing in the past. Such are the archives of the coffee table.[13]

Other recent exhibitions have displayed similar nostalgic characteristics. Presenting 254 images from twenty-seven countries, the 133rd International Exhibition of the Edinburgh Photographic Society reflected the conventional cross-section of image categories – exotic shots of faraway places, pictorial allegories with titles such as 'Temptation' and 'Isolation', portraits, street and domestic scenes. Only fifteen (6 per

[10] B. Bernard, *All Human Life: Great Photographs from the Hulton Deutsch Collection* (London: Barbican Art Gallery, 1994).
[11] Ibid., p. 9.      [12] Ibid., p. 53.
[13] A. Blaikie, 'Druggets and uglies, crotal and cailleachan: remembering the recent past', *Northern Scotland* 14 (1994), 135–45.

cent) of these photographs showed older people or relations between generations, yet of the twenty-eight plates in the accompanying catalogue, five are of older people. Interestingly, another five feature children, suggesting perhaps an editorial desire to balance the two ends of the life span.[14] Similarly, when distinguished Scots selected their seven favourite images from the National Photography Collection, older people featured in three of the chosen pictures (and 'pastness' characterises the Victorian fisher children and Victorian street scenes in two of the remaining four). While artist John Bellany chose an early (1844) Hill and Adamson calotype of a fishwife because, 'it has the stillness and silent beauty of a Vermeer', he adds: 'Perhaps more importantly I love it because it reminds me of my Auntie Nan who used to carry the creel.' Pop musician Donnie Munro selected Iain Stewart's 'Grandmother and Child', remarking that 'It's almost like the potential of youth set against a reflective image of old age.' Finally, the Bishop of Edinburgh elected an image from Grace Robertson's 'Mother's Day Off' (1954), which depicts a young girl spying into a pub window, while, in the foreground an old lady engages the attention of two middle-aged women. This picture is part of a documentary photo essay illustrating a bus outing to Clapham Common. Bishop Holloway recollects 'grannies going down for a glass of port to the Cosy Corner'. His final comment – 'I'm sorry to give you a piece of autobiographical social history but that would be the picture I would choose' – reflects the salience of images that relate to or suggest a link with one's own past. This active biographical personalisation of photographs clearly has the effect of foregrounding images of 'pastness' (rather than the present), of people (rather than buildings or landscapes), and, in particular, of people who trigger memories of childhood.[15] These images also assert mortality as a central theme of photography. As Roland Barthes has observed, photographs must remind us of death since they can only ever illustrate that which has passed and gone forever.[16] Images of old people are valuable precisely because the camera has captured them for posterity, immortalised their memory.

It is perhaps to be expected that the visual record will mirror the general marginalisation or stigmatisation of older people in our culture, with relatively few images occurring in comparison with, say, those of children, and those that are available being somewhat exceptional or

[14] Edinburgh Photographic Society, *133rd International Exhibition of Photography* (Edinburgh Photographic Society, 1995).

[15] National Galleries of Scotland, *On Photography* (Edinburgh: Education Department of the National Galleries of Scotland, 1994).

[16] R. Barthes, *Camera Lucida: Reflections on Photography* (London: Vintage, 1993), p. 79.

atypical. Indeed, recent compilations contain whole chapters on 'Growing up' but nothing on growing old.[17] Other collections emphasise (partly through what is absent) the historical invisibility of most women from the camera's gaze. To be old and female is to be doubly disadvantaged, with the domestic everyday settings of most providing the least photogenic of environments. Thus the most common everyday experience of upwards of two-thirds of the older female population – housewives at work inside their homes – is almost entirely absent from the record. Instead we have come to rely on exceptional instances for historical backdrop. A particularly good example that blends old age, dying local crafts, and rural depopulation, and, *par excellence* in this case, marginality from the mainstream is a picture of an old lady with the caption: 'Mrs Gillies, one of the last St Kildans, seated in front of her house. This photograph was taken the day before St Kilda was evacuated, in August 1930. She calmly continued to knit, using wool plucked from the local Soay sheep and spun at home. Most of her own clothes would have been dyed and woven or knitted on the island.'[18]

The problems of selectivity and representativeness in historical portraits are mirrored in the photographic record of another group chosen for their oddity, very old people: for example, six of the seven portraits in Jane Bown's collection of over-ninety-year-olds are of 'individuals whose former social role carried some kind of prestigious association . . . [and whose] media prominence quite clearly derives from factors additional to their being in their nineties'.[19] A recent feminist calendar entitled *Women Who Dare* included portraits of distinguished older women – Maggie Kuhn (of the Gray Panthers), Jane Jacobs, Elisabeth Kübler-Ross – renowned for their achievements.[20] Alternatively, the calendar from a photographic competition and exhibition mounted as part of the 1993 European Year of Older People and Solidarity Between Generations selected anonymous images of older people across Europe, but only those highlighting 'the positive face of older age'.[21] In justifying his choice of a favourite image of 1996, playwright David Hare commented:

---

[17] D. Kidd, *To See Oursels: Rural Scotland in Old Photographs* (Glasgow and Edinburgh: HarperCollins/National Museums of Scotland, 1992), pp. 119–29.

[18] L. Leneman, *Into the Foreground: A Century of Scottish Women in Photographs* (Stroud and Edinburgh: Alan Sutton/National Museums of Scotland, 1993), p. 72.

[19] Hockey and James, *Growing Up and Growing Old*, pp. 177–8. J. Johnson and Bytheway, 'Illustrating care', p. 141, cite Imogen Cunningham's photographs of old age in her *After Ninety* (Seattle and London: University of Washington Press, 1977) which were produced when she was in her nineties.

[20] *Women Who Dare*, 1995 calendar (Washington: Library of Congress, 1994).

[21] *Twelve Faces of Age*, 1994 calendar (London: Inquit, 1993).

I saw this photo in a young British art show in Paris. Most of the exhibitors were modishly nihilistic, in what is now a fairly predictable way. Only the photographs by Richard Billingham, and in particular this one of an old man being given a boiled egg, worked the proper alchemy of art. His subjects are poor and, in one sense, desperate. Yet he sees them as radiantly spirited. This is a real gift: to see vigour and beauty in what others call ugliness.[22]

### Bodies: questions of control

While Foucault recognises the body as a reference point for social control, Elias refers to the disgust that is evoked by the absence of bodily control.[23] Signs of 'datedness' – sagging flesh, wrinkles, grey hair, and so on – indicate bodily betrayals and thus tend to be stigmatised in a youth-fixated culture. The gaze of fashion rejects the naked older body as a possible site of 'beauty'. As Waters has commented: 'Most of us shrink from contemplating the ageing naked body. Lines and wrinkles in the face may be taken as signs of character and maturity. But how – without denying the flesh altogether – do we deal with that tattered coat upon a stick, the ageing body?'[24]

In a couple of rare instances the answer appears to be via direct exposure of older people doing things with their bodies quite naturally and unashamedly. Cotier's *Nudes in Budapest* presents portraits, individual and collective, of older people in the steam rooms of a large public baths, a venue which people self-evidently attend for the good of their health. The suggestion of sound maintenance is enhanced by the surrounding art nouveau decor: both appear old but well preserved.[25] In *Extracts from Harry's Diary* and *Pretty Ribbons* Donigan Cumming presents a series of images of a naked octogenarian couple in their home in Montreal. This work is more shocking because, whereas Cotier's bathers are on public display these bodies are captured in private poses and engaged in intimate acts, including scenes of lovemaking.[26] What

---

[22] 'The year in moments: how 1996 looked to 32 *Observer* readers', *Observer Life*, 29 December 1996, 4–11 (8).

[23] N. Elias, *The Civilising Process: The History of Manners*, 2 vols. (Oxford: Basil Blackwell, 1978), vol. I.

[24] M. Waters, *The Nude Male: A New Perspective* (New York and London: Paddington Press, 1978), cited in M. Hepworth, 'Positive ageing and the mask of age', *Journal of Educational Gerontology* 6, 2 (1991), 93–101 (98).

[25] J. Cotier, *Nudes in Budapest* (Budapest: Aktok, 1992). The book provoked sufficient interest for the British Sunday press to carry a photographic story – 'Naked age', *Observer Magazine*, 18 October 1992, 42–8. In his late seventies, John Coplans, a New York-based British photographer, continues to execute naked self-portraits.

[26] D. Cumming, *Extracts from Harry's Diary/Pretty Ribbons* (Montreal, December 1991–April 1992).

both sets of images share is an ability to confront us by making us feel embarrassed; we are the ones being shamed for our prejudices.

In the creation of images of disabled people David Hevey accuses photographic artists of 'enfreakment', a process of accentuating grotesqueness in order at once to enchant and repel the public. He cites Diane Arbus's deliberate exposition of physically and mentally disabled 'freaks'.[27] The offence he encounters is shared by several critics who have been upset by the absence of probity in photographing mentally retarded adults who, by definition, were unable to give their informed consent beforehand. Arbus's late work on people in care institutions may have been designed to project 'symbolic specimens of otherness',[28] to 'parody our ideas about normal' by dressing up residents in Halloween masks or posing them in invented family snapshots, but the ethical transgression remains: 'Her "freaks" here do not know they are freaks and do not know there is a game going on.'[29] Here art finds parallels with documentary photography, and, as Johnson and Bytheway have demonstrated, such practice and critique have clear resonances when applied to the depiction of older people in institutional settings, especially those affected by mental or physical disabilities.[30] On the one hand, older people, like disabled people, have been subjected to the 'enfreakment of photography' whereby their very marginality – both bodily and socially – is used to excite public fascination. Like Arbus's voyeuristic images of 'dwarfs', 'a Jewish giant', and 'retardees', one can easily see how pictures of demented or crippled old people fall into the same offending category.[31] Less obviously perhaps, the ageing enterprise abounds with images of positive ageing. While pictures of intergenerational interaction, close-ups of deeply etched faces denoting wisdom or action shots of angry pensions campaigners aim to dispel any suggestion of 'freakishness', they are none the less elements in the construction of another stereotype – that of integrated elders sorting out their own social problems. Truth is hard to come by.

This discussion raises some of the ethical and legal issues behind the use of photographs. Who owns the images and who ought to benefit from their reproduction? Should standards of informed consent be applied? In 1992, Grace Robertson was commissioned by BBC Television to photograph people in their nineties. Williams points out that, in producing the images, 'she has defined her parameters in an ethical as

---

[27] D. Hevey, *The Creatures Time Forgot: Photography and Disability Imagery* (London: Routledge, 1992), pp. 53–74.

[28] T. Lubbock, 'At the limit of exposure', *Guardian*, 29 September 1995, 6.

[29] M. Freely, 'More trick than treat', *Observer Review*, 17 September 1995, 16.

[30] J. Johnson and Bytheway, 'Illustrating care'.

[31] Hevey, *The Creatures*, pp. 53–74.

well as a visual way: "Among the hundreds of photographs I made of ninety-year-olds there were, inevitably, moments when my sitters gave me looks which, though pictorially interesting, presented a false and even unkind impression of the individuals themselves. In deciding which pictures should be selected for exhibition and publication ... I was left to answer one question: supposing I was this person, would I be happy about this likeness going on public display?" ... Forty years on, these are the ethics of *Picture Post*.'[32] Unfortunately, not all photographers are quite so conscientious.

### Playing with conventions

While images may be politically convenient, ideologically sound, or commercially successful, the idiomatic fallacy that the camera cannot lie means that the historical accuracy of photographs is rarely questioned. However, as with any source, we really ought to be more sceptical. Now that positive ageing has become a byword of political correctness, a Martian falling to Earth might find a set of celluloid images of Jane Fonda in leotard and tights with a beaming and bushy-tailed Burt Reynolds and thereby conclude that all older people looked and communicated as they do. We would know differently, but where would we find representative data? Where are the millions of ordinary people, quietly ageing with limited but sound health, restricted budgets, bare but adequate housing?

The only right response to this question is to refrain from any such search, to eschew reconstruction in favour of deconstruction, for it is the diversity of identities and relations between generations that characterises the ageing experience, not its homogeneity. Impressionistic analysis indicates an often inadvertent, none the less socially constructed imagery of the life course. However, photography as a form of art involves processes that are more readily deconstructive than reconstructive: the diversity of identities and relations between generations is emphasised, rather than any stereotypical characteristics of ageing.

A second 1994 Barbican offering is exemplary. Entitled *Who's Looking at the Family?*, the exhibition explicitly evoked the multiplicity of ways of presenting, photographing, and reading images of interaction within and across generations. The images of later life are strikingly different from one another both in intention and in effect. Jim Goldberg's technique of asking family members to comment on the shots he

---

[32] V. Williams, 'Ethics of everyday life: Grace Robertson's photojournalism, 1949–1993', essay accompanying *Grace Robertson into the Nineties* (London: Watershed Touring Exhibition, 1993).

has taken, by writing around the image 'both affirms and denies the power of documentary, contrasting appearances with reality and presenting a complex set of truths'.[33] One portrait shows a well-dressed older couple in a spacious room decorated with prints, antique furniture, and Persian rugs. He is seated, wearing suit and tie and looking composed, if slightly resigned; she stands, looking on, her right hand gently resting on an incidental table; her expression is similar. In his remarks, Edgar Goldstine has scrawled, curtly: 'My wife is acceptable. Our relationship is satisfactory', while Regina writes somewhat more fulsomely: 'Edgar looks splendid here. His power and strength of character come through. He is a very private person who is not demonstrative of his affection; that has never made me unhappy. I accept him as he is. We are totally devoted to each other . . . May you be as lucky in marriage!'[34] Social documentarist Tony O'Shea angrily makes the stark decline, illness, and death of his father the subject of a photo series whilst Liz Rideal's images of her grandmother's death aim to stress a far more serene spiritual continuity by including a picture of clouds between the final shots of the old woman closing her eyes and the still-warm corpse.

Richard Billingham grainily depicts the domestic chaos of living with an alcoholic father.[35] Meanwhile, Larry Sultan presents the complicated relationships between his parents by juxtaposing home movie stills ('a kaleidoscope of history, investing the past with both magic and pathos. Appealing to the power of photography to halt the passing of time') with a picture of his mother as she is now, posing while his father obliviously watches the television, his back to the camera.[36] While much may be gained from viewing such works, Sultan warns the would-be analyst against reading too much into them: 'Photographing my father became a way of confronting my confusion about what it is to be a man in this culture . . . [but] What drives me to continue this work is more difficult to name. It has more to do with love than with sociology, with being a subject in the drama rather than a witness.'[37]

Finally, Corinne Noordenbos's haunting close-ups of Alzheimer's sufferers' faces 'stare out at the photographer, vestiges perhaps of their former selves, but presences which cannot be denied'.[38] Ethical issues

---

[33] V. Williams, *Who's Looking at the Family?* (London: Barbican Art Gallery, 1994), p. 110.

[34] J. Goldberg, *Rich and Poor* (New York: Random House, 1985), text taken from untitled individual frame.

[35] V. Williams, *Who's Looking*, pp. 45–7.     [36] Ibid., pp. 41–4 (p. 41).

[37] L. Sultan, *Pictures from Home* (New York: Abrams, 1992), quoted in V. Williams, *Who's Looking*, p. 41.

[38] V. Williams, *Who's Looking*, pp. 98–105 (p. 100).

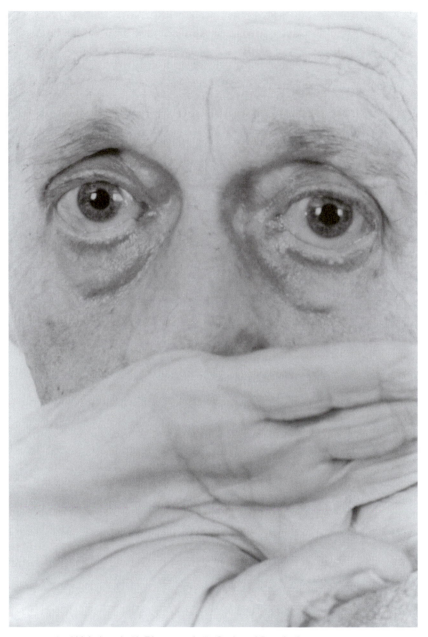

6   'Alzheimer's 4'. Photograph © Corinne Noordenbos.

arise here: is this the face of someone able to 'manage' her pose? The question arises of 'the extent to which objectivity dehumanises' the subject. Photographers frequently use 'devices of identification such as direct address to camera ... and often the use of quizzical expressions ... to create an intimate complicity between the subject and the viewer'. In the seeming bewilderment of this gaze, however, the very lack of communication between subject and viewer (and, indeed, photographer) is highlighted.[39]

Whatever we might think, in contemporary media culture, none of us is a distant or naive observer. Not only this, but each of us invests images with our own meanings, culled from experience. What we can claim with confidence is that our understanding of photographs is socially constructed. And however we might protest about the capability of visual images to convey the truth, once a moment has passed it becomes part of an ongoing rewriting of events. Almost as soon as they are taken, pictures are taken out of context. Family snapshots are a good case in point in that selected happy events – weddings, christenings, holidays – are held in aspic as a chronicle of the good old days, whereas the less joyful events – funerals, illness, divorce – are not photographed, thus absent from the memory bank.[40] By definition, memories are located in the past but considered in the present, and it follows that, since we select out the 'good times', most family archives focus on childhood and early adult life, rather than periods closer to the present when the rough edges and 'hard times' remain noticeable, or, as we age, intimations of mortality suggest themselves in the missing older relatives, facial wrinkles, and children pointing to pictures of us as 'granny' or 'grandpa'.

### The shock of the new

Perhaps not surprisingly, given the false image such snaps tend to create of domestic life, it has been women photographers who have latterly begun to set the record straight. Whereas much of this work may be dubbed consciousness-raising (see for example Andrea Fisher's *Let Us Now Praise Famous Women* which involves a resuscitation of long-forgotten archive material by Esther Bubley and other women photographers, and compares with Agee and Evans's celebrated record of the Depression in *Let Us Now Praise Famous Men*),[41] Jo Spence called her

---

[39] Achenbaum, 'Images of old age in America, 1790–1970', p. 24; J. Evans, 'A sense of self', *Ten 8* 31 (1989), 50–2 (51–2).
[40] Spence and Holland, *Family Snaps*.
[41] A. Fisher, *Let Us Now Praise Famous Women: Women Photographers for the US*

work 'unconsciousness-raising'. A retrospective exhibition held in autumn 1994 revealed significant insights into both the selectivity of family photographs and the means by which underlying contradictions in intergenerational relationships may be revealed.[42] Spence's photographs challenge the 'official' face that the family presents to itself, not only to make a political point about gender imbalance but also to suggest a means of coming to terms with long-term but hidden pain, anxieties, and tensions:

'photo-therapy' was a way in which family relationships could be explored in order to throw light on what ultimately constitutes the individual. This frequently involved dressing up and role-playing to recreate particularly painful or otherwise significant scenes, representing points in time when the 'sitter-subject' became psychologically stuck. The theory was that re-enactment could lead to resolution ... this was something that played with rituals and generations.[43]

Of 'Transformations' she remarks: 'With the help of the camera I re-enacted both of my parents. Their individual histories had never been acknowledged nor their deaths, many years before, mourned by me. Thus I began to re-embrace my forgotten roots.'[44] In this portrait she pictures herself as her mother in four frames, beginning with a sprightly young woman and ending with a resigned older lady; in the course of the sequence ageing is suggested by the posture of the shoulders which become more hunched in each shot. Superimposed over the central axis where the four images meet is the original wedding photograph of her parents as the happy couple.

The centrality of generational and family interaction in the developing therapeutic use of the photograph is clearly demonstrated in the amount of space devoted to family dynamics in recent counselling texts.[45] Certainly the possibilities of using photographs as a visual adjunct to reminiscence therapy are considerable, especially when used with people wishing to 'settle their accounts' as death becomes imminent. Indeed, it was when she was diagnosed as suffering from breast cancer that Spence, in dealing with her own illness and mortality, 'discovered she also needed to deal with the family she had "ingested"'.[46]

*Government 1935 to 1944* (London: Pandora Press, 1987); Agee and Evans, *Let Us Now Praise Famous Men*.

[42] A. Hopkinson, *Jo Spence: Matters of Concern, Collaborative Images, 1982–1992* (London: Royal Festival Hall Galleries, 1994).

[43] Ibid., leaflet.

[44] J. Spence in collaboration with R. Martin, 'Transformations', in *New Portraits From Old Exhibition* (1986).

[45] L. Berman, *Beyond the Smile: The Therapeutic Use of the Photograph* (London: Routledge, 1993).

[46] Hopkinson, *Jo Spence*.

More generally, while the late 1970s saw a turn towards oral history, and with it a re-evaluation of older people as witnesses to the events of the Second World War, the recognition of demographic shifts, and especially the growth of leisure and consumerism amongst older people now provides space for celebratory images to flourish.[47] In the mid-1960s Arbus produced a photo essay in *The Sunday Times* magazine illustrating old people living in California's Sun City. Thirty years later, from a very different perspective, Georgina Ravenscroft's *A Prime Passage* chronicles the pleasures of a group of Saga holidaymakers (see chapter 7).[48]

## Postmodern photography: juxtaposing generations

The family is a crucial constituent in a great many photographs, as the massively popular *Who's Looking at the Family?* exhibition indicated. Many of the themes we have discussed have addressed different ways of presenting and reading interaction within and across generations by experimenting with photographic images and techniques. As Pultz remarks: 'With the demise of the belief that a photograph can present a privileged window onto reality and truth, photographers have chosen instead to make pictures that admit to being artifices.'[49] While modernist documentary photographers asserted their objectivity – one that I have been at pains to undermine – artists since the 1980s have pursued their own self-conscious involvement with their subjects. The staged exploration of family relationships has been central here, and Pultz cites Sally Mann's 'Sherry and Sherry's Grandmother Both at Twelve Years Old' which poses the body of Sherry beside a cracked old photograph of her grandmother: 'Both women are represented at the age of twelve. The cultural changes in the fifty or so years that intervene between the two photographs have redefined both photography and adolescence. Unlike the dress that Sherry's grandmother wears, which is delicate and concealing, Sherry's shorts are brief, tight, and reveal[ing].'[50]

Two recent British exhibitions similarly attempt to engage the audience in biographical exploration through juxtaposition of intergenerational images. Steven MacLaurin's installation *They Saw My Age and*

[47] V. Williams, 'A new age coming', *Guardian Weekend*, 21 September 1996, 38–44 (43–4), notes the importance of Anne Noggle's *Silver Lining* which focuses on older women as 'symbols of experience and wisdom'. Noggle's work with Sue Packer, 'The Wheel of Life', is also significant. See A. Noggle, *Anne Noggle* (London: Photographers' Gallery, 1988).
[48] G. Ravenscroft, *A Prime Passage* (Leeds, Leaf Press, 1996).
[49] J. Pultz, *Photography and the Body* (London: Weidenfeld and Nicolson, 1995), p. 145.
[50] Ibid.

*Not Myself* (premiered October 1995) encourages viewers to consider their own ageing and attitudes towards older people. On a high wall five television screens project a series of shifting narratives, at any one moment featuring simultaneously: mother and children at the seaside in the 1940s, in bathing costumes; a sunny street scene with father and children; a wedding couple, c. 1930; a young woman holding a puppy; a team photo from schooldays. As each series gradually rotates to present further images, on the floor in front are projected five, life-sized images of older women. Viewers cannot but connect the running biographies on the television screens (like family albums) with the figures projected on the ground where they stand, but they are left to establish correspondences between one set of images and another, to imagine which snapshots 'belong' to which person's life.

Colin Gray's *The Parents* 'is the fruit of a fifteen-year project documenting the artist's own parents, reflecting upon domestic ritual, the waning of sexual desire, failing health, and old age'.[51] It is presented in three distinct sections. The first, 'Narratives', consists of theatrical tableaux of 'suburban surrealism' developed from Gray's fantasies, but staged with his parents' active collaboration and 'resonant with the new found freedom of early retirement' – for example, dressing up as Father Christmas and the Fairy Godmother in their own lounge.[52] Such staging, according to Gray, 'arose from the need to go beyond the limits of documentary': family portraits, he feels, only serve to conceal realities behind a facade of 'acting naturally'.[53] The second series, 'Close ups', shifts abruptly to giant wall-size microscopic enlargements: 'comparisons between the worn-out carpets, furniture, and utensils in the family home and the surface details of his parents' ageing bodies ... which expose a hidden world of translucent skin, broken capillaries and liver marks'.[54] These all share what Lowenthal calls 'the look of age'; because they bear the marks of use, weathering, and decay they appear connected to the past.[55] The link to painting is revealed in the remarks of one of Gray's critics: 'Is this the warning of the Vanitas paintings in European art, that all life is mortal and all beauty passes?'[56] Finally, in 'Scans', Gray uses magnetic resonance imaging, CAT scans, and x-rays – all medical technologies – to illuminate the insides of his parents' bodies and their possessions. The progression in *The Parents*, then, is one from subjective interaction to objectified science, signifying the

[51] 'The Parents: Colin Gray', *Art News*, September 1995.     [52] Ibid.
[53] E. McArthur, 'Foreword', in C. Gray, *The Parents* (Edinburgh: Fotofeis Ltd, 1995).
[54] 'The Parents: Colin Gray', *Art News*, September 1995.
[55] D. Lowenthal, *The Past Is a Foreign Country* (Cambridge University Press, 1995), pp. 125–82.
[56] H. Beloff, 'Family contradictions', in Gray, *The Parents*.

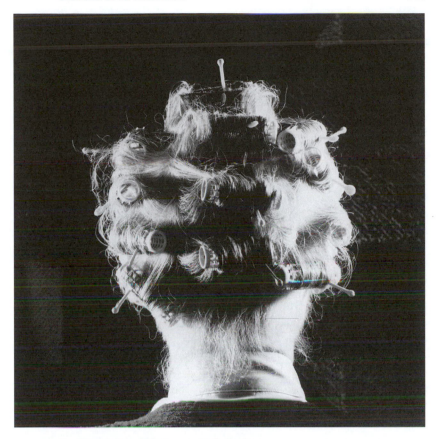

7   'Roots': from *The Parents*. © Colin Gray.

inevitability of physical betrayals and death, 'the disconcerting shift of dependence that affects each generation in time'.[57] Such apparent mimicry of medical procedures implies the limitations of a socially constructed view of the ageing body – in the end biology becomes destiny.

As with McLaurin, so with Gray, 'reconsidering our own relationships must surely be a result'. Indeed, to the extent that Gray's 'Narratives' dramatise his past memories, they may be 'allied to dream-work ... a complex use of photography in the service of self-development'.[58] In this important methodological respect, a focus on the family, connects postmodern art with the uses of photographs in both therapy and

[57] 'The Parents: Colin Gray', *Art News*, September 1995.
[58] Beloff, 'Family contradictions'.

reminiscence work.[59] They become a key resource within reflexive (post)modernity.

## Conclusion

Peter Coleman has noted that 'reflection on the nature and purpose of reminiscence in later life takes one to the heart of social gerontology ... For it leads to the examination of the dynamic and creative forces that mould what is remembered and what is forgotten, as well as of older people's potential and actual role as tenders of culture and tradition.'[60] Photography is most surely one 'trigger' in facilitating such a process. But we should bear in mind that it is a pliable medium that can be used either to create stories, or just as easily to subvert them. Thus, while it is our job as gerontologists to reconstruct the history of ageing in all its specific dimensions, we would be foolish ever to think that a single immanent truth lurks behind all the many masks. While, like a waxwork, one granny or grandad figure is being modelled, others wait their historical turn: Joan Collins, like Jane Fonda a legend in her own Hollywood lifetime, is now older than Anna Mathilda Whistler – 'the mother image of the American nation' – was when she was immortalised on canvas 130 years ago. The differences in appearance cannot fail to strike one.[61] Of course, a more sophisticated range of techniques of reproduction allows for more refined representations of later life than in the days of Victorian art. However, this does not mean that the underlying realities of ageing are more directly conveyed.[62] On the contrary, as the technology develops, so the scope for artifice grows in proportion. We must always bear in mind that visual images are never 'innocent' but, in an archaeological sense, comprise several layers of interpretation

---

[59] Berman, *Beyond the Smile*; Spence and Holland, *Family Snaps*; Age Exchange, *Lifetimes: A Handbook of Memories and Ideas for Use with Age Exchange Reminiscence Pictures* (London: Age Exchange, 1987).

[60] P. Coleman, 'Reminiscence within the study of ageing: the social significance of story', in J. Bornat (ed.), *Reminiscence Reviewed: Perspectives, Evaluations, Achievements* (Buckingham: Open University Press, 1994), pp. 8–20 (p. 8).

[61] T. Prideaux, *The World of Whistler, 1834 – 1903* (New York: Time-Life Books, 1970), p. 77. Whistler painted his famous *Arrangement in Grey and Black, No. 1: The Artist's Mother* at some time between 1866, when his mother was fifty-nine, and 1872, when she was sixty-five. For a decade she had been 'failing in sight and generally frail in health' (Prideaux, *The World of Whistler*, pp. 77, 86–7). In her portrait she sits 'in bleak contentment', an image of 'tight-lipped Puritan austerity ... dressed in black as always' (S. Weintraub, *Whistler: A Biography* (London: Collins, 1974), pp. 4, 147). Joan Collins reached sixty in 1993.

[62] See A. Blaikie and M. Hepworth, 'Representations of old age in painting and photography', in Jamieson, Harper, and Victor , *Critical Approaches*, pp. 102–17 (pp. 103–10).

and re-interpretation; as such they constitute the social imagination of old age. We also rewrite our personal biographies to suit the present context, so that old photographs often shock us into the recognition of how different our remembrance is from what was actually recorded; the intensity of unexpected encounters with the past may frequently be sharpened by the sight of oneself or one's relatives beaming out across the years from a long-lost portrait that has lain dormant amidst the domestic lumber. We are jolted into acknowledging that it is not only the image but also the memory of it that changes through time.

# 7    Beside the sea: collective visions, ageing, and heritage

This chapter develops the theme of nostalgia mentioned in our earlier discussion by concentrating on a particularly vivid aspect of photographic memory, namely the persistent emphasis on images associating age with pastness and community through the use of coastal milieux. These, as we shall see, are varied, and supply different functions. However, the following discussion attempts to derive a set of connected themes that help us to interpret the symbolic popular culture of later life.

The role of older people as inadvertent exemplars of all that was good about the nation's past is thrown into high relief when we consider representations of Britain's 'maritime heritage'. Yet such mythology has a longer pedigree than may at first be apparent. Victorian pioneers of photography championed the custom, dress, and extended family roles of elders in fishing villages since these displayed an older moral world distinct from the sins of the city. Subsequently, the conflation of positive ageing and seaside living fuelled the promotion of health products and lifestyles, whilst the rise of the seaside holiday prompted a more humorous re-evaluation of the ageing body as typified by saucy postcards and family snaps. Alongside and related to the phenomenon of retiring to the seaside, a fresh imagery is being wrought as nostalgic images of the country's seafaring history play heavily on the reminiscences of older people. Meanwhile, growing numbers of retirees opt for foreign travel. Focusing on a range of photographic materials, this chapter explores the continuities in perception that have connected ageing and older people with the morally and spiritually uplifting virtues of coastal communities.

Parts of this paper, originally published as 'Beside the sea: visual imagery, ageing and heritage', *Ageing and Society* 17, 6 (1997), 629–48, were presented to the British Society of Gerontology Annual Conference, Keele University, September 1995, and at the Center for Gerontology, Lund, November 1995. I should like to thank both audiences for constructive comments, and the Nuffield Foundation whose grant facilitated research in photographic archives.

## Introduction

Heritage has a habit of creating symbols that render otherwise disparate phenomena self-evidently related. Indeed, some would aver that this is precisely its function: to invent a strong, shared sense of 'imagined community' where history reveals little concrete evidence.[1] The present discussion speculates as to how one might solve the riddle of what connects older people with British coastal towns via an exploration of the role of visual images. The first part considers why pioneering photographers sought out the seaside and how older fisherfolk became icons of intergenerational harmony. Although this emblematic status was further developed in advertisements for health and holidays, cartoon postcards poked fun at unhealthy bodies and figures whose styles of dress and conduct were clearly outmoded. Thus both positive and negative images of ageing were apparent by the middle of the twentieth century. The second section explores the motives that may have lain behind the coastwards shift of postwar retirement migration. Whilst negative stereotypes have rather evaporated as holidaymakers have deserted the nation's beaches, nostalgic, environmental, and social reasons reflect the pervasiveness of positive perceptions of seaside towns as safe havens where, alongside the elixir of ozone, and relived holiday remembrances, exists an enticing picture of crime-free boulevards and peer-group sociability.

Rather than nostalgic 'community' having been invented *ex nihilo*, this examination reveals the supposed morality of older people living in the old order to have been a continuous referent since the early days of industrialisation. The historically new factors in the equation have been, first, the Victorian association of close-knit fishing villages with virtuous family life, and, secondly, the influx of retirees to coastal resorts in the later twentieth century. Arguably, in sustaining an image of utopian escape, the former evaluation has contributed to the latter reality. Older people are perhaps agents in the reconstruction of communities in their own desired image.[2]

## The quest for community

A fundamental distinction taught to most first-year sociology students is that made by the German sociologist Ferdinand Tönnies between

[1] B. Anderson, *Imagined Communities: Reflections on the Origin and Spread of Nationalism* (London: Verso, 1993).
[2] There is a parallel here with holiday brochures. According to Featherstone and Wernick, these are 'concerned to show images which affirm identity through an invented tradition which emphasizes communalism and collective rituals' (Featherstone and Wernick, 'Introduction', p. 10).

*Gemeinschaft* and *Gesellschaft*.[3] *Gemeinschaft* translates as 'community' and refers to pre-industrial, small-scale societies in which people were bound in harmony by extended kin relationships and a shared culture. By contrast *Gesellschaft* ('association') characterises modern relationships that are individualistic, impersonal, competitive, and calculative. As industry and urbanisation supplanted older rural society, so *Gesellschaft* replaced *Gemeinschaft*. This distinction provided a framework for explaining the problems caused by the modernisation, that is, the supplanting of traditional values and ways of life by modern urban–industrial society. Tönnies wrote in 1887, but his argument finds resonance both fifty years before, and over one hundred years later. In the history of photography, as we saw in chapter 5, the seaside is of particular significance. One reason why this was the case lies very much with contemporary social anxieties over urbanisation, and in this paper I wish to argue that these concerns continue to prevail, affecting not just ideologies of place, but also the decisions of retirees to migrate to the coast.

In 1840, William Pulteney Alison, Professor of Medicine at the University of Edinburgh, published his *Observations on the Management of the Poor in Scotland*.[4] In it he emphasised the inability of the traditional system of voluntary redistribution of church funds to cope with the problems of poverty in an increasingly urban and industrial society. In 1843, Lord Cockburn added his fears of political breakdown, noting that: 'In Edinburgh, besides its fullest complement of ordinary distress, we have a battalion of . . . "Unemployed Poor" . . . being congregated in numbers . . . can we . . . expect to be ever free of the constant risk of the occurrence of such scenes?'[5] The migration of the rural poor and the growth of the industrial slums undermined the effectiveness of the parish system and raised fears of the rioting and the mob – it was less than fifty years since the French Revolution, and Alison's and Cockburn's ideas were just two among the many voices of Victorian middle-class anxiety. They would not be out of place in some circles today, and, indeed, we shall return to this parallel. But let us continue with nineteenth-century Scotland. Against the incipient disorder, the

[3] F. Tönnies, *Gemeinschaft und Gesellschaft* (Leipzig: O. R. Reinholz, 1887; trans. C. P. Loomis as *Community and Association*, London: Routledge and Kegan Paul, 1955).

[4] W. P. Alison, *Observations on the Management of the Poor in Scotland* (Edinburgh: Blackwood, 1840).

[5] H. Cockburn, *Journal of Henry Cockburn; being a Continuation of the Memoirs of His Life, 1831–1854* (Edinburgh: Edmonston and Douglas, 1874), cited in S. Stevenson, *Hill and Adamson's The Fishermen and Women of the Firth of Forth* (Edinburgh: National Galleries of Scotland, 1991), p. 23.

Rev. Thomas Chalmers had, in Glasgow, attempted a return to the personal village scale, by dividing up a parish into twenty-five districts, each with sixty to one hundred families, patrolled by separate church elders and deacons and with a devolved system of welfare and schooling. His aim was, in his own words, to restore 'nature's own simple mechanism'. Meanwhile, one Dr George Bell, appalled by the conditions of Edinburgh's Old Town, advocated the demolition of whole streets and the recreation of small-scale, self-sufficient, and morally alive communities.

To prove the effectiveness of the latter, one did not have to look far: 'The ironic descent from the crest of the Old Town, crowned with slums to the moral example of Newhaven, a practical working community [of fisherfolk on the nearby Firth of Forth], was ... too good to miss.' And it just so happened that those two pioneers of photography Hill and Adamson took many of their earliest and certainly their best-known shots at Newhaven. Their intention was 'to make an analysis through visual art of the way Newhaven had survived and coped through the social confusion and distress of the Industrial Revolution'. The pictures were designed 'to be morally educational and uplifting'.[6] That is why, if we look at Victorian (rather than later) photographs, so few capture industrial scenes – mines and factories – or abject poverty in the cities, while so many present bucolic rural scenes. How might such be linked with images of ageing?

### Figures in a lost landscape

As pioneers of photography, Hill and Adamson began the trend towards painterly depiction of posed family groups. Indeed, they acknowledged a debt to Vermeer. The significance of their work lies in their creation of a model notion of coastal communities as utopian and prelapsarian – an alternative Eden that the modern world was passing by. As this older way of life, indicated by its ritualised work patterns, dress codes, and customs, became scarcer, so its exemplars became harder to find. And, as photography progressed, so the imagery of the seaside became, like antique-hunting, an attempt to find and immortalise in pictures the last of a dying breed, old people in particular.[7]

This can be seen clearly by returning to the vast photographic collections of Aberdeen's George Washington Wilson and Whitby's Frank Meadow Sutcliffe discussed in chapter 5. Indeed, analysis of

[6] S. Stevenson, *Hill and Adamson's*, p. 25.
[7] A. Blaikie, 'Photographic images of age and generation', *Education and Ageing* 10, 1 (1995), 5–15 (7).

these archives indicates a consistent iconography. First, photography imitated artistic convention, as seen in Frank Meadow Sutcliffe's photograph, entitled 'Peace', which clearly echoes Whistler's mother. In this image, old Ann Scarth of Glaisdale sits in the doorway of her home darning a sock. The twin focus of the picture lies with the gnarled, but precise hand threading the needle, and her etched brow and laughter lines framed by an ornate mutchkin cap. Such homely scenes built on a tradition of social realism that aimed to portray the fisherfolk and peasants as the 'salt of the earth', as in Washington Wilson's famous portrait, 'An Old Salt' or titles like 'Old Betty O' Auchmithie' – people who were deemed to be closer to Nature than either urban sophisticates or proletarians corrupted by city life. Sutcliffe's 'Retired from the Sea', an old man standing, again in a doorway, and chewing on a long clay pipe is particularly interesting because of a latter-day caption which reads: 'A fine character study . . . of Isaac Verrill of Staithes. The fishing village of Staithes on the rugged North Yorkshire coastline . . . has remained less influenced by outside pressures and changes than many such communities.'[8]

Secondly, a number of stereotypical roles existed for older people: older people as elders respected by the local youth (Sutcliffe's 'Free Education', taken on the Fish Pier, where a local fisherman 'gives an al fresco lesson to a bunch of children'); generational continuity of trades (Washington Wilson's 'Three Generations of Newhaven Fishwives' ), and happy, still-working older couples ('Fisher Folk of Auchmithie' greeting one another as they carry their creels (large wicker baskets for carrying fish)). Grandparent–grandchild bonds convey the timeless rhythm of the life cycle:

The sepia photograph, taken on Tate Hill Pier, Whitby, in 1884, depicts an old man smoking a clay pipe cuddling a small boy. They are in fact grand-nephew and great-uncle. The old man, an arm encircling his nephew's shoulder and a hand enclosing his small bare feet, draws him into a shared intimacy. The photograph is entitled, significantly, 'Morning and Evening'. Through its association with the daily temporal cycle old age and childhood are located side by side at either end of the day; as day turns into night, so each eve is followed by a new morn.[9]

Thirdly, there are what might be termed stereotypes of decrepitude, such as Sutcliffe's 'What Did You Say My Dear?' where the old man sitting, holding his stick, holds his ear to listen to a toddler. Again, the caption added later is revealing: 'Each figure has been carefully posed,

---

[8] Caption from postcard reproduction (1987), the Sutcliffe Gallery, Whitby.
[9] Hockey and James, *Growing Up and Growing Old*, p. 19.

yet the resulting photograph shows no trace of camera consciousness or tension.'[10] For this reviewer, Sutcliffe had succeeded as a realist.

Clearly, then, there are reasons why photography latched on to older people in fishing communities from its inception until the First World War. Thereafter, the popularity of the seaside holiday produced similar images. The London and North Eastern Railway commissioned a series of Frank Newbould advertising posters depicting exotic 'East Coast types' – among them 'The Scottish Fishwife' and 'The Deck-Chair Man' – and reiterating the young-learning-from-old motif (the boy with his model boat, listening to the old white-bearded man, telescope under his arm, on the harbour wall).

Meanwhile, soap manufacturers aligned the putative anti-ageing benefits of their products with the morally uplifting and patriotic example of the old salt passing on the message through the generations.[11] The singular significance attached to images of fisherfolk in the material available owes much to the circumstances in which photography first developed. Advertisers were quick to cotton on to both the touristic curiosity and wholesome salience of such stoically traditional portraits. Lifebuoy soap, making play on the old salt character ('I'm weather beaten but Lifebuoy soap is never beaten!!'), also drew heavily on the intergenerational impact of the grandparent–grandchild relationship. Their 'For Young England' poster shows the old salt, in full regalia, including lifejacket, seaboots, and sou'wester, sponging a naked child in his bath, while 'A Picture of Health' illustrates him kneeling on the harbour wall, on which sits a doll-like, bonneted child, clad in white from top to toe. He is holding a lifebelt so as to frame her rosy face. On it is inscribed the slogan: 'Lifebuoy soap for preservation of health'.[12] In 1936, the Coca-Cola Company commissioned a number of advertisements for its fiftieth birthday. One image in that year's calendar depicts an old salt sitting on the prow of his boat and holding a bottle of Coke as he talks with a young girl in her bathing costume. The caption reads: 'Through all the years since 1886'.

---

[10] Postcard caption; postcard © The Sutcliffe Gallery, Whitby, 1989 (ref.: 26-10).

[11] Hepworth suggests that 'one answer to the social and personal threat that was posed by the ageing body was to put more effort into the promotion of moralistic images of positive ageing'. The 'granny' figure who persevered 'in the proper maintenance of [rural] hearth and home' codified 'a longing for an illusory image of a timeless homeland presided over by an everlasting feminine grace'. Advertisements for Sunlight Soap and Pears Soap which juxtaposed grannies with grandchildren thus 'capitalised on the Victorian association between cleanliness, health, and morality', and 'implied a close relationship between cleanliness and positive ageing' (Hepworth, 'Where do grannies come from?', 3–4).

[12] Lifebuoy Soap Series (A), The Robert Opie Collection, Museum of Advertising and Packaging, Gloucester.

Undoubtedly, such images ramified earlier stereotypes, although the explosion in working-class trips to the cheaper resorts in the 1920s and 1930s created new images – saucy postcards – which poked fun at the older unclothed body on display as never before. The saucy postcard was, and still is, retailed as a vehicle for cheap gags featuring caricatured holidaymakers in generally embarrassing encounters, often lavatorial or ripe with sexual innuendo. Here a cardboard cut-out stereotype serves a kind of survivalist humour. Middle-aged spread is a feature. There exists a certain sort of fatalism in accepting that the body beautiful is going to seed – here many a rosy-cheeked woman whose bathing bloomers and corset are bursting at the seams as a crab lurks dangerously close to acres of posterior, and many a pigeon-chested, knobbly-kneed balding husband loitering timidly in the corners of the frame. The front cover of a retrospective digest of photographs of everyday life in Britain from the 1930s to 1950s used an illustration of an old man slumped in a deck-chair (will he ever be able to stand up again?), handkerchief knotted at the corners and worn on the head to shield out the sun.[13] By the 1960s these beach-loving figures of fun had become known colloquially as Grockles. The advent of Hollywood gave us glamour and turned the beach into a zone for bodily display, but Bournemouth and Bridlington were hardly Venice Beach, and certainly not St Tropez: the Grockle is relaxed, but he's also expanding in all the wrong areas, he's overweight (or weedy) and not at all active; the clothing is no more beachwear than gardening gear, merely work-clothes rolled up or tied up to deal with a singularly British environment.

The Grockle image was the last of the line. Meanwhile, that butt of the end-of-the-pier comedian's joke, the mother-in-law as dictatorial hag, has become a figure associated with nostalgia for the days when workingmen's clubs were just that (and, indeed, marking a time when generations were forced to live cheek-by-jowl in the same household). Its last nationally famous exponent (*sic*), Les Dawson, died in 1993, the end of a music hall lineage, including Freddie Frinton and Eric Morecambe (both pseudonyms taking the names of popular British resorts), and tracing back to before Frank Randle (see chapter 5). Thora Hird's longevity as the character actress continually associated with the part renders her more a heroine of ageing than a figure of fun.

The Grockle figure lingers on as an anachronism that equates ageing with outmoded styles. Nevertheless, the contemporary media have drawn on an intergenerational continuity image at times of national

[13] *Memory Lane: A Photographic Album of Daily Life in Britain, 1930–1953* (London: J. M. Dent and Sons, Ltd, 1980).

8  'Grockles', Bournemouth, 1946. © Topham Picture Library.

celebration. A recent newspaper image, for instance, presents an evocative portrait of an old man carrying a Union Jack, handkerchief knotted
over his head in the heat, pointing out a military flying demonstration to
his grandson. *The Times*'s caption from May 1995 read: 'Les Hammond,
formerly of the Royal Electrical and Mechanical Engineers, explains to
his grandson, Edward Parker, the sights and sounds of the VE-Day
anniversary celebrations yesterday in Hyde Park, London.'[14]

Traditional icons are indeed frequently recycled. John Gay's classic
photograph, 'Paddling at Blackpool', taken during a Wakes Week
(annual holiday) in 1930, poses an old man in the foreground, standing
barefoot in a several inches of seawater, trousers rolled up to the knee,
his boots in one hand, walking stick in the other. His back is to the
camera, as he gazes, fully dressed in dark suit and flat cap, along the
massed ranks of bathers towards the distant tower.[15] Over sixty years
later, advertising copy for Cherlin and Furstenberg's *The New American*

---

[14] *The Times*, 8 May 1995.
[15] Reproduced in C. Ford (ed.), *The Story of Popular Photography* (London: Century,
1989), p. 119.

*Grandparent* used a near-identical image.[16] This time the man's wife is on his arm, no tower looms in the distance and the bathers are fewer; otherwise, the casual observer would swear this was the same individual, captured at the same time.

Val Williams has suggested a chronological sequence in the changing imagery of old age over the past half-century that mirrors the fluctuations in intergenerational relations over the period. At some times ageing has been positively perceived, at others rather more negatively. She begins from the premiss that 'throughout photography's history, documentarists have taken older people as a focus for their feelings about society':

Photographing in the London Underground during the Blitz of the Second World War, Bill Brandt made a portrait of an elderly woman wrapped in thick clothing settling down for the night. Brandt's photograph was a study of stalwart yet fragile old age, a pertinent comment on the predicament of a nation at war. Brandt's hermetic old woman, sheltering from the bombing, engages our imaginations and becomes a symbol of survival.

She then goes on to explain that in the 1940s, 'while the young signalled hope for the future, the old became pillars of resistance, their very longevity signalling an ability to persist despite overwhelming odds'.[17] By the end of that decade, however:

The effects of bombing had fractured many inner-city communities, and this (together with the founding of 'utopian' new towns) led to the break-up of the extended family which had provided a support system for many of Britain's old people. Far from being elders, matriarchs, and patriarchs, important cogs in the wheel of the family, old people began to be perceived as social problems. This perception informed and directed much of the picturing of older people that was to appear over the next thirty years.[18]

Following the demise of *Picture Post*, photo journalism in the 1960s and 1970s portrayed older people as casualties of this fragmentation, 'not as survivors, but as victims ... as a race apart'. And, she contends, television focused the aspirations and attitudes of youth, rendering older people objects of ridicule – the three caricatured old women in Britain's longest-running popular soap serial *Coronation Street* (Ena Sharples, Minnie Caldwell, and Martha Longhurst), 'a fretful yet dynamic chorus of ancients bewailing the misdemeanours of the young'; the triple spectres of ageism, sexism, and racism incarnate in Alf Garnett, protagonist of the 1960s sitcom, *Till Death Us Do Part*, who calls all black people 'coons' and his wife 'silly old moo'; the rag-and-bone squalor of

---

[16] A. J. Cherlin and F. Furstenberg, *The New American Grandparent* (London: Harvard University Press, 1991). Advertised in Harvard University Press Sociology catalogue (1994), p. 6. Photo credit © Frank Dugan.

[17] V. Williams, 'A new age coming', 38.    [18] Ibid., 43.

Albert Steptoe (in the comedy series *Steptoe and Son*), 'an unpleasant, dirty, irksome presence in a world of chafing youth', referred to regularly by his son as a 'dirty, little old man'.[19]

Since the 1970s, Williams detects a 'revived anthropological focus', with foreign photographers 'entirely committed to a harsh black-and-white picturing of a lost and tragic Britain'.[20] In particular, she selects the works of Sirkka-Liisa Konttinen in Byker, and Markéta Luskacová in Spitalfields, both run-down inner-city areas where isolated old people appear to have been abandoned. All the imagery considered here is urban, and appears to reflect the dread effects of city redevelopment upon the old, whose familial status appears to have been usurped. In classic Marxian terms, they appear alienated, dispossessed. If such is the inevitable outcome of a quest for photographic realism, there are, as we have seen, other uses of the photograph which suggest a desire to reinstate older people within longlost rural communities. Moreover, as Featherstone and Hepworth have noticed:

In its more popular representations, and following a lingering tradition dating at least back to images of later life in Victorian painting, positive aging is intimately associated with the countryside. Rustic imagery is a pervasive characteristic of successful retirement as it is with pre-paid funeral plans such as 'Golden Charter', illustrated on the back cover of *O50* with a photograph of an enchanting woodland scene where sunlight filters through autumnal leaves on to an older woman attending on a pram and a small child on a leaf-strewn pathway.[21]

A point worth emphasising, however, is that such images, convenient though they may be in terms of metaphors of age – autumn leaves, pathways, sunsets – or association with 'retreatist relaxation' and pastimes such as gardening, painting, even photography, often represent later life in fallaciously nostalgic ways: 'It is easy to think in terms of a dichotomy between past and present, traditional and modern, and by extension to perceive that, "in the past, people looked after their own" whereas today they do not. Although such a generalisation is grossly inaccurate, modernisation theory has given spurious academic credibility to the idea of a shift from a pre-industrial Golden Age of extended family care to a present-day marginalisation of aged relatives reliant on institutional support.'[22]

This overview presents us with two issues worthy of investigation: first, in what ways do today's older people differ from the received picture; and secondly, what is the relationship between ageing,

---

[19] Ibid.        [20] Ibid.
[21] Featherstone and Hepworth, 'Images of positive aging', p. 32.
[22] Blaikie, 'Photographic images', 8.

nationhood, and the recycling of images from the past? Crucially, the intentions of photographers at the time and the motivations and responses of those who have used their images since may be very different. The heritage process might appear only elliptically linked to today's older people, but the creation of the past as a commodity has much to do with tapping the desires of its consumers. These are by no means all retired people, but their experience helps to account for the current vogue.

### Retiring to the seaside

Industrialisation and urbanisation have had major continuing effects on population geography. Although strongly biased towards young adults, and rather less numerically significant among older groups, migration has been an important factor affecting the distribution of retired people in Britain, particularly in recent decades.[23] A summary of demographic and geographical trends has noted that: 'In 1921, the areas with the highest proportions of elderly people in their populations formed a belt stretching ... from Norfolk ... to Cornwall and Central Wales ... The loss of younger people from rural areas to the big industrial centres led to these high proportions in what were then largely rural communities.' But by 1981 the pattern was quite different: the central rural belt had disappeared and areas with high proportions were mainly on the coast. These high proportions were 'a result of inflows for many years of people at or near retirement age'.[24]

The rise of British resorts began in the middle of the eighteenth century, when the health-giving qualities of sea bathing drew the nobility away from the inland spas to the coast. A connection to patriotism can be detected from the earliest days, when Queen Charlotte patronised Southend, through to Bognor becoming Bognor Regis to celebrate George V's successful convalescence there in 1929. By the 1930s, particular pockets such as the Isle of Wight had become stereotyped as haunts of the old.[25]

The initial visibility of coastal populations containing large concentrations of older people owed much to the geographical mobility of

---

[23] Detailed analysis of the OPCS Longitudinal Study revealed that 'only a small proportion of those in the retirement age groups migrate and most movers go only short distances' (E. Grundy, 'Retirement migration and its consequences in England and Wales', *Ageing and Society* 7, 2 (1987), 57–82 (78)).

[24] United Kingdom, Office of Population Censuses and Surveys and Central Office of Information, *Census Guide I: Britain's Elderly Population* (London: HMSO, 1984), pp. 3, 7.

[25] Priestley, *English Journey*, pp. 20–1.

middle-class retirees, a group who, for the first time, were living long enough, and staying sufficiently fit and active, to make such moves at this stage in the life course. However, it was the leisure and recreational possibilities provided by rail access, and more especially the rise of the paid holiday, that saw the real rise to prominence of the seaside in the 1920s and 1930s. Later, the advent of cheap holidays in Continental Europe from the 1970s onwards saw the decline of much of the traditional family trade, and 'retirement resorts' came into their own.

Yet even by 1951 some resorts had populations comprising up to one-third of people over sixty. This pattern has been consolidated as more people can expect to live longer, with the incentive to plan their retirement in relative economic independence from younger family. The consequent image of large swathes of the coastline of southern England as Costa Geriatrica is one not of saucy-postcard mirth and vulgarity but of sedate bungalows, blue rinses, and True Blue attitudes. By 1981, ten south coast districts had elderly populations of over 30 per cent, compared with a national average of 18 per cent, whilst the Isle of Wight witnessed a net gain of 40 per cent in women aged fifty-five to sixty-four and men from sixty to sixty-nine in the decade from 1971 to 1981.[26]

What then are the links between heritage, ageing, and the seaside? It helps to ask who the movers are. As Valerie Karn discovered, and as subsequent census figures continue to bear out, in most resorts proportions of retirees who formerly worked in professional and managerial occupations are well above the national average. She found that Bexhill had 41.1 per cent of retired men in classes I and II, and some resorts had over 50 per cent.[27] Furthermore, studies undertaken in the USA, the UK, and Australia each indicate retirement migrants to be relatively privileged economically.[28] There is clearly considerable variation between resorts, but the overall picture is one of middle-class social composition. Undoubtedly, some people return to the scenes of happy family holidays, but relatively few are moving to be with their families. Arguably, though, relatively affluent retirees have chosen to move to the coast because the seaside upholds an image of health, safety, and moral rectitude in comparison with the increasingly shabby suburbs of the manufacturing towns whence they came. An interesting contrast is provided in the French case where, although affluent retirees have moved to the expensive south coast, a more general quest for rural roots

[26] *New Society* Database, *New Statesman and Society*, 24 October 1986; Grundy, 'Retirement migration', 72.

[27] V. Karn, *Retiring to the Seaside* (London: Routledge and Kegan Paul, 1977), pp. 268–9, Appendix 1, table A1.9.

[28] Grundy, 'Retirement migration', 58–9.

also appears evident: considerable numbers of working-class Parisians return on retirement to the rural provinces, often far distant, of their birth.[29] Whatever the case, retirement migrants are not constrained by factors of employment location, and their decision to move to the coast, or the scenes of their youth, appears to blend both nostalgic and environmental preferences.

### Safe havens

In 1981, the *Observer Magazine* dispatched Jeremy Seabrook and Yvonne Roberts to Lytham St Anne's, a town immediately south of Blackpool, but very much at the 'posh' end of the Fylde coast. Their article was billed as being about 'Life in Torytown'.[30] Lytham St Anne's appealed to these journalists because of two elements: first, retirement (by 1981 25 per cent of the population was over sixty); secondly, by having the largest Conservative majority at the 1979 general election. Initially built by businessmen in 1874 as a resort and watering place for the bourgeoisie escaping the 'squalor and menace of the manufacturing districts' of the industrial north, the town's redbrick mansions suggest an anachronistic, rather grandiose attempt to preserve *Gemeinschaft*. But Seabrook and Roberts dispute this:

The town appears now to be an elegant and melancholy enclave of an almost extinct way of life, but it is not. On the contrary, in many ways it is a model for the future. It is at the heart of Mrs Thatcher's ambition ... slumless, well-ordered, obsessively neat. Crime and vandalism are rare, social problems hard to find. There are no down-and-outs, no drunks, no scroungers; apparently no poverty... already 80 per cent of those employed here are in service industries.

None the less, their observations and interviews appear to elicit a nostalgic vision borne of present unease. Here in the coffee shop:

In Jaeger suits, velour hats, and button earrings, [the women] carry gloves in even the warmest weather – a gesture to an old idea of gentility. They invoke dead husbands to affirm their status and to give substance to their views. 'As my husband used to say ...'.

Their sometimes long dead men are summoned to support opinions about the working man or the state of the country. 'The working man is putting a noose round his own neck' ...

The daily encounter isn't really a political dialogue, an exchange of ideas. It's a conversation between strangers who at this stage in their lives no longer wish to reveal anything of themselves or to be challenged in their opinions. Yet as

[29] Ibid., 59, citing F. Cribier, 'Migration et cycle de vie', in *Les Ages de la vie. VIIe colloque national de démographie, INED, travaux et documents* (Paris, PUF, 1982), pp. 149–58.

[30] J. Seabrook and Y. Roberts, 'Mrs Thatcher's heartland', *Observer Magazine*, 8 February 1981, 26–33.

they rise to go, each her separate way, you can see that the vigour of their opinions is at odds with their physical infirmity. The carefully made-up face is that of a woman in her late seventies. One of her legs is heavily bandaged and she walks with a stick. In the lift, her loneliness overcomes her sense of convention, and she talks with the directness of despair.[31]

In common with early Victorian Newhaven, today's Lytham St Anne's stands as a model for traditional community. Both perform a symbolic role as a critique of modern society and only manage this, of course, because they are well out of the industrial mainstream and thus cushioned from its worst effects. We can detect the features of a heritage culture, one that seeks to go 'back to the future', to trumpet the virtues the past, whilst denying or side-stepping the present. Of course, only a small minority of all older people retire to the seaside, but if the old Tories of Lytham St Anne's were in the vanguard, then perhaps the nation's prevailing obsession with its past – a new museum or visitor centre opens every two weeks – says something about the ageing of the population, as well as the demise of manufacturing, or, more germanely, the crisis of the fishing fleet and the death throes of an Empire built on Britain's ocean-going marine. This lament codifies a conservatism, deep in the British psyche, one indeed that travels across the political spectrum. Entitled 'A dose of the old salt', a newspaper profile of John Prescott, then Labour's Deputy Leader, son of Hull, who began as a waiter on Cunard liners captions a portrait of the MP with his words: 'I would emphasise that traditional values in a modern setting are still relevant to a Labour government.'[32]

### The comforts of heritage

There are two ways in which to deny the problems of the present: one is to disclaim all continuity with the past and to assert one's self-sufficiency; the other is to embrace the past so completely that a Golden Age nostalgia replaces reality.[33] Rather like the quiet, but decorously desperate old ladies of St Anne's, perhaps we try to do both at once. Heritage thus represents what Raphael Samuel memorably refers to as 'the anxiety, particularly marked among the geographically mobile and sociologically orphaned, to reaffirm family roots'.[34] The rise of the seaside holiday coincided with the advent of the cheap and easy Box Brownie

---

[31] Ibid., 27–8.

[32] E. MacAskill, 'A dose of the old salt', *Scotsman*, 11 June 1994, 11.

[33] C. Lasch, *The Culture of Narcissism: American Life in an Age of Diminishing Expectations* (London: W. W. Norton, 1991).

[34] R. Samuel, *Theatres of Memory*, vol. I, *Past and Present in Contemporary Culture* (London: Verso, 1994), p. 352.

camera, such that every family could, in the words of a 1923 Kodak advertisement, 'turn your fleeting holiday pleasures into permanent joys'.[35] Seventy years later we ransack those family albums in the search for frameable snapshots that do not so much aim to revisit the past, or hang on to it, as aim to *create* 'an allegorical space and allow us to people it with our imaginings ... when people enjoyed more "natural" ways of living', where people made their own pleasures, work was dignified; children were childlike, adults adultlike, and grandparents grandparent-like.[36] The past is no longer a prelude to the present; it is an alternative to it, one that restores the absent elements, even if these are 'about as natural as a photograph of Granny in a "kiss me quick" hat at Eastbourne when she never wore a hat and had only been to the seaside once in her life'.[37]

Heritage asserts the values of family and community at a time when more and more older people live alone. Many have moved to the coast precisely because they have (or had) the wherewithal to become in-dependent from their families. Since 1961 the number of older people living alone has more than doubled, whereas the proportion of house-holds containing three or more people has fallen by a third. In many coastal towns, younger people have moved away as service industries supplant manufacturing and fishing, notably through the provision of residential and nursing homes (often hotel conversions). Social distance and cultural autonomy are not necessarily bad things, as Jerrome's work on social networks in old people's clubs in Brighton and Hove has demonstrated, but do such age-segregated enclaves compensate for the lost sociability of the extended family living in an integrated commun-ity?[38] A moot point, perhaps, yet it might help to explain the popularity of images depicting fishermen populating quays now bereft of people, of sagacious captains revered by awe-struck boys, of generations mixing in harmony. Such heart-warming images are legion among collections small and large – in every case crowds gather only because of the presence of the photographer, but no matter the typicality or otherwise. We want to think of the past as safe streets filled with working adults, children playing, respected elders. And we forget, unless occasionally reminded by collections of local snapshots – the rare image of tired and stooped fishwives returning from selling around the doors of the locality – of the pain of carrying creels, or the loneliness of the long-distance

---

[35] National Museum of Film, Photography, and Television, Bradford.
[36] Samuel, *Theatres of Memory*, p. 357.     [37] Coward, *Female Desire*, p. 50.
[38] D. Jerrome, *Good Company: An Anthropological Study of Old People in Groups* (Edinburgh University Press, 1992).

fishwife.[39] Surprisingly, perhaps, these images are less 'historic' than many might imagine: in 1967, Mrs Gibson of Musselburgh was still carrying her creel once a week; Esther Liston, the last surviving Newhaven fishwife gave up carrying her creel in 1976 at the age of eighty; Mrs Baillie was still filling her fish basket at Nairn in 1979, and there are the pictures to prove it.[40]

The sepia memorabilia of Sutcliffe's collection are now big business, with two shops in Whitby and one in York selling nothing but his reproductions. In Captain Cook Country, they are a key ingredient in constructing The Heritage Coast (as this section of North Yorkshire and Cleveland styles itself) as part of theme-park Britain.[41] What has become of Hill and Adamson's happy hunting ground of Newhaven? Its past is certainly not forgotten. Each year here, and in several of the old Forth villages, there are still gala days and fishermen's walks in which older folk dress up in period costume. Reproduction pottery figurines ('Wemyss Ware'), and pub designs alike iconise the fishwives. On the Newhaven shorefront, the 'Old Chain Pier' public house boasts a sign depicting its most famous daughters in full regalia. The old fishmarket is home to two new enterprises: the Newhaven Heritage Centre and a branch of a national fish and chip shop chain. Last time I visited, the Heritage Centre had drawn a large crowd of elderly ladies, prompted by the videos and wall displays and absorbed in retelling their pasts to one another. Outside only leisure craft bobbed about in the harbour. Samuel remarks that, in terms of marketability, 'the more completely the environment has been destroyed, the higher the going rate', although he goes on to note that seaside photography is 'only just beginning to make its way into the archives'.[42] At Newhaven today you will no longer see any older people who conform to the stereotypes of yesteryear – but you will find plenty of pensioners eating fish and chips next door. Perhaps, like the good folk of Lytham St Anne's, or of Gorleston, a real retirement town near Great Yarmouth fictionalised by Henry Sutton, they are waiting:

A man and a woman were drinking mugs of steaming tea or coffee or soup in the Seaside Cafe. They were sitting at separate tables, but it struck Percy how similar they both looked. They seemed of the same age. Both had thin white

[39] M. Thomson, *Old Wemyss* (Ochiltree: Richard Stenlake, 1995), p. 49.
[40] National Museums of Scotland, Country Life Archive, neg. no. c. 7687.
[41] See Featherstone, *Consumer Culture and Postmodernism*, p. 102: 'One increasingly lives in a "heritage" country in which the sense of historical past gives way to myths. Hence if one crosses the north of England one moves rapidly from Wordsworth country, to Brontë country, to Herriot country, to Captain Cook country ... to Catherine Cookson country, each with tour guide, itineraries, museums and souvenirs.'
[42] Samuel, *Theatres of Memory*, p. 347.

hair and both wore thick, black-framed glasses that swamped their aged, wrinkled faces. Percy watched them through the window. They would look up at each other now and then, careful not to catch the other person's eye. Neither of them were reading newspapers or anything, but playing with their spoons and packets of sugar and the tomato-shaped ketchup dispensers. They were waiting, like Percy, for a sign that everything was how it should be, how it was before.[43]

Here bungalows huddle in serried ranks, perched – literally and metaphorically – atop cliffs that are slowly crumbling into the cold North Sea. But there are others who have no intention of waiting. The Saga holidaymakers, like the 'Snowbirds' who vacate their homes in Northern Europe for the Mediterranean resorts each winter in increasing numbers, and the more permanent emigrants have opted for something altogether more hedonistic. Certainly, 'heritage' appears to play little part in their retirement decisions. In the 1990s Georgina Ravenscroft's series of photographs, *A Prime Passage*, featured active elders on holiday, in Bournemouth, Tunisia, Madeira, Malta, Florida, and Tenerife. The message – a long way from Sontag's double jeopardy of ageism and sexism, or, indeed, from the retirement uniform of so much of the present century – is emphatically one of positive ageing:

It is a comedy [of manners] in which the major players are women, Rabelaisian almost in their commitment to enjoyment, and there is a conviction conveyed in these photographs of the bonds of convention having been loosened. It is impossible, when looking at these casually dressed holiday-makers, to determine their social background or their income. There is in these photographs an overwhelming sense of the physical mobility of those portrayed. They climb mountains, swim, and dance. They constantly gesticulate and gesture, as if reaching out to embrace experience.[44]

Like Ravenscroft's photograph of pensioners at dinner – 'one is dressed as a fairy, resplendent in a wig, tiara, and pink feathers, another wears a scarlet mask' – some have graduated to an altogether more surreal, near-carnivalesque landscape, where connections to childhood or family holidays have been severed, but where the promise of a perpetual sunny present beckons.[45] Meanwhile, seaside humour now appears to lie more in exposing the realities beneath the old archetypes. As Bernice Martin has remarked, 'Beryl Cook's fat ladies are the battle-axes from Donald McGill's seaside postcards with their sexuality miraculously restored.'[46] Since the mid-1970s, the phenomenon of summers spent lounging on the beach has all but disappeared in the wake of cheap package deals to Continental Europe. Not only have the

---

[43] H. Sutton, *Gorleston* (London: Hodder and Stoughton, 1995), p. 223.
[44] V. Williams, 'A new age coming', 44; Ravenscroft, *A Prime Passage*.
[45] V. Williams, 'A new age coming', 38.
[46] B. Martin, 'The cultural construction', p. 67.

holiday hordes been displaced to the costas, but also the archetypal 'oldie' at play is now to be found enjoying long-stay winter breaks in the Mediterranean, dressed in department-store light casual wear.

Likewise television comedy has begun to represent retirement as in some ways a form of revived adolescence, with the attendant bizarre and ambiguous experiences of that stage of life. For example, Martin notes of Roy Clarke's comedy series *Last of the Summer Wine*:

It is disarming because its images are a reworking of the stereotyped and familiar. The setting is an idyllic Yorkshire village which evokes nostalgic sentiments about moorland landscape, Englishness, and lost community while reminding its urban viewers, as a central element in the primary joke, that 'community' means that everyone knows everyone else's business. Our three heroes [old men with nicknames – Compo, Clegg, and Foggy – that reflect their schoolboy natures] either escape the prying eyes or, as often, defy them and turn every attempt at surveillance and control into an occasion for joyous resistance – a sort of raspberry blown at Michel Foucault, as it were. Indeed, since most of the community sanctions concern loss of respectability, all that is required is to follow Compo's lead and not care a toss for it. The formula only works as well as it does because the three old boys are unencumbered by wives or families. Many of the jokes have them improvising temporary escape routes for friends still caught up in the serfdom of marital obligations to monstrously powerful women.[47]

There are, of course, similar catches with real 'escapes' from the constraints of locality. As retired settlers in Spain have already discovered, dealing with the eventual physical decrements of old age, dementia, and bereavement is not easy where medical and social services are patchy and you do not speak the language.[48] It seems that not only a sense of community, but also the services that such a social institution provides, will be critical if the positive attributes of the seaside are to remain attractive. For the relatively affluent modern retiree, it appears that the British Empire on which the sun never sets, or just the Empire bingo, are things of the past. Yet for many more, in a rather phatic, unexciting but comforting manner, the proximity of like-minded, fellow retirees remains a significant factor:

'If you don't fancy the bingo at least pop round some time for a cup of tea. I live on Arnott Avenue.'

---

[47] Ibid. If youth connotes strength and virility, and mid-life the reins of power, the one image remaining for the disempowered older man to return to is 'the disruptive role of being one of the boys again' (Featherstone and Wernick, 'Introduction', pp. 8–9) – what Hepworth ('"William" and the old folks') refers to as 'positive infantilisation'. Another reading is less charitable: 'Compo is the "dirty old man" who lusts after Norah Batty, the "ill-tempered, unattractive" old woman' (M. Johnson, 'Never say die', 21).

[48] C. Betty, 'Language problems of older British migrants on the Costa del Sol', *Generations Review* 7, 2 (1997), 10–11.

'Oh really,' said Percy, 'I live just around the corner.'
'Everyone, my dear, lives just around the corner here.'[49]

Such residents have made a myth their own.

[49] Sutton, *Gorleston*, p. 28.

# 8 Landscapes of later life

## The trouble with maps

Our maps have improved in a kind of spurious precision as they have deteriorated in the amount of worthwhile information they convey ... If the Ordnance Survey were worth the paper it prints on it would be producing a special series of maps for the over-forties, the over-fifties etc. (When you reach a hundred you end up merely with an enlarged plan of your house, with the location of the lavatory clearly marked and a small arrow pointing towards the crematorium.)[1]

It's time to go feral. Tribes of feral grandmothers holed up in the hills, just imagine it, refusing to take on those time-honoured mindings and mopping up after the little ones while the big ones jaunt into the distance.[2]

Much of the sociology of later life remains uncharted territory, a Dark Continent like Victorian Africa, understood and diversely interpreted by its indigenous peoples yet still awaiting 'discovery' by the 'civilised' world. Although one hopes that our explorations will not repeat the conceits of imperialist adventures, there is already evidence that our categorisation of findings is somewhat less than accurate in judging the ontological universe of its subjects. And, as we have seen, images of older people frequently inhabit mythical spaces that bear little resemblance to lived experience.[3] Sociology may have clarified how 'being elderly' is a learned social role, but is not particularly good at explaining what it is like to become and be old, and, as Gubrium and Wallace remark, 'there seem to be two existing worlds of theory in human

---

[1] A. Maclean, *Night Falls on Ardnamurchan: The Twilight of a Crofting Family* (Harmondsworth: Penguin, 1986), p. 106.

[2] T. Astley, *Coda* (London: Secker and Warburg, 1995), p. 153.

[3] The debate about older people's sexuality and sexual activity testifies to one of the difficulties created by imputing motivation and meaning from limited or impressionistic evidence. See D. Jerrome, 'Intimacy and sexuality amongst older women', in M. Bernard and K. Meade (eds.), *Women Come of Age* (London: Edward Arnold, 1993), pp. 85–105, and H. B. Gibson, *Love in Later Life* (London: Peter Owen Publishers, 1997). Lamentably little has been written concerning older gay and lesbian experience, although see, for example, M. Adelman (ed.), *Long Time Passing: Lives of Older Lesbians* (Boston, MA: Alyson Publications, 1986), and R. Berger, *Gay and Gray* (Urbana: University of Illinois Press, 1982).

experience, one engaged by those who live the experiences under consideration, and one organised by those who make it their professional business systematically to examine experience'.[4] In what ways, therefore, might we attempt to bridge the chasm?

Laslett has already established the character of the terrain in *A Fresh Map of Life* (see chapter 3). In so far as people will seek varying routes to self-actualisation, or more constrainedly eke out strategies for survival, our discussion of symbolic representation and the appropriation of imagined worlds, as with the moral community of the seaside town, indicates the significance of visual resources in discerning a social backdrop. The cultural landscape known as retirement can be understood as a series of intersections, informed by imaginative operations – fictional, photographic, ideological, and otherwise. As we have seen, however, rather than providing straightforward avenues to enlightenment, the signs by which we interpret ageing tend to reduce persons to types and experiences to anecdotes. Images rarely illuminate paths to meaning, but they do sharpen our awareness of the symbolic labelling and demarcation of ages and stages.

Our current perception sees children as precious individuals to be nurtured and socialised before they can become adults. However, in *Centuries of Childhood*, Philippe Ariès contends that there was no concept of childhood prior to the seventeenth century and that a recognition of children as anything other than adults in miniature arose only following increased interest in education and developments in the notion of the family. Given the socially malleable character of the life course and our perception of the roles of children, perhaps a further rethinking has become necessary. Meyrowitz suggests that, via television culture and the fashion market, children are now more adultlike than previously while adults are becoming more childlike. He observes that adults wear 'playclothes' (T-shirts and trainers), while children wear designer dresses. Meanwhile, 'uni-age' styles (jeans, shell suits) synthesise high fashion and play.[5] Education is no longer a stage that comes only before work – it can be chosen in mid-life. We have moved, then, beyond the era of progressive, linear stages of development, where age is assumed – 'naturally' – to determine a child's behaviour and how it relates to adults. What this demonstrates is that age-appropriate behaviour is a system of roles that have been socially constructed. We must therefore distinguish between the biological existence of phases of

---

[4] J. Gubrium and B. Wallace, 'Who theorises age?', *Ageing and Society* 10, 2 (1990), 131–50 (147), cited in B. Bytheway, 'Ageing and biography: the letters of Bernard and Mary Berenson', *Sociology* 27, 1 (1993), 153–65 (154).

[5] Meyrowitz, 'The adultlike child and the childlike adult'.

physical immaturity, maturity, and decline and the social meanings that we give to each.

Hendrick argues that at different historical periods politically convenient ideologies informed varying social constructions of childhood. By 1800, the idea that the child was inherently sinful and thus required punishing was replaced by the notion of childhood innocence, hence the 'romantic child'. Secondly, came a notion of the 'evangelical child' which challenged the naturally good, optimistic vision of the Romantics, arguing that education had a role in correcting the naturally sinful disposition of children. If children were to be educated, then was this compatible with their employment in the mills and the mines? Thus, the problematisation of the 'factory child' was highlighted by the Factory Acts, and these, in turn, 'heralded the transformation of the working child into the school pupil'. Significantly, this marked a moment in the construction of a notion of universal childhood, whereby the 'nature' of childhood was seen as distinct from that of adulthood. Having begun to split childhood apart from labour, reformers sought two further developments in separation. The 'delinquent child' was distinguished – the 'precocity' of working children who had 'much to unlearn'. The desire to propel the working-class child into the classroom, supported by the images, if not the realities, of vagrancy and delinquency, resulted in restructuring of the child's identity towards that of the 'schooled child'. The classroom became a laboratory for scientific research into mental and physical conditions. With this change came concerns over deprivation. New discourses on 'psycho-medical' and 'welfare' children were launched.[6]

A similar exercise may be conducted with regard to later life, applying cultural, scientific, or political periodicity to a sequence of archetypes – say, the wise elder, aged pauper, pensioner, geriatric, senior citizen ... These possible models present a limited range of ideological scripts, inscribed in social policies, which older people may or may not have followed, and from which a number of stereotypes, or caricatures, have been developed. However, as well as this historical succession, at any one time a number of categories coexists within the retired population which is fragmented according to cohorts/health status (Third and Fourth Ages, mid- and later life, young old and old old), class, race, ethnicity, gender, and geography. One way in which such differentiation has been addressed is through the concept of lifestyle.[7]

---

[6] Hendrick, 'Constructions and reconstructions of British childhood', pp. 41, 43, 44.

[7] The following discussion is diagnostic rather than descriptive. Consequently, no attempt has been made to incorporate a full range of lifestyles: for example, the literatures on older gay and lesbian lives and on race and ethnicity are not considered, while rural/

### Lifestyles and later life

Over a generation ago, Anne-Marie Guillemard attempted to classify retirement lifestyles.[8] In near-equal measures her subjects fell into six categories, each of which remains observationally relevant, though impressionistic. The 'withdrawn' she characterised as 'surviving from day to day, with few interests beyond housekeeping'; the 'spectators' were more active – with interests in television and food – but again had a very limited network of relationships or activities outside the domestic home. By contrast the 'leisured' exhibited a strong orientation towards clubs and organised activities, with involvement in a range of pastimes; the 'family-centred' were similar, but demonstrated a greater penchant for extended family relationships. 'Challengers and claimants' were 'the grey power people who see old people as a group with common interests, a potential pressure group', clearly an active group with political concerns, and were the only category positively interested in settling in residential homes, as well as retirement villages. Finally, the 'third age living group' were characterised less by their diversity of interests (not especially great) than by the intensity with which they pursued chosen activities, roles, and contacts.[9]

We have also seen how, latterly, market researchers have produced an alternative spectrum of social categories through which lifestyle products may be marketed – Woopies, Jollies, Glams, and other acronyms – with consultants dividing the over-45s into five phases: Retire Aware, Wind-Down, Lifestyle Adjustment, Leisure Years, and Inactive, the last of which begins at around seventy-five.[10]

These are but two attempts to pigeonhole through generalisation, and like all generalisations they end up reducing the life-worlds of their chosen populations to reflexes which can be read off from systems of superficially measurable social preferences. 'Psychographic segmentation' of the 'mature market' via lifestyle analysis is simply another sociological approach, albeit one geared to commercial ends rather than objective scholarship. Thus American cohorts born in each decade since 1900 have been allocated 'time signatures' from which consumption styles may be gauged:

urban and gender differences are alluded to only in passing. The institutional environments inhabited by half a million British elders are not detailed. On these 'special settings', see the synopsis in Fennell, Phillipson, and Evers, *Sociology of Old Age*, pp. 136–59.

[8] A.-M. Guillemard, *La Retraite: une mort sociale* (Paris: Mouton, 1972).

[9] Ibid., pp. 33–4.

[10] M. Gwyther, 'Britain bracing for the age bomb', *Independent on Sunday*, 29 March 1992, 16–17 (17).

1910–1920 – "Those of the Dream Deferred" have a time signature of disappointment and deferred compensation. Now they are the mainstream aged, attempting, in their own way, to make up for the past. They are often caught between wanting to give and to take. They feel they have earned their retirement and will not let anyone take it away from them.

Key point: the Great Depression has had a profound impact on the attitudes that many of today's 65+ers have about spending and managing money. These seniors are extremely concerned about their financial security and independence. As a result they tend to behave in ways that bolster their economic wellbeing – such as accumulating large savings accounts and buying medical insurance policies – while avoiding behaviors that might jeopardize their financial welfare.[11]

The notion of 'time signatures' prescribes a different mindset for each cohort as it moves through time carrying with it sets of values specific to the period of its own socialisation. In chapter 3, I argued that this means the market will trail the babyboomers as they age. They are a particularly large cohort, with plenty of disposable income and, since they have a firm cultural orientation towards 'youth', they are especially prone to purchasing goods and services designed to 'combat the signs of ageing'. However, in terms of consumption patterns and lifestyle preferences, the hegemonic group is not determined simply by demographics. As Featherstone and Hepworth elaborate, cultural capital, 'the possession of or knowledge about valued cultural goods', is strongly influenced by social class:

The value an individual places on his or her body, for example, is not simply a matter of personal choice or taste, but is determined by what Bourdieu describes as the class habitus.

Class habitus comprises the unconscious dispositions, taken-for-granted preferences, and attitudes towards the world which are displayed in the individual's natural sense of the correct behaviour and bodily order; taste for cultural goods, e.g., holidays; view of morality; sense of time, and so on. These together are the product of his or her social group, class, or class fraction's relation to other groups.[12]

Social mobility, prestige, and the maintenance of social distance depend on being able to demonstrate distinctions through the exercise of 'taste'. Whereas the upper social strata are unselfconsciously assured of their social position and the traditional working class are resigned to fatalistic acceptance of such things as 'belief in the naturalness of overweight as one gets older', the petite-bourgeoisie's social aspirations

---

[11] Ostroff, *Successful Marketing*, pp. 156–7, citing J. O. Gollub, SRI International.
[12] M. Featherstone and M. Hepworth, 'New lifestyles in old age?', in Phillipson, Bernard, and Strang, *Dependency and Interdependency*, pp. 85–94 (pp. 89–90); P. Bourdieu, *Distinction: A Social Critique of the Judgement of Taste* (London: Routledge and Kegan Paul, 1984).

have accustomed them to self-consciousness – watching, checking, correcting themselves. This class fraction will be attracted to cosmetics, exercises, and body maintenance techniques 'ostensibly designed to deliver the ideal body' and to involvement with 'symbolic goods and services', because it is through such consumption that differentiation may be sustained. Unfortunately for the rest, these are the very processes which perpetuate the stigma of ageing. In terms of their cultural effectivity, Featherstone and Hepworth argue that 'the new petite-bourgeoisie will have an upward trajectory as they increase numerically, and increase their relative social power', being in 'a stronger position to legitimise their view of the body and its uses and the acceptability of their own particular habitus'. Consequently, an ex-panding new middle class largely composed of babyboomers will dictate a trend towards increased age-denial.[13]

Acknowledging lifestyle as the basis of social differentiation, Bellah *et al.* use the term 'lifestyle enclave' to refer to a network 'formed by people who share some feature of private life. Members of a lifestyle enclave express their identity through shared patterns of appearance, consumption, and leisure activities, which often serve to differentiate them sharply from those with other lifestyles. They are not interdepen-dent, do not act together politically, and do not share a history.'[14] The lifestyle enclave provides identity symbols which define its members as distinct from others, both within an age group and between generations. It also operates as a vehicle of incorporation:

The newer kind of lifestyle enclave was perhaps first visible after World War II in what was called the 'youth culture'. Patterns of recreation, dress, and taste in matters such as music or food characterised young people more or less independently of ethnic or class background. These emerging youth patterns were interpreted as reactions to the 'strain' of prolonged education and delayed participation in the adult world. Whether the emergence of lifestyle enclaves in mid-life and among the retired can be interpreted as a reaction to the 'strain' the adult occupational system places on older people is an open question. Certainly we have some evidence that that is the case. We might consider the lifestyle enclave an appropriate form of collective support in an otherwise radically individualising society.[15]

Against this, however, they contend that, 'whereas a community attempts to be an inclusive whole, celebrating the interdependence

[13] Featherstone and Hepworth, 'New lifestyles', pp. 91–4. The grey market is also widening its parameters by encroaching on younger age groups. The Aberdeen annual 50+ Lifestyle Festival flyer (1997) appealed: 'If you are over 45 then the 50+ Lifestyle Festival is for you.'

[14] R. Bellah, R. Madsen, W. M. Sullivan, A. Swidler and S. M. Tipton, *Habits of the Heart: Middle America Observed* (London: Hutchinson Education, 1988), p. 335.

[15] Ibid., p. 73.

of public and private life and of the different callings of all, lifestyle is fundamentally segmental and celebrates the narcissism of similarity':

a life composed mainly of work that lacks much intrinsic meaning and leisure devoted to golf and bridge does have limitations. It is hard to find in it the kind of story or narrative, as of pilgrimage or quest, that many cultures have used to link private and public; present, past, and future; and the life of the individual to the life of society and the meaning of the cosmos.[16]

Clearly, in lifestyles alone, there is insufficient fuel for constructing meaning in later life. Meanings, however, are not the only issue, for as Saul Bellow once wrote: 'We need to see how human beings act after they have appropriated or assimilated the meanings. Meanings themselves are a dime a dozen.'[17]

## Old lives, new landscapes

Some gerontologists claim that 'in the years after retirement leisure is the functional equivalent of work'.[18] Leisure and consumption play an important symbolic role in affirming personal identities, a point that chimes in with the morality of diet and exercise discussed in chapter 4.

Ekerdt speculates that the expansion of time spent in retirement has led people to carry the work ethic through into later life in the form of what he calls the 'busy ethic', a vocabulary of motive that 'legitimates the leisure of retirement, [since] it defends retired people against judgements of senescence, and it gives definition to the retirement role'.[19] The extent to which this acts as the basis for new cohort norms requires investigation, but common beliefs and activities do appear to be characteristic of ThirdAgers. For example, in retirement communities high value is placed upon strenuous involvement in leisure activities. Advertising copy for Del Webb's Sun City West in Arizona highlights the 'diverse array of recreational choices' to stimulate 'active adult living':

Imagine golfing every day. Or becoming more physically fit that ever before. Or playing in your hometown symphony orchestra. Or finding others who share your enthusiasm for antique cars. Or softball. Or quilting. Learn to make a

---

[16] Ibid., pp. 72, 83.
[17] S. Bellow, 'Deep readers of the world, beware!', *New York Times Book Review*, 15 February 1959, 1, 34, quoted in S. Cohen and L. Taylor, *Escape Attempts: The Theory and Practice of Resistance to Everyday Life* (2nd edn, London: Routledge, 1992), p. 31.
[18] J. Hendricks and S. J. Cutler, 'Leisure and the structure of our life worlds', *Ageing and Society* 10 (1990), 85–94 (91).
[19] Ekerdt, 'The busy ethic', 243.

lamp, use a computer, or develop and print your own photos ... Join the club. We have 150 in Sun City West.[20]

Alternatively, such activities may be construed as opportunities for leisure denied by a hectic working life: 'For people who have worked hard all their lives, life in a "retirement community" composed of highly similar people doing highly similar things may be gratifying. As a woman who had lived fourteen years in Sun City Center, Florida, told Frances FitzGerald, "It's the long vacation we wished we'd always had." '[21]

As the 'land of old age' is redeveloped, 'the ways in which new built environments of aging match shifts to a postmodern lifecourse' require evaluation. Part of the shift towards new lifestyles in old age is a corresponding cultivation of designer landscapes, be these bungalows, or congregate-care complexes that have 'the appearance, both in exterior detail and in lobby decoration, of grand-deco hotels, and explicitly offer "hotel lifestyle"', or (in Vancouver) 'golf-and-country-club estates with secured perimeters, such as Arbutus Ridge, a seaside adult village'. The development of specialised housing submarkets has heightened a tension between 'a built environment still dominated by a legacy of the modernist preoccupation with order and segregation and a postmodern society which is increasingly moving away from a strict model of chronological age scheduling'. Under modernity, each life course stage was dominated by a particular built environment: school, workplace, home, and poor house/institution. In the postmodern city, property developers have exploited the discretionary wealth of some older people to redesign the built environment at the expense of poorer, young, and old households: 'The reconstruction of old age and its spatial corollaries thus signal the potential for intergenerational and class conflicts over the distribution of urban resources ... to refit suburbia for lives of leisure but lives of gradual frailty, as distinct from the lives of child-rearing and commuting for which they were first built.' Traditional old people's homes serve a population of frail elders 'largely excluded from the new construction of the life course'. They are becoming marginalised 'relics' since their regimes reflect a modernist rigidity of ideology and because of land use pressures on their sites, which were once peripheral but are now locations ripe for redevelopment. Meanwhile, in North America, the elderly poor have remained consistent consumers of squalid city-centre hotels.[22]

---

[20] Del Webb's Sun City West (1986), brochure.
[21] Bellah, Madsen, Sullivan, Swidler, and Tipton, *Habits*, p. 83.
[22] D. W. Holdsworth and G. Laws, 'Landscapes of old age in coastal British Columbia', *Canadian Geographer* 38, 2 (1994), 174–81 (174, 176, 179, 181). G. Laws, 'Spatiality

Yet, paradoxically, while the postmodern blurring of chronological boundaries would appear to favour age-integrated living, age segregation is fundamental to housing markets which are clearly trying to capture niches. Further, retirement resorts, Sun Cities, and Sunbelt migration destinations all explicitly reflect a desire to live separately from younger people, a shift perhaps motivated by an effort to hold on to an identity which is under threat. A big part of the sales pitch in attracting elders to American retirement communities is an emphasis on security. As with British seaside towns, the survival strategy is one of 'encrustation', a barricading in which has 'become increasingly common as senior adults find themselves in a world that does not seem to understand and respect the values they so long cherished'.[23] Del Webb's Sun City West advertises: 'A friendly hometown. With rolling greens and community spirit' in its 'planned small town atmosphere'. Residents claim to have been attracted to 'the happiest place on earth' – population 40,000, mean age seventy-seven, and no one under fifty-five allowed – by 'sun and safety'. Indeed, such is the desire for the latter that regular police patrols are augmented by volunteer vigilantes.[24]

While permanent migration to the Sunbelt states, particularly Arizona and Florida, has been considerable, nascent North–South trends are also evident in Europe. Presently 28,000 UK pensions are paid to people living in Spain, 19,000 in Italy, and 12,000 in France.[25] Meanwhile, seasonal migration on both sides of the Atlantic comprises mostly relatively young, healthy, and affluent people who, because of these characteristics, tend to create cohort-based norms within the destination communities. They are also likely to be married, and better educated than non-movers, and almost entirely white.[26] Such selectivity, like its permanent equivalent, can have a destabilising effect by, for example, placing a strain on local health services, bringing an influx in spending power, or creating a boom in demand for private residential care. However, less than 1 per cent of Canadian 'snowbirds' spending the winter months in Florida use social services such as special

and age relations', in Jamieson, Harper, and Victor, *Critical Approaches*, pp. 90–101 (p. 96), refers to Sun Cities as 'a landscape to be consumed'.

[23] R. Kastenbaum, 'Encrusted elders: Arizona and the political spirit of postmodern aging', in T. R. Cole, A. Achenbaum, P. Jakobi, and R. Kastenbaum (eds.), *Voices and Visions of Aging: Toward a Critical Gerontology* (New York: Springer, 1993), pp. 160–83 (p. 180), cited in Holdsworth and Laws, 'Landscapes of old age', 176.

[24] *3D* documentary/magazine programme, ITV, 1 May 1997.

[25] R. Sharpe, 'Property. An A to Z of modern manors: N is for the North', *Observer Life*, 11 May 1997, 45.

[26] C. F. Longino and V. W. Marshall, 'North American research on seasonal migration', *Ageing and Society* 10 (1990), 229–35 (230).

transportation, meal delivery, homemaker services, visiting nurses, home health aids, or adult day care. Indeed, any deterioration in circumstances appears to trigger a return to the strongly preferred Canadian health system. More generally, Longino and Marshall note: 'They were nomadic in the sense that their social ties were primarily with the same migrants in the communities they shared at both ends of the move. Their ties were not to places but to the migrating community itself.'[27]

One of the great ironies of postmodernity is that an enhanced range of choices brings with it the possibility of opting for a culturally homogeneous lifestyle enclave in which sameness rather than diversity is of the essence. Our examples thus far suggest attempts to reconcile the apparently conflicting desires for individualism and freedom on the one hand, and commitment to community on the other. Unfortunately, lifestyle enclaves, while providing support networks for their members, none the less appear to erode the cohesiveness of place-bound social relations. Indeed, such affinities appear to fracture the kinds of integration fostered by family ties. The segregationist impulse suggests a willingness to cut generational ties, voiced quite clearly in such things as bumper stickers reading: 'We're spending our children's inheritance.' The estimated 3 million older Americans who live on the road in their towed trailers and motor homes known as recreational vehicles (RVs) and who have become permanent nomads push the paradox one step further.

In their detailed monograph, Counts and Counts claim that because they appear to challenge 'mainstream values of "rootedness", permanence, land-ownership, and community', RVers are cast as deviants. Many have no fixed address and some, such as those who are flea marketers, avoid regulations and taxes by participating in an underground economy. Space constraints within mobile homes mean they collect very few possessions. This is anxiously regarded as a rejection of the consumer ethic, a fact celebrated by RVers themselves as evidence of 'Zen affluence' (finding happiness by desiring little). They also contradict the old age stereotype. In turn, they are labelled as 'gypsies':

They are homeless and cheap, they violate the consumer ethic, they threaten community and 'family values', and they are trailer-trash and slobs. At the same time they are seniors who do not act their age. They are selfish, immature, gadget-ridden consumers. They pollute the atmosphere, spend their children's

[27] Ibid., 232, 234. For these and other reasons, conflicts between incoming and indigenous elders have provided useful ethnographic fodder. See J. M. Okely, 'Clubs for le troisième age: communitas or conflict?', in Spencer, *Anthropology and The Riddle*, pp. 194–212.

inheritance, and selfishly consume scarce resources. They are having fun instead of vegetating in their rocking chairs.[28]

Counts and Counts argue that RVers constitute a subculture: 'They have their own system of values, their own social networks, their own symbols and metaphors to explain who they are to themselves and to others ... their own jargon.' This is manifestly evident in an analysis of the Escapees (the title speaks volumes), founded in 1978 as the first club for serious, full-time RVers and, by 1995, claiming a membership of 37,000, over two-thirds of whom were aged sixty and above. Escapees claim to maintain their individuality whilst being part of a community that shares activities and helps one another. RVers, like the wagon-convoys who opened up the Western frontier, epitomise the ideology on which the United States was founded, 'the values that reveal themselves in the pioneer lifestyle: freedom, independence, self-reliance, community, and mutual assistance'. Meanwhile, mobility enables some to make lengthy or regular visits to widely dispersed family and friends, thus strengthening, rather than weakening, primary social ties. In these ways individualism is 'fulfilled in community rather than against it'.[29]

Having control over how and where time is spent is a key aspect of leisure. The lifestyles I have discussed imply a liberationist perspective whereby older people freely experiment with new ways of living. However, for many, carving out acceptable lives depends upon confrontation with an overarching dominant culture which devalues ageing. To understand these challenges, we need to examine the evidence which is available on the localised level at which these problems are encountered.

### Not feeling old

Ethnographic research provides considerable scope for establishing the diversity of later life, and much of this work has accentuated the efforts of individual agents actively to construct and lend meaning to everyday life. To this extent, it presents an antidote to functionalist arguments whereby older people are simply the passive subjects of structural determinants, such as dependency ratios and institutionalised ageism.

---

[28] Counts and Counts, *Over the Next Hill*, pp. 53, 56, 71, 61. Interestingly, the only previous research of note on RVing was a Ph.D thesis by the renowned gerontologist Donald O. Cowgill ('Mobile homes: a study of trailer life', University of Pennsylvania, 1941). RVing began in 1930s, but the surge in attraction came later. Between 1980 and 1992 RV ownership among householders aged fifty-five and over increased by 50 per cent (Counts and Counts, *Over the Next Hill*, p. 27n).

[29] Counts and Counts, *Over the Next Hill*, pp. xiii, 26, 68, 64, 75 (quoting Bellah, Madsen, Sullivan, Swidler, and Tipton, *Habits*, p. 162).

At this remove political economy debates are far less important than interactionist or narrative accounts. Life course perspectives have been influential here.[30]

Adopting a life history approach, based on over 600 interviews and autobiographies and spanning 150 years, Thompson *et al.* suggest that, although class and income determine the range of choices available in retirement, the ways in which later life is approached depend more on individual personality, spirit, and sense of purpose than material circumstances. In retirement, all share in a freedom from the imposed structure of the workplace, and the quality of later life 'seems to be associated with an ability to use that freedom positively'.[31] Retirement from work is only one of an number of probable life-events that force adjustment in later life. Resilience and adaptability are crucial competencies in dealing with the loss of intimates, bereavement, and loneliness, as well as in finding fulfilment through dancing, gardening, or simply in constructing a regular pattern of living.[32] The researchers found that most old people felt uncomfortable with people of their own age, perhaps because of fears of confinement within the ghetto of residential care, or of being patronised by club organisers.[33] Many enjoyed the mutuality provided through intergenerational links, although this frequently involved sensitive negotiations over when and when not to intervene in family life and dealing with anachronistic images of grandparenthood as the preserve of the truly ancient.

Such positive attitudes appear to continue until very late in life. Between 1900 and 1990 the numbers of persons in the UK aged ninety and over have increased dramatically from 10,000 to 250,000.[34] In

[30] See, for example, R. Butler, 'The life-review: an interpretation of reminiscence in the aged', *Psychiatry* 26 (1963), 65–76; M. Johnson, 'That was your life: a biographical approach to later life', in V. Carver and P. Liddiard (eds.), *An Ageing Population* (Sevenoaks: Hodder and Stoughton in association with Open University Press, 1978), pp. 99–113; S. H. Matthews, *Friendships Through the Life Course: Oral Biographies in Old Age* (London: Sage, 1986).

[31] Thompson, Itzin, and Abendstern, *I Don't Feel Old*, p. 244. Thompson *et al.* are conscious of the seemingly gender-neutral limitations of such a position and accordingly address these. See also M. Bernard and K. Meade, 'A Third Age lifestyle for older women?', in Bernard and Meade, *Women Come Of Age*, pp. 146–66.

[32] The benefits gleaned from simple activities may be manifold. For example, dancing has been characterised as 'exercise, and a skill, and companionship and a romantic echo of youth all in one' (P. Thompson, Itzin, and Abendstern, *I Don't Feel Old*, p. 164).

[33] Hockey and James, *Growing Up and Growing Old*, pp. 152–3, note that children and elderly people are the only two groups who are confined to 'play' with peers. Whilst they are regarded as a solution to problems of isolation, clubs therefore constitute the imposition of social exclusion through leisure.

[34] Centre for Policy on Ageing, *Over 90 in the 1990s* (London: CPA, 1990). A large proportion of the increase depends upon declining infant mortality: in 1900, 156,000 died before reaching age one; in 1990 only 130,000 died before the age of sixty-five.

Coleman's evocative phrase, these nonagenarians have become 'pioneers in the art of long living'.[35] Although a proportion of these very old people suffer from poor health, Bury and Holme's research indicates that subjective wellbeing does not necessarily tally with objective quality measures. Some interviewees who were in good health had low life satisfaction, whereas others who were disabled or in pain nevertheless remained optimistic.[36]

These views may be surprising because of the freight of conventional stereotypes, which Saul suggests arise from two myths: the negative 'inevitability' myth regards older people as being in a state of irremediable physical, mental, and social decline, whereas the positive 'tranquillity' myth sees them as resigned, gracious, and passive.[37] Lifespan psychology ramifies such thinking through cognitive personality theory, which, following Jung, argues that the concerns and satisfactions of 'life's afternoon' will differ from those of its morning. Hence, for Erikson, 'ego-integrity' happens only when the older individual accepts adversity by acknowledging limitations: 'A wise decrease of former aspirations and unavailable goals and ideals will provide a peace of mind.'[38] For the very old respondents discussed above, feeling old is clearly associated with disengagement, 'feeling exhausted in spirit, lacking the energy to find new responses as life changes ... giving up'. Thus to say 'I don't feel old' is to dissociate oneself from dependency and decline, the great swathe of experience that remains invisible from such accounts. As the researchers observe: 'Because inevitably it is only survivors whose stories we can hear, it is much easier to show the strategies through which they manage, and the kinds of meaning they find, than to disentangle the factors in earlier as well as present life which influence why some succeed while others do not.'[39] In sympathy with this statement, the remaining discussion considers some of the barriers to the development of successful survival strategies and how they may be overcome.

---

[35] P. Coleman, 'Last scene of all', 4.
[36] M. R. Bury and A. Holme, *Life After Ninety* (London: Routledge, 1991).
[37] S. Saul, *Aging: An Album of People Growing Old* (New York: Wiley, 1974).
[38] F. Dittmann-Kohli, 'The construction of meaning in old age: possibilities and constraints', *Ageing and Society* 10 (1990), 279–94 (291).
[39] P. Thompson, Itzin, and Abendstern, *I Don't Feel Old*, pp. 250, 246. Although L. Rosenmayr, 'Objective and subjective perspectives in life span research', *Ageing and Society* 1 (1981), 29–49 (46), claims that 'cumulating disadvantages' may be internalised and cause 'a progressive reduction of chances of the deprived of coping' in later life, di Gregorio, 'Understanding the "management" of everyday-living', demonstrates how older women who have dealt with crises in the past may be better able to cope with changes in later life than those who have not.

## Language games

Because stereotypes, particularly those associated with consumer culture, focus attention on superficial appearances, the old are reduced to their observable physical attributes. We fail to see beneath the surface. In an attempt to deconstruct such myth-making, much of this book deals with images. Nevertheless, it is important to take note of what Hazan refers to as the 'ocularcentric gaze'.[40] The effects of privileging the visual are paradoxical, for while 'unlike some other forms of deviation [social ageing] is extremely difficult to conceal',[41] much of the experience remains socially invisible.[42] Meanwhile, a good deal of the 'hidden work' of ageing, involving exercise, diet, cosmetics, is aimed at disguising stereotypical signs. For this reason he argues: 'The quest of the elderly (or of their advocates) to eliminate at least some of the burden of representation and find ways of counter-expression can be better realised through speech rather than vision.'[43] However, the language we use to describe age can be just as reductive.

While institutional ageism such as employment legislation is explicit, the social world of later life is constrained by communicative barriers enshrined within language. For example, *Roget's Thesaurus* (1982–4 English edition) cites the following synonyms for 'elderly':

old age, anno domini; pensionable age, retirement age; advanced years; grey hairs, white hairs, old person; senescence, declining years, vale of years, evening of one's days, winter of life, weakness; second childhood, dotage ... senility, deterioration ... matured; overblown, run to seed; not so young as one was; no chicken, past one's prime, getting on ... hoary-headed, long in the tooth ... moribund ... drivelling, doddering, gaga.[44]

Hockey and James illustrate how metonymy and metaphor play important roles in the social construction of old age stereotypes. In its part-to-whole function (e.g., through 'wrinkly' the wrinkled skin comes to signify the whole person), metonymy selectively highlights a particular aspect of ageing and generalises from this.[45] On the British traffic

---

[40] Hazan, *From First Principles*, p. 27.
[41] Hepworth, 'Positive ageing: what is the message?', p. 184.
[42] Hence titles like D. Unruh, *Invisible Lives: The Social Worlds of the Aged* (Beverly Hills, Sage, 1983).
[43] Hazan, *From First Principles*, p. 27.
[44] Tyler, 'Structural ageism', 44. The American edition included: 'passé, effete, doddering, decrepit, superannuated ... stricken in years, wrinkled, marked with the crow's foot, having one foot in the grave'.
[45] Hockey and James, *Growing Up and Growing Old*, p. 41. Stereotyping age according to solely corporeal attributes reflects the problems with mind/body dualism highlighted by the mask of age (see pp. 189–90 below). As one interviewee commented to Thompson, Itzin, and Abendstern, *I Don't Feel Old*: 'It's just my legs that feel old, not me head. I don't feel nearly eighty' (p. 112).

sign a pair of bent figures with a walking stick means elderly people. Meanwhile, metaphor conceives one thing in terms of another. Of particular import is the way in which, having constructed deep old age as the mirror image of infancy through metaphors of 'second childhood' and forms of 'babytalk', infantilisation becomes a pervasive cultural strategy of dependence conditioning both attitudes and practice among carers.

Language is also significant where personal and social identities of older people are constructed through conversations with younger people. Focusing on the relationship between 'diachrony and decrement', Coupland, Coupland, and Giles demonstrate how 'old age' and 'elderliness' constitute collective subjectivities reproduced through talk. Their videotaped linguistic analyses make comparisons between peer–elderly conversation and intergenerational conversation, each type giving rise to different definitions of elderliness: when May (seventy-nine) talks to Nora (eighty-two) she defines her experience of old age in a positive way, laying stress on coping strategies and helping roles (e.g., charity work at local hospices). However, when May talks to Jenny (thirty-eight), her elderly identity is defined for her in negative terms, with Jenny's stereotypes focusing on notions of physical and financial dependency, decrement, and assumed loneliness. Age identity is thus managed differently according to different interpersonal contexts, with 'painful self-disclosure' (revelation of intimate information about bereavement, ill-health, loneliness, and immobility) tending to be more positively accented in peer conversation. The language we have available to us structures our thinking and leads to unwitting collusion by younger people in drawing out 'problematic' interactional behaviour from older people. Furthermore, otherwise neutral aspects of conversation, such as slow speech, poor pronunciation, or silence may be read off as signs of confusion. This can also lead to self-stereotyping amongst older people, whilst younger people may be unwittingly sealing their own developmental fate by internalising expectations of what 'being older' will mean to them.[46]

## Sites of struggle

The rise of an income-rich over-50s generation, as well as a large group of poor pensioners, means that the transitional phase from work to retirement takes on new meaning as regards both consumerism and discontent. However, finding oneself through community is not easy.

---

[46] N. Coupland, J. Coupland, and H. Giles, *Language, Society and the Elderly: Discourse, Identity and Ageing* (Oxford: Basil Blackwell, 1991).

The effects of age classification are such that adolescence and the Third Age ('middlescence') share a liminal status. In both cases individuals are considered to be out of the previous age category, but not yet into the next.[47] Such ambiguity is seen as giving rise to problems – teenage trauma or mid-life crisis – as well as providing the social licence to experiment with norms, values, and personal conduct. However, while youth involves strongly institutionalised socialisation processes, there are no such clear procedures for the transition from mid- to later life, hence the notion of retirement as 'the roleless role'.[48] Enhanced possibilities for self-styling have to be balanced against the added risk of anomie.

Although I have discussed the need for individuals to develop personal strategies, group support is a crucial means of avoiding social exclusion. As with religious faith, lifelong commitment to a political cause can provide both a clear sense of belonging and a rationale for life.[49] However, with the ardent exception of Dame Barbara Castle (first elected to Parliament in 1945 on a pensioners' ticket), few have devoted themselves to the pensioners' cause until they themselves have retired. Alongside liminality, social fragmentation has meant that older people have had relatively little direct influence on policymaking. First, as we saw when discussing lifestyles, each cohort within the older population exhibits a different awareness; secondly, horizontal inequalities (of income, gender, race, ethnicity, and health) divide older people internally; and, thirdly, the disqualification from employment wrought by retirement effects a vertical separation from people in work. For these reasons collective organisation as 'pensioners' *per se* has arguably had limited impact.[50]

Against the model of political lobbying for rights and resources, organisations such as the University of the Third Age have sought a 'civic' route, aimed at cultural innovation. To this extent they resemble some of the lifestyle-based new social movements which have coagulated around environmental issues. New social movements are defined as

[47] This compares with the firmly demarcated structured dependency common to early childhood and deep old age.

[48] Hazan, *From First Principles*, pp. 33, 3.

[49] M. Andrews, *Lifetimes of Commitment: Ageing, Politics, Psychology* (Cambridge University Press, 1991).

[50] Blaikie and Macnicol, 'Ageing and social policy', p. 77. The reasons why political campaigns have failed to impact on policymaking are discussed at length in Blaikie, 'Emerging political power'. Political scientists have discussed the mechanics of political activity in detail – see especially H. J. Pratt, *Gray Agendas* (Ann Arbor: University of Michigan Press, 1993), and J. Miles, 'Slow progress: why a political framework is necessary for the evaluation of pensioners' campaigns', *Generations Review* 4, 1 (1994), 4–7, but analysis of cultural dialogue in pensioner organisations is seriously lacking.

attempts to further common interests collectively using tactics which are outside the political mainstream. They are particularly concerned with non-material values and keener to redefine culture and lifestyle than to pursue legislative change. Most members belong to the new middle class, and are motivated by frustration caused by their political exclusion or economic disadvantage relative to their high levels of educational attainment.[51]

We have already seen how new lifestyles have emerged through the efforts of this class fraction to establish a social distance via the acquisition of cultural capital. In adopting the 'University' tag, the University of the Third Age (U3A) is clearly attempting to reappropriate both knowledge and learning and to present itself as authoritatively in the vanguard of cultural change, 'the *avant garde* of society, setting an instructive example of leadership'.[52] The current priorities of the British education system, not yet geared to lifelong education, are regarded as obsolescent. In 1981, the Cambridge U3A declared as its first object: 'to educate British society at large in the facts of its present constitution and of its permanent situation in respect of ageing'. The document went on to accentuate the aim of making older people aware of their 'intellectual, cultural, and aesthetic potentialities' and 'to assail the dogma of intellectual decline with age'.[53] Flowing from the pen of Peter Laslett, a leading historical sociologist, these were no idle aspirations. And, according to Hazan's analysis of this albeit unrepresentative local group, conducted in the 1990s, they have succeeded in creating 'a setting for generating knowledge about themselves which does not entail an adverse effect on their lives'.[54] It is indeed rare to find a situation which reverses the medicalised norm of outsiders' expertise being used to analyse and thus claim power over older people.

As chapter 3 explained, the unprecedented expansion of the Third Age means that nowadays most people in the Western world can expect to live for between twenty and thirty years after they have retired. While this has been heralded as a major social attainment,[55] the fact that most ThirdAgers are eager to put ever more clear blue water between themselves and the Fourth Age suggests that old age itself remains

---

[51] L. Martell, *Ecology and Society: An Introduction* (Cambridge: Polity, 1994), pp. 113–16.

[52] Hazan, *From First Principles*, p. 72.

[53] Reprinted in Laslett, *A Fresh Map*, pp. 177–9.

[54] Hazan, *From First Principles*, p. 141. Declining health for some and geographical mobility for others forced a high turnover of members, and ensured that 'emergent bureaucratic properties' remained absent. In this respect, the organisation (as a social movement, but not as a campaigning unit) has perhaps made a virtue out of necessity.

[55] See the various outputs from the Carnegie Inquiry into the Third Age, for example T. Schuller and A. M. Boston, *Learning: Education, Training and Information in the Third Age* (Dunfermline: Carnegie United Kingdom Trust, 1992).

problematic.[56] Laslett has emphasised that, as well as being active in the sense of developing 'leisure as distinct from idleness', the U3A also pursues a 'doctrine of withdrawal ... from those engagements with society [work and parenting] which are the essence of the Second Age'.[57] Rather than trying to reclaim mid-life, U3A has succeeded in carving out a niche to explore Third Age living as a distinctly different experience. However, Hazan asserts that this has been accomplished only by denying the transition to the Fourth Age and death. By emphasising the freedom of the mind, U3A have effectively obliterated concern for the body from their discourse. His anthropological study of the Cambridge U3A found that causes of disappearance from the group – hospitalisation, institutionalisation, and family care – were never discussed. An attempt to research television-viewing in geriatric institutions collapsed through lack of volunteers. And, when, during a party, a member died on the premises after a heart attack, those who had attended to him returned to the gathering without letting the secret be known to the rest. Thus, Hazan advances the alarming claim that 'the U3A's reason for existence was in its power to banish death from its midst'.[58]

Parallels between the rise of the Third Age in general and the emergence of youth culture are not difficult to find, although cultural studies have yet to explore these. The teenage consumer was 'discovered' in the 1950s when market researchers found an opportunity to exploit fresh disposable income which could be spent on goods – records, clothes, motorcycles – expressing pleasure at 'not being grown up'.[59] By the same token, the grey market of today encourages expenditure on leisure items, holidays, and health – all in the service of not growing old. In both cases consumption, not production, forms the basis for lifestyle. However, while the refusal to 'mature' or maturing 'too early' has occasioned recurrent moral panics over torn cinema seats, pitched battles between Mods and Rockers, gymslip mums, or children murdering toddlers, we have yet to see senile delinquency assert itself on a grand scale. Instead, the threat from old age is presented ideologically as a 'burden of dependency', to be financed by taxing the non-aged. Meanwhile, the costs of educational provision for children are taken for granted since these are regarded as an investment in future producers. Hence youth subcultures are threatening in ways that older people cannot be because they undermine or deflect the

[56] Pilcher, *Age and Generation*, p. 100.    [57] Laslett, *A Fresh Map*, p. 157.
[58] Hazan, *From First Principles*, pp. 111–15, 141.
[59] S. Frith, *The Sociology of Youth* (Ormskirk: Causeway Books, 1984).

progress of potential – rather than former – workers and parents on whom economic and social stability will depend.

Old age is clearly a period of leisure for growing numbers of people, and following Matza we might expect delinquency (and the attendant risk of law-breaking) to arise as a means of solving the leisure problem (boredom).[60] But to call an action delinquent is to describe the social reaction to it, and a deviant becomes one only after the label has been successfully applied by others.[61] Reported acts of deviance on the part of older people have not, to date, manifested themselves in collective rituals of gang warfare, sexual promiscuity, or drug-based musical gatherings. Headlines such as 'Oldies' barney at the bingo! OAPs riot as caller flees' fail to terrify precisely because the rioters are pensioners and remain contained within their age-appropriate domain, the bingo hall.[62] Any imagined rebellion has been cast as harmless shenanigans – the beleathered bikers called 'Hell's Grannies' in the *Monty Python* sketch, or the comedy capers of three bored elderly criminals who rob a bank in the movie *Tough Guys*. Yet neither scenario is as improbable as the humorous fantasy suggests. The drinking, mayhem, and gang fights in Hollister, California, on which the Brando film *The Wild One* (1953) was based happened fifty years ago, and in 1997 a (peaceful) commem-orative rally was staged there. Many of the bikers were still Hell's Angels, only much greyer.[63] Meanwhile, in 1980s Britain, 'two pen-sioners, wearing wigs and balaclavas and packing a Walther automatic pistol, tried to solve their desperate financial problems by carrying out a Bonnie and Clyde-style robbery'.[64] Had they been younger, a Mertonian criminologist would doubtless have rationalised their non-standard means of getting the money to pay the mortgage as an example of action motivated by blocked access to social rewards. Like un-employed teenagers ramraiding shops in order to steal videos, they were simply acquiring the necessary but – since work was not an option – by an illegal route. But this was clearly not the message conveyed by the

---

[60] D. Matza, *Delinquency and Drift* (New York: Wiley, 1964).

[61] H. S. Becker, *Outsiders: Studies in the Sociology of Deviance* (New York: Free Press, 1966), is the classic interactionist text on how deviance develops and is amplified.

[62] R. Notarangelo, 'Oldies' barney at the bingo!', *Scottish Daily Mirror*, 18 December 1996, 1.

[63] *Observer*, 6 July 1997.

[64] A. Clements, 'Pensioners turn "Bonnie and Clyde" to pay off mortgage', *Scotsman*, 27 May 1989, 1. In May 1998, two brothers aged sixty and sixty-six appeared in court charged with 'conspiracy to possess home-made firearms with intent to endanger life, conspiring to blackmail Barclays Bank, and also conspiring to blackmail Sainsbury'. This followed a police investigation into thirty-six attacks mainly against branches of Barclays and Sainsbury's supermarket, the so-called Mardi Gra (*sic*) bombings ('Mardi Gra charges', *Independent*, 1 May 1998, 4).

press. Rather, as Hockey and James claim, referring to the same story, 'the account doubly marginalises the elderly people. Through seemingly trivialising their attempt, however misguided, to accrue money, the report mockingly re-classifies the pensioners' marginal act of robbery.'[65] Perhaps, in such a climate, older people prefer alternative modes of expression.

## The resistant self

Being old, visible, and on the street usually indicates poverty, depicted as 'silent suffering'. However, often symbolic forms and social actions that are apparently non-political are, in fact, resistances. Morinis argues that the Native Americans living on Skid Row in Canadian cities are not simply deprived and undersocialised, but, through drinking very heavily, scavenging from and sleeping in garbage bins, they are succeeding in offending wider society and thus compelling others to take notice. There is a clear parallel here with youth lifestyles and 'resistance through rituals' via dress 'statements', body piercing and tattooing, music, slang, and drugs. Such politics do not flourish in the organised political arena, but take place 'through life-styling on the stage of their personal minds and bodies. Their lives are their manifestos. Their politics is the politics of self.'[66] Arguably, this reasoning applies to a number of deliberate attempts to 'grow old disgracefully', be this by being difficult with carers, flaunting sexuality, being a bag lady, or fashioning other 'repertoires of resistance'. In the form of the fictional Betty Spital ('Pensioner, Activist, and Radical Granny') such types are turned into a compound figure of fun, although we laugh with her, not at her.[67] Meanwhile, accenting the idiosyncratic, Alan Bennett recounts his everyday encounters with Miss Shepherd, the old lady whose outlandish wardrobe was matched only by her bizarre reasoning, and whose chaotic home was a series of vans parked opposite the playwright's London house for almost twenty years.[68]

In the above examples the behaviour of an individual is evoked, rather than collective actions. However, outsiders frequently exhibit subcultural traits, if not self-consciously regarding themselves as members of a

[65] Hockey and James, *Growing Up and Growing Old*, p. 139.

[66] A. Morinis, 'Skid Row Indians and the politics of self', in F. R. Manning and J.-M. Philibert (eds.), *Customs in Conflict: The Anthropology of a Changing World* (Peterborough, Ont.: Broadview Press, 1990), pp. 361–86 (p. 362).

[67] C. Meade, *The Thoughts of Betty Spital: Pensioner, Activist and Radical Granny* (London: Penguin, 1989).

[68] A. Bennett, 'The lady in the van', in Bennett, *Writing Home* (London: Faber and Faber, 1997), pp. 83–130.

wider group. Joyce Stephens's study of single-room occupancies in an American slum hotel revealed how elderly tenants strove to preserve their autonomy and individuality in ways not entirely dissimilar to Morinis's Skid Row Indians. All felt threatened by the potential loss of physical or mental abilities since this would destroy the one crucial factor in their lives – independence.[69]

One can appreciate why these elders were so apprehensive when one learns of the fate of Pat Moore, a researcher who during her twenties spent three years travelling to 200 cities throughout the United States and Canada camouflaged as an 85-year-old.[70] To simulate the normal sensory degeneration associated with ageing, she wore a latex mask, wax in her ears to impair hearing, dabs of baby oil in the eyes to blur her vision, balsa wood splints at the back of each knee to restrict flexion, taped her fingers together to simulate arthritic hands, and applied salt and water paste at the back of her throat to ensure a rasping voice. Her experience was not a happy one: 'shortchanged by shopkeepers, verbally abused when she got in the way, and assaulted and left for dead by a gang of youths out for drugs money. Police pleaded with her to give up her double life ... Irascible behaviour became almost a Pavlovian response to her "aged" appearance'. Pat commented: 'I was always painfully aware the disguise was just a shell for me.' However, she was surprised to discover that 'when she voiced this guilt to her elderly friends, they confirmed the feeling. They too felt they were in a shell – young minds trapped behind old faces.'[71]

The implications of this mind/body dichotomy are developed in Hepworth's concept of the 'mask of age'. In the above instances the true – perpetually youthful – self is disguised behind an old skin. However, there is a contrastingly revelatory sense in which, as we have seen, cosmetics and other props are employed to project an inner persona ('the self we would like to be') that belies a person's real age. Both cases illustrate the role of outer, physical appearance in social interaction and communication. As the individual ages, the 'familiar (and more youthful) identity exists in a delicate state of balance, dependent for its

---

[69] J. Stephens, *Loners, Losers and Lovers: Elderly Tenants in a Slum Hotel* (London: University of Washington Press, 1976).

[70] Pat Moore is a founder of the Universal Design movement in the USA and of Moore Design Associates, institutions dedicated to the development of new products (such as soap powder boxes with resealable flaps or laser distance sensors to aid car parking), environments, services, and marketing strategies for older consumers.

[71] L. Young, 'The incredible ageing woman', *Guardian*, 1 August 1989, 16–17 (16). See also 'How TV stunner Carol grew old before her time', *The People*, 27 February 1993, 5, which reports a similar experiment with comparable results, conducted by television personality Carol Smillie, who remarked: 'I was shocked by the way old people are ignored. I felt totally anonymous.'

survival on his ability to convince others that he is still the person he once was: to persuade those around him to reflect back and publicly confirm his private image of his inner self'. Such persuasion involves considerable backstage work, as Hepworth notes in the case of the satirist Max Beerbohm:

Beerbohm's biographer recalls the style of self-presentation favoured by the elderly artist when receiving his constant stream of celebrated visitors.

Now he was so old, Max liked to prepare himself before making the effort to meet a new person. Generally the visitor was introduced into the drawing-room where he was met by Florence [Beerbohm's wife]. She then took him up to the terrace where Max was waiting. He was dressed with all his old care ... his appearance still mattered to him. Cecil Beaton visited him during these years and took some photographs. After he had finished. 'You'll let me see them?', Max asked. 'And you'll destroy any horrors.'[72]

Where self-image and that of the artist conflict the result can be catastrophic – witness Winston Churchill's destruction of his portrait by Graham Sutherland. For those with less social prestige and fewer props, the tasks can be awesome.

The very existence of the 'mask of age' testifies to the vulnerability of an unchanging inner consciousness, the 'ageless self', in the face of stereotyped assumptions and expectations held by the non-aged.[73] In Cohen's terminology, it is a prime example of the individual's resistance to 'subordination-by-categorisation'.[74] And, as a de-stigmatising process, upholding the mask demands unstinting application to 'the hidden work of everyday life', the efforts required to sustain the value structure through which relationships are maintained as fully human. Both self-consciousness and self-control are essential to such a tenacious, but tenuous undertaking.[75]

Resistance to categorisation can take several forms. First, developing Goffman's notion of 'passing', full adult status is best preserved if one can indeed mask the realities of one's ageing by, for example, refusing to

[72] M. Hepworth, 'Positive ageing and the mask of age', 95–6, citing D. Cecil, *Max: A Biography* (London: Constable, 1964). Cecil Beaton is reported to have said: 'Fashion provides the means not only to find an identity but to escape one too' (*Undressed: Fashion in the Twentieth Century*, Channel 4, 22 February 1998). The comment might equally apply to any mask.

[73] See S. Kaufman, *The Ageless Self: Sources of Meaning in Later Life* (Madison: University of Wisconsin Press, 1986).

[74] A. P. Cohen, *Self Consciousness: An Alternative Anthropology of Identity* (Routledge: London, 1993), p. 104. Cf. carers who regard as 'difficult' older people who insist on their rights.

[75] See B. G. Myerhoff, *Number Our Days* (New York: Simon and Schuster, 1978); C. Wadel, 'The hidden work of everyday life', in S. Wallman (ed.), *Social Anthropology of Work* (London: Academic Press, 1979), pp. 365–84; Okely, 'Clubs for le troisième age'.

state one's true age, or avoiding physically demanding activities in which one's frailty would be exposed. The consequences can, however, be self-delusory: for instance, isolation from family could be rationalised as being due to their children's 'busy success'. Further, constant fabrication of disguises can lead to denial of selfhood in that 'our true identity, never acted out, can lose its substance, its meaning, even for ourselves'.[76]

Secondly, whereas the mask of age seeks to harmonise mind and body as equally young, some older people accept bodily decline but assert forcibly the continuance of a healthy intellect. Arguably, given the 'double jeopardy' of ageism and sexism thesis, this is easier for men, for whom physiological signs of age may be esteemed, or insignificant, than for women, who remain under pressure to satisfy the male gaze or risk social invisibility by dint of losing their physical attractiveness.

Late life transitions require strategies of self-management. First, the person may manipulate reality. For example, 'they could interpret things contrary to common sense, and identify so strongly with the past self that a photograph from the past could be vividly presented as evidence for the present self'. Secondly, they can assimilate by developing 'instrumental and compensatory activities aimed at preventing or alleviating losses in areas of life central to self-esteem and identity'. Artur Rubinstein managed to perform at an advanced age by restricting his repertoire (selection), practising more (optimisation), and enhancing the impression of speed in fast passages by slowing down preceding passages (compensation). Finally, Coleman suggests an accommodative acceptance of change, 'to disengage from blocked commitments and to adjust aspirations to what is feasible'.[77]

## Status passage

Building on the idea of *rites de passage*, Glaser and Strauss claim that the life course involves a series of transitions from one social state to the next. Each status passage consists of a negotiated process in which both the properties of the passage and the awareness of each participant will vary. Among the properties cited are: desirability; inevitability;

---

[76] Hockey and James, *Growing Up and Growing Old*, p. 165, citing B. Macdonald and C. Rich, *Look Me in the Eye: Old Women, Aging and Ageism* (London: Women's Press, 1982), p. 55. See also S. H. Matthews, *The Social World of Old Women* (Beverly Hills: Sage, 1979).

[77] P. Coleman, 'Last scene of all', 3; P. B. Baltes and M. M. Baltes, 'Psychological perspectives on successful aging: the model of selective optimisation with compensation', in P. B. Baltes and M. M. Baltes (eds.), *Successful Aging: Perspectives from the Behavioural Sciences* (New York: Cambridge University Press, 1990), pp. 1–34.

reversibility; repeatability; whether the passage occurs alone, collectively, or in aggregate; whether or not it is voluntary; the degree of control the central figure has over the process; legitimisation by others; the clarity or disguised nature of the signs; centrality of importance of events for persons involved; and the duration of passage. Each passage has a 'trajectory' (a managed period featuring the chronological sequence of events and a sequence of shifts in self-image) during which the individual combines a number of roles to establish their own career paths or role career.

Persons may not be aware that they are experiencing the same passage. For instance, many people suffer depression on retirement, but they suffer separately because they no longer have the workplace as a common meeting ground. There are also situations where, although individuals are aware of what is going on, they cannot communicate their awareness to others – dying and possibly dementia are examples. Thus patterns of interaction will differ according to the level and type of awareness that is or is not shared.[78] The model is clearly applicable to many later life transitions: for example, retirement may or may not be desirable or voluntary; the 'mask' of age indicates attempts to disguise signs of ageing, although mental and physiological decline are generally irreversible; dying is inevitable.

Legitimacy and control are important aspects since the status passage into deep old age depends upon social permissions to broach moral categories. Williams, for instance, has shown how in everyday theorising a group of older Aberdonians considered it a moral obligation to resist the onset of the signs of ill health. It was a duty to remain active and disengagement was sanctioned only after serious illness had been diagnosed. Only then did it become legitimate to give up.[79] Likewise, Jerrome's study of old people's clubs in 'Seatown' [Hove] notes that: 'Responses to [old age] are a matter of virtue and moral strength or weakness. To be happy and to make the best of things in spite of pain and hardship is a moral and social obligation attached to the status of the old or handicapped person. Those who fail are blameworthy, and tend to blame themselves.'[80] Thus the policing of deviance occurs internally, amongst older people themselves. Through this mechanism, resistance to decline becomes the expected norm, the individual being blamed for any 'failure' to attempt to stay healthy. Indeed, Jerrome

[78] B. Glaser and A. L. Strauss, *Status Passage* (London: Routledge and Kegan Paul, 1971), pp. 1–13.
[79] Rory Williams, *A Protestant Legacy: Attitudes to Illness and Death Among Older Aberdonians* (Oxford: Clarendon Press, 1990).
[80] Jerrome, *Good Company*, p. 142, cited in Hepworth, 'Positive ageing: what is the message?', p. 181.

suggests that the continual discussion of illness in the clubs reflected a need to monitor the social implications of altered health status.[81]

The fact of retirement marginalises all older people. To this extent, they are excluded both socially and economically, but the very legitimacy of retirement as a political institution means that retirement is itself a normative expectation of reaching a particular age. Retiring at, say, thirty-five or ninety-five would be regarded as abnormal. Deviance within retirement requires departures from the standard script. Where these are partial and temporary they signify little, since the individual remains, for the most part, a conformist. A pensioner who enjoys motorbiking may be regarded as eccentric, but no more than that, since when they are not biking they will do similar things to other pensioners. However, should the deviance become a matter of lifestyle – say, joining a motorcycle gang and living on the road – then he or she will have become an outsider.[82] In this respect older people are no different from others. Where old age differs from adulthood in general is in the system of constraints that gradually enforce conformity. As one becomes more entrenched, so it becomes increasingly difficult to resist. By the same token, minor forms of rebellion will have far greater impact on others. Jenny Joseph's poem *Warning* is so often quoted because the hypothetical woman who decides she will be subversive when she gets old by wearing purple, spending her money on brandy, and learning to spit is seen as advocating behaviours that are shocking in an old lady, but would be scarcely noteworthy in a young woman.[83] Her deviance, for all the effort in achieving it, reads as humorous rather than dangerous.

### Late life passages

Partly because it can be trivialised in such ways, effective resistance becomes increasingly difficult with the transition from Third to Fourth Age. Indeed, the fact of such a transition implies a degree of failed intersubjectivity, referred to in the doubly meant phrase 'the unbecoming self'.[84] Personhood requires the individual to have acquired physical, cognitive, and emotional maturity. Thus children become persons when they grow up. By the same token, the loss of any of these attributes means that old people can un-become persons (hence become un-persons) as they grow old. The socially manufactured relationship between personhood, infantilisation, and the life course ensures that

---

[81] Jerrome, *Good Company*, p. 145.　　[82] Becker, *Outsiders*.
[83] J. Joseph, *Rose in the Afternoon* (London: Dent, 1974).
[84] Personal communication, from discussion with Nikolas Coupland and John Nussbaum.

bodily betrayals invoke disgust while, in the face of diminishing communicative competence, stigma follows on their declining ability to reciprocate, to fulfil the obligation to socialise.[85]

In a study of Alzheimer's disease, Kitwood graphically demonstrates how a 'malignant social psychology' operates through a series of threats to personhood. These he enumerates as: (1) treachery: dishonest representation used by others to secure the sufferer's compliance with their wishes; (2) disempowerment: deskilling and diminution of agency since things are done for the sufferer; (3) infantilisation: an extreme version of (2) accompanied by messages of childlike mental capacity and capability; (4) intimidation: impersonal head scans and psychological assessments; (5) labelling by being given a diagnosis, e.g., 'primary degenerative dementia'; (6) stigmatisation, labelling with connotations of exclusion; (7) outpacing: lack of compensation/consideration by caregivers for a slower rate of mental functioning; (8) invalidation: experiences and feelings ignored or overlooked rather than understood, accepted, and sympathised with; (9) banishment: deprivation of sustaining human contact since physically or psychologically removed from the human milieu; (10) objectification: being treated as an object rather than a person. He claims that each of these is 'remarkably common in the lives of older people who are confused, who inhabit "the borderlands of dementia"'.[86] Evidence of personal resistance against such onslaughts is brittle, since it is, of course, methodologically well nigh impossible to find out how a dementia sufferer feels. However, McIsaac suggests that interaction between residential home staff and residents is rendered problematic by dint of a 'medical model' of confusion that fails to appreciate the experience of the resident's changing sense of self. While 'confusion' implies failure to communicate, it may sometimes be a surface manifestation of a coping mechanism by which the older person willingly withdraws into subjective control of their own status passage.[87]

Hockey and James note that 'tiny gestures of defiance and small acts of personal insurrection' can take on particular significance in institutional settings where residents are more likely to run up against infantilisation. A tactic frequently observed here is to adopt appropriately childlike characteristics, such as sticking out tongues, manipulating

[85] B. S. Turner, 'Ageing, status politics and sociological theory', *British Journal of Sociology* 40 (1989), 588–606.

[86] T. Kitwood, 'The dialectics of dementia: with particular reference to Alzheimer's disease', *Ageing and Society* 10 (1990), 177–96 (181–4).

[87] S. J. McIsaac, 'How nursing home residents live while in the sub-passage of confusion: the battle of dignity and respect versus deterioration and decline', Ph.D thesis, University of Aberdeen, 1993, p. 296.

orderly sequences by refusal to hurry, kicking other residents under the dining table, and general being 'disobedient'. In this way residents are able to 'undermine the power of the adult [nursing staff] as metaphoric "parent"'.[88] Far from indicating institutionalised behaviour, the fact of such gestures suggests a high degree of reflexivity. In so far as they know how to play the game, these residents are able to distance themselves mentally from the roles they are playing. This does not mean, however, that they have any option but to interact according to the rules.

The pervasiveness of such rules depends on the degree to which old age has become the master status in one's life. As I have argued earlier, deep old age may be replacing death as the great contemporary taboo. Certainly, the boundaries fencing off the Fourth Age from the rest of society are comparable. Institutions effect both temporal and spatial segregation.[89] Ariès has argued that whereas in the pre-industrial past people of all ages died at home, in the bosom of their family, modern medicine has both improved life expectancy so that dying at any point prior to old age is uncommon and shifted the site of dying to the hospital or nursing home.[90] Similarly, and relatedly, old age is now regarded as the appropriate time to suffer specific maladies prior to death and the old people's home is considered the appropriate place. Thus social marginalisation relates to medical control where the organisation of both time and space is in the hands of the institution.[91] Beginning with the petty bureaucratic intrusions of the welfare system, the 'geriatric gaze' widens to embrace all aspects of daily life.

The poem *Kate*, written by an elderly woman in a nursing home but discovered only after her death, begins with a plea:

What do you see nurse, what do you see? / What are you thinking when you look at me? / A crabbit old woman, not very wise, / Uncertain of habit with far away eyes, / Who dribbles her food, and makes no reply / When you say in a loud voice, 'I do wish you'd try', / Who seems not to notice the things that you do, / And forever is losing a stocking or shoe, / Who, unresisting or not, lets you do as you will / With bathing and feeding, the long day to fill. / Is that what you're thinking, is that what you see? / Then open your eyes you're not looking at me.[92]

---

[88] Hockey and James, *Growing Up and Growing Old*, pp. 131, 172–3, 175.

[89] J. Hockey, *Experiences of Death: An Anthropological Account* (Edinburgh University Press, 1990), pp. 27–55. Hockey also discusses the significance of linguistic boundaries in constructing stereotypes.

[90] P. Ariès, *The Hour of Our Death* (London: Penguin, 1983).

[91] See D. M. Willcocks, S. M. Peace, and L. A. Kellaher, *Private Lives in Public Places: A Research-Based Critique of Residential Life in Local Authority Old People's Homes* (London: Tavistock, 1987).

[92] 'Poem found with the belongings of an elderly lady who died in a nursing home in Ireland', in E. S. Johnson and J. B. Williamson, *Growing Old: The Social Problems of Aging* (New York: Holt, Reinhart and Winston, 1980), pp. 131–2.

She duly goes on to reveal her life story, but by now it is too late. In deep old age difficulties of communication may become so severe that no form of attention-seeking will work. Even the resources for communicating may be withheld, as with the protagonist in May Sarton's novel *As We Are Now* who begins her copybook: 'I am not mad, only old. I make this statement to give me courage. Suffice it to say that it has taken two weeks for me to obtain this notebook and a pen. I am in a concentration camp for the old, a place where people dump their parents or relatives exactly as though it were an ash can.'[93] Forced to resort to undercover messages, which may or may not be found later, she is indeed imprisoned.

Such depersonalisation and consequent effacement have sinister implications, particularly in a political atmosphere of concern over the fiscal 'burden' of growing numbers of very old people demanding scarce health resources. Arluke and Levin foresee that 'stereotyped images of the elderly may one day include less emphasis on infantilisation and more emphasis on dehumanisation. There is a tendency to view some aged people as mere "vegetables" – totally beyond the age of productivity and usefulness. They are viewed as no longer alive in the sense that we understand what it means to be human and therefore not worthy of the medical and social services available to those who are younger.'[94] The translation of such views into medical practice, through, for example, the rationing of dialysis according to age, has attracted comment, with one writer referring to the legitimisation of 'a hidden programme of cost-induced euthanasia', and another adding that 'chronological cleansing is the ultimate act of ageism'.[95] Such is the paradox of achieving longevity. Beyond the gloom of societal rejection or incarceration lies the stark inevitability of death.[96] Is it any wonder that our elders should be so diligent and ingenious in their attempts to escape while they can?

---

[93] M. Sarton, *As We Are Now* (London: Women's Press, 1983), p. 1.

[94] A. Arluke and J. Levin, 'Another stereotype: old age as a second childhood', *Aging* (1984), 7–11 (11).

[95] H. Diessenbacher, 'The elderly in the health care system: ethic and economy of the generation conflict in the medical system', *Generations* 4 (1986/7), 1–7 (6); Bytheway, *Ageism*, p. 27.

[96] There is a voluminous literature on the sociology of death and dying. For a brief overview of relevant aspects, see Fennell, Phillipson, and Evers, *Sociology of Old Age*, pp. 160–8.

# 9    Conclusion: the struggle of memory against forgetting

The relationship between older people, history, and imagery is neatly encapsulated by a recent critique of popular televisual culture:

Bryan Appleyard ... writing in *The Sunday Times* (5 January 1997), raised the question of the changing nature of moral communities as indicated by the changing imagery of the characters of *Coronation Street* [Britain's longest-running and most popular television soap opera]. Appleyard took the view that the essence of The Street is its fictional celebration of a kind of world we have lost: a nostalgic recreating, larger than life, of the enduring values of life on a small and intimate scale where survival is based on interpersonal accommodation and respect. Such values were reflected in the pride of place occupied by the older characters ... But in today's piping times these figures represent not only ageing individuals but ageing social values.[1]

Two important questions arise from this observation: first, what are the roots of people's elaboration of ideal moral communities; secondly, do these represent 'ageing social values', or are they part of a vision appropriate to the present or an aspiration for the future? Contrary to the apparent message conveyed by older people retiring to the seaside (chapter 7), Appleyard's analysis suggests that, as people age, both their tastes and their values travel with them, so that they become an anachronism. Whichever claim one prefers, the argument requires reference to an imagined community held up as the reflection of a particular world view. This ideological device is 'imagined' in the sense that actual interaction with all those who might people it – television characters, deceased relatives, identikit archetypes – is impossible; it is a 'community' in that, regardless of any actual degree of inequality, its relationships are always those of 'deep horizontal comradeship'. Imagined communities are important because they provide the sense of continuity on which identities are premised. Benedict Anderson applies this reasoning to the 'biography of nations', nations, he argues, being inherently social constructs. Yet the necessity for such construction applies equally to the individual:

[1] 'Free radicals', 25.

All profound changes of consciousness, by their very nature, bring with them characteristic amnesias. Out of such oblivions, in specific historical circumstances, spring narratives. After experiencing the physiological and emotional changes produced by puberty, it is impossible to 'remember' the consciousness of childhood. How many thousands of days passed between infancy and early adulthood vanish beyond direct recall! How strange it is to need another's help to learn that this naked baby in the yellowed photograph, sprawled happily on rug or cot, is you. The photograph, fine child of the age of mechanical reproduction, is only the most peremptory of a huge modern accumulation of documentary evidence (birth certificates, diaries, report cards, letters, medical records, and the like) which simultaneously records a certain apparent continuity and emphasises its loss from memory. Out of this estrangement comes a conception of personhood, *identity* (yes, you and that naked baby are identical) which, because it cannot be 'remembered', must be narrated.[2]

Like Kundera's plea for national identity, ageing thus involves 'the struggle of memory against forgetting', the resources with which the battle is waged being products of the modern urge to individuate.[3] Nevertheless, as chapter 8 has illustrated, belonging to a wider entity is also critical. If we consider history not as Great Men, Great Battles, and Grand Themes, but as lived experience, biographies of each of us as social beings in different groups in different times and places, then we must acknowledge that context is very important. Our identities are caught at the intersections. Of course, each individual will have a different profile and most of us will inhabit several different places in the course of our lives. Tamara Hareven stresses the multiplicity of influences on each individual life course: whereas 'historical time' is linear and chronological, 'family time' relates to the transitions around marriage, childbirth, leaving home, retirement, and death, while 'industrial time' considers changing patterns of work.[4] The individual strands woven through these interrelated sequences are as many and varied as the persons caught up in them; hence the researcher must construct bridges between biography and the social structure. This chimes in with a willingness on the part of some sociologists and gerontologists to shift perspective from functionalist theories of old age towards interactionist and ethnographic interpretations of becoming old.[5]

Identity is created, confirmed, maintained, and changed by a person's interaction with other people. It follows that neither models focusing on

---

[2] B. Anderson, *Imagined Communities*, pp. 204–5.

[3] M. Kundera, *The Book of Laughter and Forgetting* (London: Faber and Faber, 1989).

[4] Hareven, 'Family time and historical time'; T. K. Hareven, 'The history of the family and the complexity of social change', *American Historical Review* 96, 1 (1991), 95–124.

[5] See, for example, Bytheway, Keil, Allatt, and Bryman, *Becoming and Being Old*; A. Blaikie, 'Whither the Third Age?: implications for gerontology', *Generations Review* 2, 1 (1992), 2–4.

inner psychological processes of individuals nor those stressing broad cultural attitudes will be sufficient in themselves since neither fully captures the interaction between these levels of meaning. We all construct our own microcosm of the world. The loss of one's sense of historical understanding of oneself may provoke identity crisis – as when a wife becomes a widow – while the absence of a sense of present identity provokes existential anxieties. A new status has to be negotiated at an intermediate level between that of the broad cultural scale and that of the individual personality. That intermediate world is constituted by the social network. Therefore, the self is reconstructed through formal or informal social contacts within a limited community.

However, if our identities derived solely from where we are at any one time, we would become extremely confused, not to say mentally exhausted, with the effort of placing ourselves. On the other hand, to feel placeless is to be lost, to have no handle on how to define oneself. So we reconstruct for ourselves workable biographies, like CVs, that we know to be selective, less than whole, but sufficient for us to tell our own stories as personal odysseys.[6] Diaries and letters represent private attempts to chronicle and reflect on our lives, and through these devices we interpret our ageing as it happens rather than retrospectively.[7] Nevertheless, part of who we are is where we are from, even if that gets mythologised as something better than it really was in the process. At an autobiographical level, each of us needs to connect, or strives to reconnect, with our own past. Many of us are trying to recover something of the sensibility that made us who we are, or we have a deep curiosity to understand what made our parents or grandparents tick, the better to comprehend our own state of mind. You cannot know where you are going until you have worked out where you are coming from.[8] We also learn to adopt and adapt as we move through different settings in the course of our lives. Thus we become familiar with the cultural codes by which different groups survive. Indeed, we have to do this ourselves in order to survive. Context is all-important but this does not limit us to one time and one place.

---

[6] For theoretical and methodological clarification, see D. Bertaux (ed.), *Biography and Society* (Beverly Hills: Sage, 1981); N. Denzin, *Interpretive Biography* (Newbury Park: Sage, 1988); and K. Plummer, *Documents of Life* (London: Allen and Unwin, 1983).

[7] Bytheway, 'Ageing and biography'.

[8] Here I take issue with Evelyn Waugh, who opens his own autobiography with the remark: 'Only when one has lost all curiosity about the future has one reached the age to write an autobiography' (E. Waugh, *A Little Learning* (London: Chapman and Hall, 1964), quoted in M. Evans, 'Reading lives: how the personal might be social', *Sociology* 27, 1 (1993), 5–13 (5).

### Meanings of home and family

Gubrium discusses self-construction as an everyday practice based on three sets of resources: the locally shared, the biographical, and 'meaningfully available material objects'. Agency is assembled from whatever is enduringly available within each particular setting and 'from what we have done, been, or experienced'.[9] Frequently, this will involve the interplay of resources, for example the meaning of 'home' combines objects and memory: 'a widow might affirm her "wonderful" marriage by pointing to the frayed armchair she cherishes despite its shabbiness because, as she explains, its sustains her view of herself as having been a good wife and reminds her daily of her husband, who sat in it "on those many pleasant evenings we spent together"'.[10]

Because houses are full of memories and objects which help to maintain identity, idealised pictorial images of age often site grandparents by the fireside hearth. Home is also sacredly construed as a place of privacy and of spirituality.[11] Amongst the present older generation, home is perhaps more important for women, who have inhabited the domestic sphere as wives, mothers, and carers, than for men, whose preserve has been the workplace. Some women continually redecorate, as a way of changing with the times and moving to the future, whereas for others holding on to memories, thus keeping a sense of identity intact, means steadfastly preserving an unchanged environment full of objects from the past. Home can be a source of shame as well as pride, especially if falling into disrepair (when built form might mirror the decay of its occupant). Indeed, although remaining at home as one ages is associated with independence, leaving home is not always stressful or traumatic. Being moved to an institution may be regarded as betrayal by one's children, and cause anger at being labelled dependent; on the other hand, it might provide relief from maintenance problems and costs, or vulnerability – home can be a site of perceived or actual danger (particularly from burglars), rather than a safe refuge. Or again, home can hold bad memories (e.g., nursing a husband who died), and the transition to residential care could mean leaving solitary loneliness for peer-group sociability and interaction with staff.[12] A disengagement

9  J. F. Gubrium, *Individual Agency, the Ordinary and Postmodern Life*, Centre for Ageing and Biographical Studies, School of Health and Social Welfare, Open University, 24 April 1995 (printed text of inaugural lecture), pp. 8–11.

10  Gubrium, *Individual Agency*, p. 8, citing R. Rubinstein, 'The significance of personal objects to older people', *Journal of Aging Studies* 1 (1987), 225–38.

11  M. Csikszentmihalyi and E. Rochberg-Halton, *The Meaning of Things: Domestic Symbols and the Self* (Cambridge University Press, 1981).

12  On the transformation of household objects from 'material' to 'memorable', see

argument also considers preparation for withdrawal by requiring increasingly few material goods and giving away possessions. Equally, by
doing this the ageing individual retains control over allocation (who gets
what), whilst fulfilling a wish to see younger generations enjoy their
inheritance while their parents or grandparents are still alive.

Desire for genealogical rootedness and family continuity appears to
be an important facet of ageing. In her study of 1980s Mass-Observation
autobiographies, Jerrome found that some respondents, invited to list
relatives, included the deceased, adding that 'for some people the sense
of family history is almost overwhelming. There is the fascination of old
photographs, and accounts of deeds and misdeeds.'[13] Plath uses the
metaphor of shoals of fish sailing down the biographical current to
indicate how siblings – by extension other significant contemporaries –
move along on separate tracks which at various points intersect.[14]
However, increasing numbers of people experience radical discontinuities through migration, marriage outside their religious or cultural
group, or divorce, and the childless would appear not to engage in the
transmission of family traditions.[15] Moreover, in the public domain of
cultural super-ego, some stories are central, others more marginal.
Thus, in *Landscape for a Good Woman*, Carolyn Steedman tries to
account for her mother's experience as a child in the 1920s, as a single
mother in the 1950s, and as an older woman, dying of cancer, in the
near-present. She finds it difficult to place a woman with no wish for
children within psychoanalytic theory; to place a father who is insignificant in the world outside the household within a patriarchal interpretation; to locate a woman who grew up in East Lancashire in the 1920s,
then moved to South London, within a Hoggartian framework of (male-
orientated) working-class culture; to situate an old person dying alone
in poverty within the frame of reference that enveloped Simone de
Beauvoir's wealthy mother.[16] This takes us beyond the normal and
the deviant, the social construction of conventional interpretations, to
the far more challenging terrain where autobiography is accommodated
to collective memory, where 'the irreducible nature of all our lost

E. Fairhurst, 'Recalling life: analytical issues in the use of "memories"', in Jamieson,
Harper, and Victor, *Critical Approaches*, pp. 63–73 (pp. 68–71).

[13] D. Jerrome, 'Time, change and continuity in family life', *Ageing and Society* 14, 1
(1994), 1–17 (10–11).

[14] D. Plath, 'Resistance at forty-eight: old-age brinkmanship and Japanese lifecourse
pathways', in T. K. Hareven and K. J. Adams (eds.), *Ageing and Life Course Transitions:
An Interdisciplinary Perspective* (London: Tavistock, 1982), pp. 109–25.

[15] Some migrations, or diaspora, have the effect of strengthening cultural ties. Moreover,
as survivors of the Shoah have testified, memories can carry a very heavy burden.

[16] Steedman, *Landscape for a Good Woman*; S. de Beauvoir, *A Very Easy Death*
(Harmondsworth: Penguin, 1969).

childhoods'[17] finds resonance in the phenomenal sales of department store reproductions of L. S. Lowry's paintings, or, indeed, in the popularity of sepia postcards of old fishermen, the shared 'contemplation of time passing without meaning'.[18]

Without roots, the sense of self remains clouded. Thus, the effort to restore meaning involves attempts to explain family dispersal. Rather than this being perceived as a cyclical process common to each generation, the hiving off of one's own family may be seen as part of a historical development from an extended family system peopled by a cohesive range of relatives to a scattered set of sub-nuclear arrangements:

> There is a popular belief that the family as an institution is in a state of transition and that the range of relatives described by older people will disappear ... People typically experience diminution in the strength of their 'own' family (i.e., of origin) ties through the lifespan. But for each cohort it is the same ... In part, the conviction that it is otherwise is a product of nostalgia and childhood ignorance ... Children acquire an idealised image of the family through idyllic childhood visits in which the visiting child is protected from adult gossip and tensions between the different units.[19]

Here Jerrome offers an intriguing interpretation, developed out of 'everyday theorising', for a central myth of modernisation. It is testimony perhaps to a conviction that popular culture creates its own historical sociology of ageing.

### Fragments of selfhood

If, as Williams's research indicates, the continuing commitment of today's elders to the work ethic is a legacy of their lifelong beliefs, market researchers have a strong hunch that future generations such as the babyboomers likewise may carry their values with them into retirement.[20] Their lifestyles, radicalism, and reflexivity will doubtless conflict with the generational preferences of those before them.[21] This will not necessarily entail a less materialist ethos; rather, 'if there is a change, it may be less a move away from activity and achievement as basic cultural codes than a transition from values and duty to self-actualisation and growth'.[22] Either way, retirement entails a principle of deferred

---

[17] Steedman, *Landscape for a Good Woman*, p. 144.
[18] Ibid., p. 142, quoting J. Berger, *About Looking* (London: Writers and Readers, 1980), p. 94
[19] Jerrome, 'Time, change and continuity', 12–14.
[20] Rory Williams, *A Protestant Legacy*; Ostroff, *Successful Marketing*.
[21] The difference between 1970s feminists and their predecessors is a case in point. See B. Caine, 'Generational conflict and the question of ageing in nineteenth- and twentieth-century feminism', *Australian Cultural History* 14 (1995), 92–108.
[22] Kohli, 'Ageing as a challenge', 384.

gratification, be this as legitimate leisure earned through a lifetime of effort or as personal expansion gained by 'wisdom'. As we have seen, the latter, speculative model has been extended from personal fulfilment to social service by those who favour the Third Age as a cultural vanguard: 'Old age would become the field of symbolically enacting the social values and concepts; as in traditional societies, the elderly would again appear as the symbolic leaders or at least the symbolic conscience of society. Moreover, such a synthesis would allow for a solution of the cultural contradiction between achievement and leisure, by offering a convincing sequential model.'[23] It would also involve the assumption of the responsibilities as well as the rights of citizenship, hence a reincorporation of 'values of duty'.

Both theories, indeed any conceptualisation of the contingencies of the life course, highlight the point that cultural shifts will be understood properly only by reference to biographical perspectives. Chapter 8 has indicated that surviving retirement requires not just the internalisation of cultural norms but also an ability to respond to the structural requirements of later life. As Kohli elaborates, understanding such accommodation may be aided by regarding reminiscence as a socialisation process of validating past experiences. And, he adds, 'biographical socialisation is a function not only of individual but also of collective memory (and of the ways by which it is institutionalised)'.[24] Such reasoning helps to explain the existential importance of artefacts such as photographs. The 'material culture' of life – house, furniture, heirlooms, photographs – constitutes a set of objects which become symbols of one's past. Inasmuch as these are culturally generalised, they are localised parts of a universal, intersubjectively acknowledged 'heritage'; that is, some memories evoke shared symbols with an attendant vocabulary of meanings. Nevertheless, we have also recognised the importance of diversity in imaging both ageing and the past. It is at this juncture that negotiated definitions (or redefinitions) of culture become most apparent. Again, Kohli cites cases that find resonance in our earlier discussions:

In a study of women moving to old-age facilities, Redfoot has found that middle-class women, having established strong attachments to place, often cope with relocation by making their new rooms into museums of their lives, while the lower-class women, who were likely to have moved many times in their lives and were unlikely to have owned their houses, often experienced relocation as simply one more in a long succession of moves. Thus, the middle-class women remained committed to their former life by conserving its material culture,

---

[23] Ibid.      [24] Ibid., 387.

while for the lower-class women, it was the life-long experience of change (and not being in control) itself that was re-enacted and represented by relocation.[25]

Here we see strategies for dealing with late life passage (cf. McIsaac), some of which draw upon life course experiences (cf. di Gregorio) and utilise domestic objects as symbolic resources (cf. Csikszentmihalyi and Rochberg-Halton) but which differ according to class (cf. Thompson *et al.*). The model might equally apply to our analysis of the role of the seaside in explaining the migration decisions of retirees, although clearly the relevance of such anchorage is diminished in the case of those who relocate to destinations far removed from the memories of their earlier years, the Northern Europeans shifting to the Mediterranean sunbelt, or, indeed North America's nomadic RVers. Their identities have to be constructed from other sources, although their motivations and aspirations are perhaps similar. For those whose lives are restricted within the walls of an institution, location is firmly fixed, but – for some, at least – remembrance of things past provides sustenance.[26]

This acknowledgement of pluralism is very much in line with the postmodern assault on the authority of a monolithic societal metanarrative. Unfortunately, however, in overthrowing established authority we are in danger of devaluing the authenticity and weight of experience that formerly constituted the wisdom of old age. Foucault, Elias, and Weber, to name but three major social theorists, agree that the concept of the individual emerges and is transformed through modernisation.[27] Thereafter, Ulrich Beck argues, the attenuated development of industrial society has led to 'reflexive modernisation', whereby individuals become increasingly detached from ties of family, class, and locality.[28] As a consequence, we fashion our own choices, identities, and biographies and are related to others only through the market, or, as Bellah *et al.* would have it, via lifestyle enclaves.

The self of the Victorian era was one who struggled to improve him- or herself through acquiring culture, becoming part of the civilising process. The aristocracy wrote the script, and gave us a notion of elite culture that could only be painstakingly learned through education in the classics, literature, music, and the arts. Manners had to be acquired and an authentic integrity of character developed. But as we move into

---

[25] Ibid., citing D. Redfoot, 'On the separatin' place: social class and relocation among older women', *Social Forces* 66 (1987), 486–500.

[26] Within total institutions, all types of inmates are forced to depend on inner resources. As the incarcerated Hannibal Lecter put it in the film *The Silence of the Lambs*, 'memory . . . is what I have instead of a view'.

[27] Kohli, 'The world we forgot', p. 283.

[28] U. Beck, *Risk Society: Towards a New Modernity* (London: Sage, 1992).

the twentieth century, we see the rise of the performing self.[29] Whereas before the integrity of character within was all-important morally, now the inner self gives way to the outwards and visible display of personality, of self-conscious, narcissistic selves. Undoubtedly, the rise of visual culture, and particularly Hollywood, helped to emphasise outward appearance, looks, bodyshape, and body language. The morality shifted away from one determined by dominant elite culture to the popular culture of the cinema and department store to one stressing the maintenance of the body beautiful. As chapter 4 has indicated, if your body was not in shape, then you were to blame for being a slob and not keeping up that exercise routine, and it showed. We are all performers, but in postmodern consumer culture we have also to be negotiating selves; that is, actors capable of knowing what to select from the multiplicity of choices available to us. If the old hierarchies have collapsed, we need to be wary of competing interests in the marketplace and to become increasingly refined consumers. In this sense citizenship is guaranteed only by the possession of capital – financial, corporeal, and cultural.

This growing individualisation is particularly stressed by Lasch, who considers both the medical emphasis on prolongevity and the humanistic attempt to combat ageism as indicative of a decadent 'culture of narcissism', the societally endorsed obsession with self characteristic of Western individualism. He argues that the prospect of bodily decay has become repugnant, while fear of death has increased in intensity as religion and an interest in posterity have declined. Given the instrumental view of knowledge whereby rapid technological change renders previously accumulated experience obsolete, it is realistic to feel apprehensive about later life. However, in the 'premature' fears of growing old exemplified by the mid-life crisis, Lasch sees irrational panic. This, he argues, reflects

the emergence of the narcissistic personality as the dominant type of personality structure in contemporary society. Because the narcissist has so few inner resources, he looks to others to validate his sense of self. He needs to be admired for his beauty, charm, celebrity, or power – attributes that usually fade with time. Unable to achieve satisfying sublimations in the form of love and work, he finds that he has little to sustain him when youth passes him by. He takes no interest in the future and does nothing to provide himself with the traditional consolations of old age, the most important of which is the belief that future generations will in some sense carry on his life's work ... When men find themselves incapable of taking an interest in earthly life after their own death,

---

[29] Featherstone, 'The body', pp. 187–93.

they wish for eternal youth, for the same reason they no longer care to reproduce themselves.[30]

The logic here carries echoes of the British population panic of the 1930s when the 'acquisitive society' was blamed for the desire of couples to postpone or reject parenthood (see chapter 2). But what is more recent is that the dilemma is being defused through an increasingly hegemonic therapeutic sensibility (including reminiscence and photo therapy). In the works of such popular gurus as Alex Comfort and Gail Sheehy, Lasch whiffs a conformist capitulation where 'wisdom' is encouraged as a consolation for those in mid- and later life who have become superfluous. Not only this, but as Bellah *et al.* elaborate:

If it is to provide any richness of meaning, the idea of a life course must be set in a larger generational, historical, and, probably, religious context. Yet much popular writing about the life course (Gail Sheehy's *Passages*, for example), as well as much of the thinking of ordinary Americans, considers the life course without reference to any social or historical context, as something that occurs to isolated individuals. In this situation, every life crisis, not just that of adolescence, is a crisis of separation and individuation, but what the ever freer and more autonomous self is free *for* only grows more obscure. Thinking about the life course in this way may exacerbate rather than resolve the problem of the meaning of the individual life.[31]

As Lasch concurs, this is because the historical continuity between generations, implicit in the value placed on accumulated wisdom, has been severed. Moreover, 'the growth experts compound the problem by urging people past forty to cut their ties to the past, embark on new careers and marriages ("creative divorce"), take up new hobbies, travel light, and keep moving. This is a recipe not for growth but for planned obsolescence.' Humanistic psychology – the entire lifespan developmental perspective after Jung – thus provides the means by which 'people can prematurely phase themselves out of active life, painlessly and without "panic"'.[32] While Bellah *et al.* acknowledge a degree of redemption through structured sociability – 'There are truths we do not see when we adopt the language of radical individualism. We find ourselves not independently of other people and institutions but through them' – Lasch would castigate all 'escape attempts' in mid-life and after – 'doing a Gauguin' by starting a new life, taking the RV road, cyberbodies, or just makeovers and masks aimed at prolonging 'youth'

[30] Lasch, *Culture of Narcissism*, pp. 210–11.
[31] Bellah, Madsen, Sullivan, Swidler, and Tipton, *Habits*, p. 82.
[32] Lasch, *Culture of Narcissism*, pp. 207–14; A. Comfort, *A Good Age* (London: Mitchell Beazley, 1977); G. Sheehy, *Passages: Predictable Crises of Adult Life* (New York: Dutton, 1976).

– as ultimately futile.[33] Decline can be held at bay, but the inevitability of death makes it unavoidable. And in a secular epoch that realisation is not cushioned so effectively by mass belief in the afterlife or by a sense of 'living on' through our children. Since, 'the tendency to forget what we have received from our parents seems, moreover, to generalise to a forgetting of what we have received from the past altogether', life becomes a constant present.[34]

At this juncture, it is appropriate to invoke Bauman's distinction between pilgrims and nomads. In the past, he argues, identity was built up, layer on layer, from experience, so that modernists were 'pilgrims through life', guided by a 'life project' and belief in progress. But postmodern identity-seekers are simply nomads who 'hardly ever reach in their imagination beyond the next caravan-site'.[35] Destiny has been supplanted by uncertainty. For Lasch 'reality is experienced as an unstable environment of flickering images'.[36]

### Postcards from the edge

Of course, to the on-the-road RVers, on their way to that next caravan site, the whole point is to keep moving through the landscape of evanescence. Uncertainty provides the constant spur to fend off the dullness and despair that resting might engender. Our analysis suggests that this is not simply a facet of some modern malaise: these images and lifestyles, like maps or identity cards, embellish our identities and the ways in which we see the world. Rather than being temporary straws at which we might clutch, remembered experiences old and new, some from deep in our consciousness, some recollected in more tranquillity than others, help to frame coherent narratives, the myths we live by. Though biography re-enacts sequences, memory is closer to montage. In picturing the simultaneous coexistence of images from different times and places it facilitates reorientation to suit the context of the moment. Without it, like the dementia sufferer, we cannot see the whole picture. Authorship – both owning and articulating one's self-conscious thoughts – is of the essence. For the narrator this can force an existential conclusion, a moment of aloneness where, regardless of institutional and societal constraints, fear of self-disintegration may lead to resignation. Thus, near the end of his life Jean-Paul Sartre asked

[33] Bellah, Madsen, Sullivan, Swidler, and Tipton, *Habits*, p. 84; Hepworth and Feather-stone, *Surviving Middle Age*; S. Cohen and Taylor, *Escape Attempts*.
[34] Bellah, Madsen, Sullivan, Swidler, and Tipton, *Habits*, p. 82.
[35] Z. Bauman, *Mortality, Immortality and Other Life Strategies* (Cambridge: Polity, 1992), p. 167.
[36] Lasch, *Culture of Narcissism*, p. 249.

his consultant: 'How will it all end? What is going to happen to me?' But, says his partner, Simone de Beauvoir, 'it was not death that made him uneasy; it was his brain ... In two years at the outside the brain would have been affected and Sartre would no longer have been Sartre.'[37]

Yet, like Berger and Mohr's 150 photos which attempt to mimic flashes in the mind of an old French woman considering her life, images are not just documents from an inner life. They often include scenes never directly witnessed by the participants, yet critical in explaining the generality of their experience. Berger and Mohr note that 'in the long sequence concerning the impact of the metropolis on an emigrant born in a village, we have used not only images of Paris but also images of Istanbul'.[38] In the same way, 'heritage' constructs simulacra, imagined communities we could never have inhabited because their referents come from a period predating our birth, into which we willingly and imaginatively insert ourselves. More crucially, there is no shortage of images of old age on which the non-aged draw. A more sympathetic set of representations of the present may endear us more to the notion of our future selves, whilst a less soft-focused rendition of the past might restrain the impulse to nostalgia. Yet neither would succeed in supplanting fantasy with an incontestable reality, for if history, ageing, and popular culture tell us anything it is that all three, like the images they retail, are socially constructed. We are born, we live, we die; biology is destiny. But our understanding of what happens along the way depends less on who tells the story or the way it is told than how we choose to read it.

## The end of old age?

The implications of such a biographically informed view for the future sociology of ageing are several. In the last quarter of the twentieth century we have witnessed a shift towards an increasingly individualised, consumer-driven culture in which the evasion of old age can apparently be accomplished through a range of youth-preserving techniques and lifestyles. Although this strategy has origins in the Victorian desire to 'repress all but the most sentimentally optimistic images of later life', such as the benign granny figure, today's moralistic pressures to 'age well' have promoted clear distinctions between the 'heroes of ageing', who paradoxically appear not to have aged, and the villainous

---

[37] S. de Beauvoir, *Adieux: A Farewell to Sartre* (London: André Deutsch and Weidenfeld and Nicolson, 1984), p. 124.
[38] J. Berger and Mohr, 'If each time ...', p. 134.

persistence of decline.[39] Cole notes that, 'during the 1970s, an emerging consensus among health professionals, social workers, and researchers insisted on a view that was the mirror opposite of ageism: old people are (or should be) healthy, sexually active, engaged, productive, and self-reliant'.[40] Ironically, positive ageing has produced its own tyrannical imperative: unless you work at being 'liberated' from chronological destiny, you are less than normal.

Much that I have written suggests that the Third Age, at least, depends on denial. However, it may equally plausibly be argued that enhancing one's bodily appearance, social acceptability, or personal esteem through cosmetic or therapeutic interventions is simply availing oneself of contemporary resources, and that the real denial is by those who resist such accoutrements in the name of 'purity' and 'natural ageing'. Even so, these practices of positive ageing effectively transform physical and mental problems associated with biological ageing into social deviance, which, in turn, becomes evidence of clinical pathology. In this way, reasons Hepworth, 'If the ills of ageing can be attributed to physical pathology (biological deviation) then ageing itself is positively normal.'[41] By extension, to age 'successfully' is to fail deliberately to accommodate death and dying as anything other than sudden and painless; hence Cole's stress on the requirement to jettison such a bankrupt ideal in favour of a transcendent spirituality which, like religion, will allow us to find 'renewed sources of social and cosmic connection'.[42]

Unsurprisingly, given the emphasis on appearance, superficial self-presentation has become ever more prominent, while concern for the fate of the soul within has receded in the popular imagination. This transformation has not simply been a consequence of consumerism and its associated imagery. Rather, it reflects a complex field of interaction between the individual and the political economy of Western civilisation in which the mobilisation of a particular concept of the life course has been crucial.

Kohli contends that modern bureaucracies have created a number of structural problems to which the institutionalisation of a 'moral economy of the life course' has been a solution: 'Chronological age is apparently a very good criterion for the rational organisation of public services and transfers. It renders the life course – and by that, the

---

[39] Hepworth, 'Where do grannies come from?', 3.
[40] Cole, *Journey of Life*, p. 229.
[41] Hepworth, 'Positive ageing: what is the message?', p. 187.
[42] Cole, *Journey of Life*, p. 239.

passage of individuals through social systems – orderly and calculable.'[43] As children, we are educated in schools; as adults we pursue careers through successive hierarchical steps within the labour market, where vacancies occur as we retire to receive pensions. This sequencing is a mechanism for social control, whereby retirement is legitimised as deferred gratification. As well as performing a macro-structural function, the life course perspective has powerfully influenced everyday life. Rather than individual life patterns being ascribed according to our positions in family and community (as in pre-industrial times), status and identity are achieved by successfully negotiating the expectations of each life stage. The pre-modern 'annalistic' mentality, where external seasonal rhythms and rituals determined life, has been supplanted by a logic of self-development, focused on the 'life plan' as the basic organising principle. It is the narrative yardstick by which we account for our actions and project our futures, and against which we measure our progress relative to others; hence the diary, the curriculum vitae, biography, obituary, and the novel.[44]

I have already discussed the existential price of such a shift in terms of the disaffection of the individual. Even before Freud, the psychological traumas of competitive individualism had been recognised, as the religious vision of life as a spiritual journey declined and the crises of life instead became problems for expert therapeutic intervention.[45] On the basis of such a secular and personalised project, old age has been redefined as a scientific problem. Thus, while both medical and economic conditions have improved the objective quality of later life very markedly, the penalty has been cultural disenfranchisement – 'a loss of meaning and its vital social roles'.[46]

To talk of the 'end of old age' is perhaps to overstate the issue, yet we do appear to have arrived at a postmodern impasse where neither lifelong socialisation to a series of socially approved goals, nor individualised departures from the script offer coherent guidelines for how we might collectively confront life-ending. If the appropriate metaphor is no longer one of life as a clearly defined journey but of a bewildering

[43] Kohli, 'The world we forgot', pp. 286–7; see also M. Minkler and T. R. Cole, 'Political economy and moral economy: not such strange bedfellows', in Minkler and Estes, *Critical Perspectives on Aging*, pp. 37–49.

[44] P. L. Berger, B. Berger, and H. Kellner, *The Homeless Mind: Modernization and Consciousness* (New York: Random House, 1973), pp. 73–5; S. Cohen and Taylor, *Escape Attempts*, pp. 46–65; Kohli, 'The world we forgot', p. 288.

[45] T. R. Cole, *Journey of Life*, p. 220. L. Sugarman reviews the panoply of ideas since in her tellingly titled *Life-Span Development: Concepts, Theories and Interventions*.

[46] Cole, *Journey of Life*, pp. xix, 220; Kohli, 'The world we forgot', p. 287, phrases this in Weberian terms as presenting 'an uneasy tension between the formal rationality of such procedures and the substantive rationality that they are supposed to provide'.

maze, then moving beyond this impasse will mean rejecting macro-level models, such as political economy, under which individuals are at best ciphers of structural forces, and Parsonian or Foucauldian theories where agents simply internalise or refract age-norms. In what ways can the tension between the ageing individual and the social structure be resolved? And, other than through born-again religion, how might meaning be reintroduced? The search for a humanistic alternative has led to fiction and art.

The heroine in Alison Lurie's novel *Foreign Affairs* remarks that, in classic fiction, almost the entire population is below fifty.[47] However, since the publication in 1975 of Saul Bellow's *Humboldt's Gift* and Margaret Drabble's *The Realms of Gold*, a genre of progress novels has emerged in which 'life-affirming plots and thoughts can be given to mid-life characters'.[48] Such meliorism brushes against the grain of Western literature, which has long associated mid-life with the disillusion of lost innocence and wisdom with pessimism. Whereas decline with age had become an essentialist belief, Gullette argues that, in the spirit of the *Bildungsroman*, where early life is charted as a progressive learning process, mid-life development novels now suggest possibilities for active review and reconstruction. Mid-life novels are replete with possibilities for sexual reawakening, constructive retirement, and satisfying relationships, and, unlike decline fiction, they do not evade living through and confronting major challenges like bereavement. We are shown how, with resilience and imagination, we might absorb suffering, move on, and plot survival. Nevertheless, such thinking colludes with the therapeutic consensus that development is a lifelong process in which taking responsibility for one's story involves becoming protagonist rather than victim. And as the basis for a cultural programme, it has similar flaws. These novels may provide sociological illumination, but unlike earlier didactic models such as *Pilgrim's Progress*, 'they fail precisely for us now as developmental guides, if only because the old ideal of a single, spiritual goal for all has started to wither in the expansion of our own modern, secular idea of adult goals as necessarily individualistic . . . and, most of all, progressive, multiple, and shifting'.[49]

There is some evidence of ongoing life review being extended into late life – for example in Thea Astley's *Coda* – and a genre based on

---

[47] A. Lurie, *Foreign Affairs* (London: Abacus, 1986); J. Newman, 'Fifty something' (review of Gullette, *Safe at Last* (see n. 48)), *Times Higher Educational Supplement*, 14 April 1989, 14.

[48] M. M. Gullette, *Safe at Last in the Middle Years* (Berkeley and Los Angeles: University of California Press, 1988), p. xiii; Anita Brookner and Anne Tyler are perhaps the best-known current exemplars.

[49] Ibid., p. 170.

completion of life, the *Vollendungsroman*, has been mooted.[50] However, it is notable that a central figure such as Grandma in Margaret Forster's *Have The Men Had Enough?* is objectified by dint of her condition (dementia). Unlike the younger family members, she does not reflect; she presents no internal dialogue with which to voice her thoughts. All we know of her comes from what she says aloud. Her sporadic reminiscences suggest the significance of past experiences but the reader remains puzzled as to how, if at all, she connects these to the present. Grandma as narrator of her own life is absent.[51]

Here, in the assertion that the individual with dementia and the self that is accounted for are different, lies a crucial distinction. In so far as postmodernity asserts the decentring of the self and its replacement by multiple selves, society may be said to be in a state of cultural dementia. However, at another level, each of our personal narratives suggests that we are purposeful, comprehending agents capable of actively managing our own identities – unless, that is, we are diagnosed as mentally ill. My discussion of postmodern photography considered the reappropriation of images to overturn stereotypes and construct fresh messages. Similarly, Cole discusses the 'resymbolization of the ages and journey of life' in the paintings of Jasper Johns.[52] In either case we make sense of what we see because we read into the image a deliberate artifice on the part of its creator: somebody is trying to make a point. Transposing ideas from art to life, theorists of the postmodern suggest that a workable model of society consists of 'taking valuable bits and pieces of our cultural inheritance and arranging them in new ways to meet current needs, circumstances, and particular communities'.[53] Selves are also constructed through a process of 'bricolage', 'in which agency is produced from what is enduringly available'. The resources used will vary depending on the setting, and clearly those of the private household will differ from those of the residential home, or the street. 'Local culture', claims Gubrium, 'is not so much a fixed repository of shared meaning as it is a dynamic, partially predefined assemblage of interpretative possibilities.'[54]

Nevertheless, Gubrium also acknowledges that without roots 'a clear sense of self appears to be problematic'. I would further aver that personal narratives will be meaningless unless they are validated by their listeners.[55] Where members of one generation attempt to explain

---

[50] Cole, *Journey of Life*, p. 242.
[51] M. Forster, *Have the Men Had Enough?* (London: Chatto and Windus, 1989).
[52] Cole, *Journey of Life*, pp. 244–51 (p. 244).
[53] Ibid., p. 243, cited in Hepworth, 'Consumer culture', 27.
[54] Gubrium, *Individual Agency*, p. 9.    [55] Ibid., p. 12.

themselves to members of another, younger generation, interpretation is made difficult by the fact that their accounts are by definition 'anachronistic' since they derive from what has been learned through past experience. Dowd argues that, because to younger generations old people have strange bodies and often appear old-fashioned in their values, clothing styles, or entertainment preferences, they become 'strangers in their own land', their identity being regarded as 'past-situated'.[56] And, as we have seen, historians of the Industrial Revolution have noted how rapid technological change rendered the skills of older workers obsolete. Given the pace of technological change in the 'information revolution', what our elders tell us about their experience is likely to be dismissed as idiosyncratic reflection rather than received as wisdom. Where knowledge is power, old knowledge becomes redundant. The requirement for the knowledge of expert others – financial advisers, doctors, social service providers – generally increases as the stock of 'useful knowledge' declines.

Yet this recurrent devaluing of status under conditions of high modernity does not necessarily imply the same in a postmodern consumer environment, where production is less significant than lifestyles, social meanings become increasingly ambiguous and biographies appeal because in such rationalisations we might find 'models of people who knew what they were doing'.[57] Moreover, in recent decades society has switched definitively from being production-led to being consumer-determined. In 1991, Hobman remarked that: 'Within a decade, the politics of old age may well shift from the consequences of individual poverty to the impact of combined purchasing power.'[58] Nothing in the foregoing analysis would detract from his prediction.

From this perspective, it is not older people who think anachronistically, but the providers of goods and services. As the numbers of young people continue to decline we hear fears expressed that echo the 1930s population panic: 'Driving instructors may become an endangered species; and sport shoe manufacturers could find that the trainer race up to now has been like a stroll in the park.'[59] But in the consumer culture of the 1990s the potentially lucrative grey market demands a constructive response to the flip-side of this demographic coin – the growth in older consumers. For the first time ever, older people en masse are in a

---

[56] J. Dowd, 'The old person as stranger', in Marshall, *Later Life*, p. 184.
[57] M. Evans, 'Reading lives', 12.
[58] D. Hobman, *The Political Challenge of an Ageing Society*, Age Concern Coming of Age Campaign Rights and Choices Resource Paper RC9 (Mitcham: Age Concern, 1991), p. 10.
[59] Gwyther, 'Britain bracing for the age bomb', 17.

buyer's market. Advertising agencies have latterly woken up to the fact that their model of family life is twenty years behind the times and, for instance, begun to feature grandparents and grandchildren together in commercials for breakfast cereals, washing-up liquid, and underwear. While designers have acknowledged such everyday constraints as worsening eyesight and arthritic joints and have begun to create imaginative solutions (adaptable, but uni-age spectacles, spoons, furniture, bathrooms), planners need to consider our civic landscape: it is important to be both energy- and comfort-conscious with in-car design and home heating, but entire transport systems and integrated living environments for whole communities require blueprints.[60] Later life has to be incorporated in the same way that design now 'naturally' embraces the needs of previously excluded categories such as women and children. It means both recognising the special disabilities that might come with age and minimising the impact of these impairments on daily living.

## The Dorian Gray complex

The director of business development at McVitie, part of United Biscuits ... notes with relief that as consumers cross the generation zones, they are taking expensively promoted brands, such as her Hob Nobs, with them. 'As people move through the age brackets, they keep values which are youth-oriented', she says.[61]

Mme Calment had her cigarettes, the good folks of Gorleston their tea, and us mid-lifers our biscuits, small objects of oral desire that tell us more than may be immediately apparent about our place in history.

Cohorts tend to retain values of their youth throughout life, and it just so happens that the purportedly self-centred Me Generation – the one that 'shopped itself into social history' – possesses all the requisite qualities of competitive individualism.[62] The extent to which this generation as it ages manages to shift the balance of power in society – and, by extension, its age consciousness – will be critical. They, after all, were the teenagers 'discovered' in the 1950s and assiduously cultivated as 'trendsetters' in the 1960s. But, if we wish to abandon ageism, then we have to start by providing an underlying equality of opportunity for all. We need to be careful not just to plan for the fortunate few or, indeed, for the unfortunate minority at death's door. Most older people stand to be neither particularly affluent, nor desperately infirm: they are

[60] See R. Coleman (ed.), *Working Together: A New Approach to Design* (London: Royal College of Art, 1997).
[61] Ibid., p. 17.    [62] White, 'The new age no age woman', 7.

relatively poor but also fit and active, with partial, remediable disabilities and dependencies as they grow older.[63]

Political economists have emphasised constraints, whilst cultural theorists celebrate diversity, and by extension choice. Indeed, 'reflexive gerontologists' regard contemporary consumer culture as a landscape providing opportunities for personal development. As Hepworth remarks, 'it is precisely because the old rules no longer apply that we are now free to explore the sheer diversity of cultural resources in order to create life-enhancing images of later life'. Older people might thus be enabled to construct 'a plurality of responses' to the traditional constraints of ageism.[64] The present may be welcomed as deliverance from the toil of work and childrearing, but the future holds fears, either of decline and decrement, or simply of interminable boredom. In place of fear we must put not just security in old age, but also excitement, challenge, and opportunity. This may, of course, mean trading the benefits of welfare for the added risks of self-determination.

The culture of ageing, then, is beset by a series of tensions: between memory and forgetting, looking backwards and looking forwards, continuity and fragmentation, security and risk. Paradoxically, these emergent contradictions make more urgent the requirement to broach what Sartre called 'the necessity of our contingency', the fact that as individuals we each own a past, present, and future and that one set of experiences inevitably impacts upon the next.[65] Ironically, it appears that as we move to the future we have done much to accommodate the past within the present, personally, socially, and philosophically, but the spiritual connection to death and beyond has become ever more frayed. In Aldous Huxley's novel *After Many a Summer*, ageing Californian millionaire Jo Stoyte has everything money can buy, but is haunted by a morbid fear of death. To discover the secret of longevity, he hires the devious Dr Obispo, who, in a parody of Voronoff's monkey-gland experiments, recommends preparations including the intestinal flora of carp. Obsession leads Stoyte eventually to a labyrinthine dungeon where the Fifth Earl of Gonister and his housekeeper, aged over 200 and become 'foetal apes', are urinating on the floor, bellowing guttural growls, and screaming as they attack one another.[66] If the implications of tampering with our natural lifespan are so sinister, it remains the case that, in a secular society without collective visions of the afterlife, death

[63] Falkingham and Victor, *The Myth of the Woopie*.
[64] Hepworth, 'Consumer culture', 27. On 'reflexive consumption', see S. Lash and J. Urry, *Economies of Signs and Space* (London: Sage, 1994).
[65] S. de Beauvoir, *Old Age*, trans. P. O'Brian (Harmondsworth: Penguin, 1985), p. 599.
[66] A. Huxley, *After Many a Summer* (London: Chatto and Windus, 1939).

is unattractive and illness and lingering decline even less appealing. More and more people perceive deep old age as a twilight zone, uncoupled from both the land of the living and the domain of the departed. ThirdAgers desperately attempt to evade sliding into the Fourth Age, while our society ritualistically denies the problem by regarding health as 'a form of secular salvation'.[67] The only end we wish for is instantaneous and uncomplicated. Thus the images, lifestyles, discourses, and forms of interaction discussed in this book may be read as a qualification to Keynes's famous riposte that 'in the long run we are all dead'. What the popular culture of ageing appears to be saying today is: in the long run we're all just older, but with attention this can be delayed – and nothing motivates quite like enlightened self-interest. Until the last stage happens to us, if a confidence trick relying on the willing suspension of disbelief works, then why not? Cryogenics may freeze us, like insects in amber, but what we really want is immortality in life, to look into the mirror, and, like Dorian Gray in Oscar Wilde's parable, appear always young even while the images in our portraits decay.[68]

But, of course, there is a sting in the tail. As Zeilig comments, 'the basic problem with using *The Picture of Dorian Gray* to explicate notions around eternal youth is that youth is used in the novel primarily as a symbol of superficiality and decadence'.[69] When agelessness becomes the elixir, the meaning of life evaporates.

[67] Cole, *Journey of Life*, p. 239.
[68] O. Wilde, *The Picture of Dorian Gray* (Oxford University Press, 1974; orig. London: Lippincott's Monthly Magazine, 1890).
[69] H. Zeilig, 'The uses of literature in the study of older people', in Jamieson, Harper, and Victor, *Critical Approaches*, pp. 39–48 (p. 45). See also R. Kastenbaum, *Dorian, Graying: Is Youth the Only Thing Worth Having?* (Amityville, NY: Baywood Press, 1995).

# Postscript – 2158

In the *fin de siècle* 1990s, as a century before, a millennial decadence prevailed. The new cabaret was a virtual world on the Internet, touted as 'a magical realm like Oz, where age simultaneously does and does not exist'.[1] Until then, identities and self-esteem in later life had always been sustained through a sense of place, tradition, and biographical continuity. But given 'the liberatory potential of the new technology to alter the bodily infrastructure of human beings', older people began to escape the restrictive conceptual dualisms of mind and body.[2] Meanwhile, obsessed with bodily reinvention, plastic surgery, and the rest, Californians (where else but Hollywood?) claimed that 'within the next thirty years the fear that we may not be able to distinguish real humans from replicants will no longer be just science fiction'.[3]

Holidays in space were a gleam in the eye of astronaut Buzz Aldrin, who, in a television commercial for Equitable Life, enjoined us to invest wisely now to ensure a post-global leisured retirement: 'Thirty years ago I went to the moon; thirty years from now you could go too.' For all the speculation, a blend of nostalgia and a certain patriotic pride remained strong. The year had opened on a commemorative note with John Glenn, the first American to orbit the earth, '[striking] a blow for the elderly everywhere ... with the news that he is to return to space in October aged seventy-seven':

The Ohio senator, whose freckled, crew-cut good looks and ice-cool demeanour enamoured him to Americans thirty-six years ago when he orbited the earth three times in Friendship Seven, is to fly again to allow detailed experiments on the ageing process.

Mr Glenn's first flight came when the US was seen to be trailing the Soviet Union in a space race conducted at the height of the Cold War. It was a

---

[1] D. Glanz, 'Seniors and cyberspace: some critical reflections on computers and older persons', *Education and Ageing* 12 (1997), 69–81 (69). See Third Age Web Site (1997), http://www.thirdage.com, and Third Age Media Web Site (1997), http://www.thirdagemedia.com. Sun Cities now advertise on the Internet.

[2] Featherstone, 'Virtual reality, cyberspace and the ageing body', pp. 280–1.

[3] Deitch, *Post Human*, p. 17.

rejuvenating moment for America, making him, in the words yesterday of Dan Goldin, Nasa's administrator, 'one of the great heroes of the twentieth century'. The new flight meant Glenn would be 'America's first hero of the twenty-first century' ... His decision to risk his life again in the interests of science showed the senator undeniably had 'the right stuff'.[4]

This all appears rather quaint now. The year is 2158 AD, 'and Lou and Emerald Schwarz [are] whispering on the balcony of Lou's family apartment on the 76th floor of Building 257 in Alden Village, a New York housing development'.[5] Lou is 112, Em just 93. Behind the screen-door Gramps, 172, is becoming a problem. They are both still working hard, but 'the whole thing practically is taxed away for defence and old age pensions'. The anti-ageing wonder drug has ensured that nobody need die. Consequently, population centres have become clogged: New York has engulfed New Jersey and Delaware, Chicago stretches through Iowa. Em surveys her prospects, looking out over 'a thousand asphalt-paved, skyscraper-walled courtyards: "Lou, hon, I'm not calling you a failure. The Lord knows you're not. You just haven't a chance to be anything or have anything because Gramps and the rest of his generation won't leave and let somebody else take over."'

'Sometimes I get so mad, I feel like just up and diluting his anti-gerasone,' said Em.

'That'd be against Nature, Em,' said Lou.

Em sighs: 'Sometimes I wish they'd left a couple of diseases kicking around.'[6]

---

[4] N. Timmins, 'John Glenn: "heroic" senator redefines space age', *Financial Times*, 17 January 1998, 2.

[5] K. Vonnegut, 'Tomorrow and tomorrow and tomorrow', in T. Boardman (ed.), *Connoisseur's Science Fiction* (Harmondsworth: Penguin, 1964), pp. 64–6, reprinted in Carver and Liddiard, *An Ageing Population*, pp. 47–9 (p. 47).

[6] Ibid., pp. 47–9. See J. Swift, *Gulliver's Travels* (Oxford: Blackwell, 1941; orig. published 1726), in which the Struldbruggs are endowed with immortality but confound Gulliver's expectations of happiness since, rather than possessing perpetual youth, they are condemned to suffer the ills and deformities of extreme old age in abundance. Not least among these is the loss of memory.

# Bibliography

*3D* documentary/magazine programme, ITV, 1 May 1997.

Abercrombie, N., Hill, S. and Turner, B. S., *The Penguin Dictionary of Sociology*, 3rd edn, Harmondsworth: Penguin, 1994.

Aberdeen annual 50+ Lifestyle Festival flyer (1997).

Abrams, M., *The Teenage Consumer*, London: Routledge and Kegan Paul, 1959.

  *Beyond Three Score and Ten: A First Report on a Survey of the Elderly*, Mitcham: Age Concern, 1978.

  'Changes in the life-styles of the elderly, 1959–1982', in United Kingdom, Central Statistical Office, *Social Trends No. 14*, London: HMSO, 1984, pp. 11–16.

Abrams, P., *Historical Sociology*, Shepton Mallet: Open Books, 1982.

Achenbaum, W. A., 'The obsolescence of old age in America, 1865–1914', *Journal of Social History* 8 (1974), 48–62.

  *Old Age in the New Land: The American Experience Since 1790*, Baltimore and London: Johns Hopkins University Press, 1978.

  'One United States approach to gerontological theory building', *Ageing and Society* 9 (1989), 179–88.

  'Images of old age in America, 1790 to the present: after a second look', paper prepared for working conference on Images of Aging, Luxembourg, June 1991.

  'Images of old age in America, 1790–1970: a vision and a re-vision', in Featherstone and Wernick, *Images of Aging*, pp. 19–28.

  'Critical gerontology', in Jamieson, Harper, and Victor, *Critical Approaches*, pp. 16–26.

Achenbaum, W. A. and Kusnerz, P. A., *Images of Old Age in America: 1790 to the Present*, Ann Arbor, MI: Institute of Gerontology, 1978.

Achenbaum, W. A. and Stearns, P., 'Old age and modernization', *Gerontologist* 18 (1978), 307–12.

Adelman, M. (ed.), *Long Time Passing: Lives of Older Lesbians*, Boston, MA: Alyson Publications, 1986.

'After 108 years, three days still make all the difference', *Herald*, 22 August 1997, 2.

Age Exchange, *Lifetimes: A Handbook of Memories and Ideas for Use with Age Exchange Reminiscence Pictures*, London: Age Exchange, 1987.

Agee, J. and Evans, W., *Let Us Now Praise Famous Men*, Boston, MA: Houghton Mifflin, 1939; reprinted 1980.

Alison, W. P., *Observations on the Management of the Poor in Scotland*, Edinburgh: Blackwood, 1840.

Altmann, R., 'Incomes of the early retired', *Journal of Social Policy* 11 (1981), 355–64.

Amulree, (Lord), *Adding Life to Years*, London: Bannisdale Press, 1951.

Anderson, B., *Imagined Communities: Reflections on the Origin and Spread of Nationalism*, London: Verso, 1993.

Anderson, F., *Practical Management of the Elderly*, Oxford: Basil Blackwell, 1967.

Anderson, M., *Family Structure in Nineteenth-Century Lancashire*, Cambridge University Press, 1971.

   'The emergence of the modern life-cycle in Britain', *Social History* 10 (1985), 69–88.

Anderson, M. and Morse, D., 'The people', in Fraser, W. H. and Morris, R. J. (eds.), *People and Society in Scotland*, 3 vols., vol. II, *1830–1914*, Edinburgh: John Donald, 1990, pp. 8–45.

Andrews, M., *Lifetimes of Commitment: Ageing, Politics, Psychology*, Cambridge University Press, 1991.

Arber, S. and Ginn, J., *Gender and Later Life*, London: Sage, 1991.

   'The invisibility of age: gender and class in later life', *Sociological Review* 39 (1991), 260–91.

Ariès, P., *Centuries of Childhood*, Harmondsworth: Penguin, 1962.

   *Western Attitudes Toward Death: From the Middle Ages to the Present*, Baltimore: Johns Hopkins University Press, 1974.

   *The Hour of Our Death*, London: Penguin, 1983.

Arluke, A. and Levin, J., 'Another stereotype: old age as a second childhood', *Aging* (1984), 7–11.

Armstrong, D., *Political Anatomy of the Body: Medical Knowledge in Britain in the Twentieth Century*, Cambridge University Press, 1983.

Astley, T., *Coda*, London: Secker and Warburg, 1995.

Baltes, P. B. and Baltes, M. M., 'Psychological perspectives on successful aging: the model of selective optimisation with compensation', in Baltes, P. B. and Baltes, M. M. (eds.), *Successful Aging: Perspectives from the Behavioural Sciences*, New York: Cambridge University Press, 1990, pp. 1–34.

Barber, R., 'I love being Joan Collins', *Sunday Post Magazine*, 9 January 1994, 20–1.

Barthes, R., 'The world of wrestling', in Barthes, R., *Mythologies*, St Albans: Paladin, 1976, pp. 15–25.

   *Camera Lucida: Reflections on Photography*, London: Vintage, 1993.

Bauman, Z., *Thinking Sociologically*, Oxford: Basil Blackwell, 1990.

   *Mortality, Immortality and Other Life Strategies*, Cambridge: Polity, 1992.

Beauvoir, S. de, *A Very Easy Death*, Harmondsworth: Penguin, 1969.

   *Adieux: A Farewell to Sartre*, London: André Deutsch and Weidenfeld and Nicolson, 1984.

   *Old Age*, trans. P. O'Brian, Harmondsworth: Penguin, 1985.

Beck, M., 'The new middle age', *Newsweek*, 7 December 1992, 50–6.

Beck, U., *Risk Society: Towards a New Modernity*, London: Sage, 1992.

Becker, H. S., *Outsiders: Studies in the Sociology of Deviance*, New York: Free Press, 1966.

'Do photographs tell the truth?', in Becker, H. S., *Doing Things Together: Selected Papers*, Evanston, IL: Northwestern University Press, 1986, pp. 273–92.

Bellah, R., Madsen, R., Sullivan, W. M., Swidler, A. and Tipton, S. M., *Habits of the Heart: Middle America Observed*, London: Hutchinson Education, 1988.

Bellow, S., 'Deep readers of the world, beware!', *New York Times Book Review*, 15 February 1959, 1, 34.

Beloff, H., 'Family contradictions', in Gray, *The Parents*.

Bender, M. P., 'Bitter harvest: the implications of continuing war-related stress on reminiscence theory and practice', *Ageing and Society* 17, 3 (1997), 337–48.

Benjamin, M., 'Picturing the silences', *New Statesman and Society*, 25 June 1993, 32–3.

Benjamin, W., *Illuminations*, London: Fontana, 1973.

Bennett, A., 'The lady in the van', in Bennett, A., *Writing Home*, London: Faber and Faber, 1997, pp. 83–130.

Benson, A. J., *Prime Time: History of Middle Age in Twentieth-Century Britain*, Harlow: Longman, 1997.

Berger, J., *Ways of Seeing*, Harmondsworth: BBC/Penguin, 1972.

*About Looking*, London: Writers and Readers, 1980.

Berger, J. and Mohr, J., 'If each time . . .', in Berger, J. and Mohr, J., *Another Way of Telling*, London: Readers and Writers, 1982, pp. 131–275.

Berger, P. L., Berger, B. and Kellner, H., *The Homeless Mind: Modernization and Consciousness*, New York: Random House, 1973.

Berger, P. and Luckmann, T., *The Social Construction of Reality: A Treatise in the Sociology of Knowledge*, Harmondsworth: Penguin, 1991.

Berger, R., *Gay and Gray*, Urbana: University of Illinois Press, 1982.

Berman, L., *Beyond the Smile: The Therapeutic Use of the Photograph*, London: Routledge, 1993.

Bernard, B., *All Human Life: Great Photographs from the Hulton Deutsch Collection*, London: Barbican Art Gallery, 1994.

Bernard, M. and Meade, K., 'A Third Age lifestyle for older women?', in Bernard and Meade, *Women Come of Age*, pp. 146–66.

Bernard, M. and Meade, K. (eds.), *Women Come of Age*, London: Edward Arnold, 1993.

Bertaux, D. (ed.), *Biography and Society*, Beverly Hills: Sage, 1981.

Bertaux, D. and Thompson, P., *Between Generations: Family Models, Myths, and Memories*, Oxford University Press, 1993.

BEST Limited, *The Grey Market: A Golden Opportunity* (conference mailing, 1989).

Best, F., *Flexible Life Scheduling: Breaking the Education–Work–Retirement Lockstep*, New York: Praeger, 1980.

Betty, C., 'Language problems of older British migrants on the Costa del Sol', *Generations Review* 7, 2 (1997), 10–11.

Biggs, S., *Understanding Ageing: Images, Attitudes and Professional Practice*, Buckingham: Open University Press, 1993.

Biggs, S., Phillipson, C. and Kingston, P., *Elder Abuse in Perspective*, Buckingham: Open University Press, 1995.

Birren, J. E., 'My perspective on research on aging', in Bengtson, V. L. and Shaie, K. W. (eds.), *The Course of Later Life: Research and Reflections*, New York: Springer, 1989.

Birren, J. E. and Bengtson, V. L. (eds.), *Emergent Theories of Aging*, New York: Springer, 1988.

Blaikie, A., 'The emerging political power of the elderly in Britain, 1908–1948', *Ageing and Society* 10, 1 (1990), 17–39.

'Whither the Third Age?: implications for gerontology', *Generations Review* 2, 1 (1992), 2–4.

'Ageing and consumer culture: will we reap the whirlwind?', *Generations Review* 4 (1994), 5–7.

'Druggets and uglies, crotal and cailleachan: remembering the recent past', *Northern Scotland* 14 (1994), 135–45.

'Photographic images of age and generation', *Education and Ageing* 10, 1 (1995), 5–15.

Blaikie, A. and Hepworth, M., 'Representations of old age in painting and photography', in Jamieson, Harper, and Victor, *Critical Approaches*, pp. 102–17.

Blaikie, A. and Macnicol, J., 'Towards an anatomy of ageism: society, social policy and the elderly between the wars', in Phillipson, Bernard, and Strang, *Dependency and Interdependency in Old Age*, pp. 95–104.

'Ageing and social policy: a twentieth-century dilemma', in Warnes, A. M. (ed.), *Human Ageing and Later Life*, London: Edward Arnold, 1989, pp. 69–82.

Blakemore, K., 'Ageing and ethnicity', in J. Johnson and Slater, *Ageing and Later Life*, pp. 68–75.

Blakemore, K. and Boneham, M., *Age, Race and Ethnicity: A Comparative Approach*, Buckingham: Open University Press, 1994.

Blanchard, T., 'Not fade away', *Independent Magazine*, 19 October 1996, 30–3.

Blau, Z., *Old Age in a Changing Society*, New York: New Viewpoints, 1973.

Blumer, H., *Symbolic Interactionism: Perspective or Method*, Englewood Cliffs, NJ: Prentice Hall, 1969.

Blythe, R., *The View in Winter: Reflections on Old Age*, Harmondsworth: Penguin, 1979.

Bolton, R., 'In the American east: Richard Avedon Incorporated', in Bolton, R. (ed.), *The Contest of Meaning: Critical Histories of Photography*, London: MIT Press, 1992, pp. 261–82.

Bond, J., Briggs, R. and Coleman, P., 'The study of ageing', in Bond and Coleman, *Ageing in Society*, pp. 17–47.

Bond, J. and Coleman P. (eds.), *Ageing in Society: An Introduction to Social Gerontology*, London: Sage, 1990.

Bourdieu, P., *Distinction: A Social Critique of the Judgement of Taste*, London: Routledge and Kegan Paul, 1984.

Branson, N. and Heinemann, M., *Britain in the Nineteen Thirties*, London: Weidenfeld and Nicolson, 1971.

Brass, W., 'Is Britain facing the twilight of parenthood?', in Joshi, H. (ed.), *The Changing Population of Britain*, Oxford: Blackwell, 1989, pp. 12–26.

Bromley, D. B. (ed.), *Gerontology: Social and Behavioural Perspectives*, London: Croom Helm, 1984.

*The Broons annual*. London: D. C. Thomson & Co. Ltd, 1985.

Burgess, E. W. (ed.), *Aging in Western Societies*, University of Chicago Press, 1960.

Burn, G., 'Jagger pushing 50', *Observer Magazine*, 10 January 1993, 17–23.

Burrow, J., *The Ages of Man: A Study in Medieval Writing and Thought*, Oxford: Clarendon Press, 1986.

Bury, M. R., 'Social constructionism and the development of medical sociology', *Sociology of Health and Illness* 8, 2 (1986), 137–69.

Review of Katz, *Disciplining Old Age*, *Ageing and Society* 17 (1997), 353–5.

Bury, M. R. and Holme, A., *Life After Ninety*, London: Routledge, 1991.

Butler, R. 'The life-review: an interpretation of reminiscence in the aged', *Psychiatry* 26 (1963), 65–76.

*Why Survive?: Being Old in America*, New York: Harper and Row, 1975.

Bytheway, B., 'Ageing and biography: the letters of Bernard and Mary Berenson', *Sociology* 27, 1 (1993), 153–65.

*Ageism*, Buckingham: Open University Press, 1995.

'Progress report: the experience of later life', *Ageing and Society* 16 (1996), 613–24.

Bytheway, B., Keil, T., Allatt, P. and Bryman, A. (eds.), *Becoming and Being Old: Sociological Approaches to Later Life*, London: Sage, 1989.

Caine, B., 'Generational conflict and the question of ageing in nineteenth- and twentieth-century feminism', *Australian Cultural History* 14 (1995), 92–108.

Carter, A., *The Sadeian Woman: An Exercise in Cultural History*, London: Virago, 1979.

Carter, I., 'Kailyard: the literature of decline in nineteenth-century Scotland', *Scottish Journal of Sociology* 1, 1 (1976), 1–13.

Carver, V. and Liddiard, P. (eds.), *An Ageing Population*, Sevenoaks: Hodder and Stoughton in association with Open University Press, 1978.

Cave, A., 'The portrayal of the family relationships of older people in films of the 1980s as compared with films of the 1920s, 1930s and 1940s', Diploma in Gerontology dissertation, Centre for Extra-Mural Studies, Birkbeck College, University of London, 1991.

Cecil, D., *Max: A Biography*, London: Constable, 1964.

Centre for Policy on Ageing, *Over 90 in the 1990s*, London: CPA, 1990.

Charles, E., *The Menace of Under-Population: A Biological Study of the Decline of Population Growth*, London: Watts & Co., 1936; orig. pub. as *The Twilight of Parenthood* (1934).

Cherlin, A. J. and Furstenberg, F., *The New American Grandparent*, London: Harvard University Press, 1991.

*Choice*, December 1996, 3.

Chudacoff, H. and Hareven, T. K., 'Family transitions into old age', in Hareven, *Transitions*, pp. 217–43.

Clarke, J. and Critcher, C., *The Devil Makes Work: Leisure in Capitalist Britain*, London: Macmillan Education, 1985.

Clements, A., 'Pensioners turn "Bonnie and Clyde" to pay off mortgage', *Scotsman*, 27 May 1989, 1.

Clio Co-operative, *Let's Not Forget: Women's Memories of Islington*, London: Clio Co-operative, 1984 (video).

Cockburn, H., *Journal of Henry Cockburn; being a Continuation of the Memoirs of His Life, 1831–1854*, Edinburgh: Edmonston and Douglas, 1874.

Cohen, A. P., *Self Consciousness: An Alternative Anthropology of Identity*, Routledge: London, 1993.

Cohen, S. and Taylor, L., *Escape Attempts: The Theory and Practice of Resistance to Everyday Life*, 2nd edn, London: Routledge, 1992.

Cole, T. R., *The Journey of Life: A Cultural History of Aging in America*, Cambridge University Press, 1993.

Coleman, A., *Preparation for Retirement in England and Wales*, Leicester: NIACE, 1990.

Coleman, A. and Chiva, A., *Coping With Change: Focus on Retirement*, London: Health Education Authority, 1991.

Coleman, P. G., *Ageing and Reminiscence Processes: Social and Clinical Implications*, Chichester: Wiley, 1986.

'Reminiscence within the study of ageing: the social significance of story', in Bornat, J. (ed.), *Reminiscence Reviewed: Perspectives, Evaluations, Achievements*, Buckingham: Open University Press, 1994, pp. 8–20.

'Last scene of all', *Generations Review* 7, 1 (1997), 2–5.

Coleman, R. (ed.), *Working Together: A New Approach to Design*, London: Royal College of Art, 1997.

Comfort, A., *A Good Age*, London: Mitchell Beazley, 1977.

Conservative Party Annual Conference Report, 1937.

Cooper, J., 'If life begins at 40, let it rip at 60', *World of Retirement* (Summer 1997), 5–7.

Cooper, M. and Bornat, J., 'Equal opportunity or special need: combating the woolly bunny', *Journal of Educational Gerontology* 3, 1 (1988), 28–41.

Cotier, J., *Nudes in Budapest*, Budapest: Aktok, 1992.

Counts, D. A. and Counts, D. R., *Over the Next Hill: An Ethnography of RVing Seniors in America*, Peterborough, Ont.: Broadview Press, 1996.

Coupland, N., Coupland, J. and Giles, H., *Language, Society and the Elderly: Discourse, Identity and Ageing*, Oxford: Basil Blackwell, 1991.

Coward, R., *Female Desire: Women's Sexuality Today*, London: Paladin, 1984.

Cowgill, D. O., 'Mobile homes: a study of trailer life', Ph.D thesis, University of Pennsylvania, 1941.

'The aging of population and societies', *American Association of Political and Social Science* 415 (1974), 1–18.

Cowgill, D. O. and Holmes, L. (eds.), *Aging and Modernization*, New York: Appleton-Century-Crofts, 1972.

Cribier, F., 'Migration et cycle de vie', in *Les Ages de la vie. VIIe colloque national de démographie, INED, travaux et documents*, Paris: PUF, 1982, pp. 149–58.

Csikszentmihalyi, M. and Rochberg-Halton, E., *The Meaning of Things: Domestic Symbols and the Self*, Cambridge University Press, 1981.

Cumming, D., *Extracts from Harry's Diary/Pretty Ribbons*, exhibited Montreal, December 1991–April 1992.

Cumming, E. and Henry, W. E., *Growing Old: The Process of Disengagement*, New York: Basic Books, 1961.

Cunningham, I., *After Ninety*, Seattle and London: University of Washington Press, 1977.

Dail, P. W., 'Prime-time television portrayals of older adults in the context of family life', *Gerontologist* 28 (1988), 700–6.

Dalley, G. and Denniss, M., *A View of the Century: Centenarians Talking*, London: Centre for Policy on Ageing, 1997.

Dalrymple, J., 'Dietrich: the last take', *The Sunday Times*, 10 May 1992, Focus section, 11.

Davis, R. H. and Davis, J. A., *TV's Image of the Elderly: A Practical Guide for Change*, Lexington, MA: Lexington Books, 1985.

Deacon, A., 'Thank you, God, for the means-test man', *New Society*, 25 June 1981, 519–20.

Deitch, J., *Post Human*, New York: Distributed Art Publishers, 1992.

Del Webb's Sun City West (1986), brochure.

Demos, J., 'Old age in early New England', *American Journal of Sociology* 84 (1978), 248–87.

  *Past, Present, and Personal: The Family and the Life Course in American History*, Oxford University Press, 1986.

Denzin, N., *Interpretive Biography*, Newbury Park: Sage, 1988.

Diessenbacher, H., 'The elderly in the health care system: ethic and economy of the generation conflict in the medical system', *Generations* 4 (1986/7), 1–7.

Dillon, K. M. and Jones, B. S., 'Attitudes toward aging portrayed in birthday cards', *International Journal of Aging and Human Development* 13, 1 (1981), 79–84.

Dittmann-Kohli, F., 'The construction of meaning in old age: possibilities and constraints', *Ageing and Society* 10 (1990), 279–94.

Donaldson, L. and Johnson, M., 'The health of older Asians', in J. Johnson and Slater, *Ageing and Later Life*, pp. 76–83.

Dowd, J., 'The old person as stranger', in Marshall, *Later Life*, pp. 147–89.

Dressler, M., *The Life Story of an Ugly Duckling*, New York: Robert McBride & Co., 1924.

Durie, A., 'Tourism and commercial photography in Victorian Scotland: the rise and fall of G. W. Wilson & Co., 1852–1908', *Northern Scotland* 12 (1992), 89–104.

Dyer, G., 'Accentuating the negative', *Observer Review*, 17 August 1997, 4.

Edey, M., *Great Photographic Essays from LIFE*, Boston, MA: New York Graphic Society, 1978.

Edinburgh Photographic Society, *133rd International Exhibition of Photography*, Edinburgh Photographic Society, 1995.

Ekerdt, D. J., 'The busy ethic: moral continuity between work and retirement', *Gerontologist* 26 (1986), 239–44.

Elder, G. H., *Children of the Great Depression*, University of Chicago Press, 1974.

Elder, G. H. and Clipp, E. C., 'Introduction to the special section on military experience in adult development and aging', *Psychology and Aging* 9 (1994), 3–4.

Elias, N., *The Civilising Process: The History of Manners*, 2 vols., Oxford: Basil Blackwell, 1978, vol. I.

*The Loneliness of the Dying*, Oxford: Basil Blackwell, 1985.

Elliott, J. C., 'The daytime television portrayal of older adults', *Gerontologist* 24 (1984), 628–33.

Erikson, E. H., *Identity and the Life Cycle: A Reissue*, New York: W. W. Norton, 1980.

Estes, C. L, *The Aging Enterprise*, San Francisco: Jossey-Bass, 1979.

European Resource Unit, *Older People in Europe Oct. '96 Report*, London: Age Concern England, 1997.

Evans, J., 'A sense of self', *Ten 8* 31 (1989), 50–2.

Evans, M., 'Reading lives: how the personal might be social', *Sociology* 27, 1 (1993), 5–13.

Fairhurst, E., 'Recalling life: analytical issues in the use of "memories"', in Jamieson, Harper, and Victor, *Critical Approaches*, pp. 63–73.

Falkingham, J. and Victor, C., *The Myth of the Woopie: Incomes, the Elderly, and Targeting Welfare*, STICERD/LSE Welfare State Programme, Discussion Paper No. 55, London: LSE, 1991.

Featherstone, M., 'The body in consumer culture', in Featherstone, Hepworth, and Turner, *The Body*, pp. 170–96.

*Consumer Culture and Postmodernism*, London: Sage, 1991.

'Virtual reality, cyberspace and the ageing body', in Hummel and Lalive D'Epinay, *Images of Aging*, pp. 246–86.

Featherstone, M. and Hepworth, M., 'Changing images of retirement: an analysis of representations of ageing in the popular magazine *Retirement Choice*', in Bromley, *Gerontology*, pp. 219–24.

'Ageing and old age: reflections on the postmodern life course', in Bytheway, Keil, Allatt and Bryman, *Becoming and Being Old*, pp. 143–57.

'New lifestyles in old age?', in Phillipson, Bernard, and Strang, *Dependency and Interdependency in Old Age*, pp. 85–94.

'Images of ageing', in Bond and Coleman, *Ageing in Society*, pp. 250–75.

'The mask of ageing and the postmodern life course', in Featherstone, Hepworth, and Turner, *The Body*, pp. 371–89.

'Images of positive aging: a case study of *Retirement Choice* magazine', in Featherstone and Wernick, *Images of Aging*, pp. 29–48.

Featherstone, M., Hepworth, M. and Turner, B. S. (eds.), *The Body: Social Process and Cultural Theory*, London: Sage, 1991.

Featherstone, M. and Wernick, A., 'Introduction', in Featherstone and Wernick, *Images of Aging*, pp. 1–15.

Featherstone, M., and Wernick, A. (eds.), *Images of Aging: Cultural Representations of Later Life*, London: Routledge, 1995.

Fennell, G., Phillipson, C. and Evers, H. (eds.), *The Sociology of Old Age*, Milton Keynes: Open University Press, 1988.

Fielding, H., *Proposal for Making an Effectual Provision for the Poor*, London: A. Millar, 1753.

Finch, J., *Family Obligations and Social Change*, Oxford: Polity Press, 1989.

Fischer, D. H., *Growing Old in America*, New York: Oxford University Press, 1977.

Fisher, A., *Let Us Now Praise Famous Women: Women Photographers for the US Government 1935 to 1944*, London: Pandora Press, 1987.

Foner, N., *Ages in Conflict: A Cross-Cultural Perspective on Inequality Between Old and Young*, New York: Columbia University Press, 1984.

Ford, C. (ed.), *The Story of Popular Photography*, London: Century, 1989.

Ford, J. and Sinclair, R., *Sixty Years On: Women Talk About Old Age*, London: Women's Press, 1987.

Forster, E. M., *Aspects of the Novel*, London: Edward Arnold, 1927.

Forster, M., *Have the Men Had Enough?*, London: Chatto and Windus, 1989.

Foucault, M., *Madness and Civilization*, London: Tavistock, 1971, orig. published 1961.

  *Power/Knowledge: Selected Interviews and Other Writings, 1972–1977*, ed. Gordon, C., Brighton: Harvester, 1980.

'Free radicals', *Generations Review* 7, 2 (1997), 24–5.

Freely, M., 'More trick than treat', *Observer Review*, 17 September 1995, 16.

Friedan, B., *The Fountain of Age*, London: Jonathan Cape, 1993.

Fries, J. F. and Crapo, L. M., *Vitality and Aging: Implications of the Rectangular Curve*, San Francisco: W. H. Freeman, 1981.

Frith, S., *The Sociology of Youth*, Ormskirk: Causeway Books, 1984.

Gantz, W., Gartenber, H. M. and Rainbow, C. K., 'Approaching invisibility: the portrayal of the elderly in magazine advertisements', *Journal of Communication* 30 (1980), 56–60.

Geertz, C., *Local Knowledge: Further Essays in Interpretive Anthropology*, London: Fontana, 1993.

Gibson, H. B., *Love in Later Life*, London: Peter Owen Publishers, 1997.

Giddens, A., *Central Problems in Social Theory*, London: Macmillan, 1979.

*Giles, Sunday Express & Daily Express Cartoons*, Forty-fourth Series, London: Express Newspapers, 1990.

  Forty-sixth Series, Risborough: Annual Concepts Limited, 1992.

Gilleard, C. and Higgs, P., 'Cultures of ageing: self, citizen and the body', in Minichiello, V., Chappell, N. and Kendig, H. (eds.), *Sociology of Aging: International Perspectives*, Melbourne: International Sociological Association, 1997, pp. 82–92.

Glanz, D., 'Seniors and cyberspace: some critical reflections on computers and older persons', *Education and Ageing* 12 (1997), 69–81.

Glaser, B. and Strauss, A. L., *Status Passage*, London: Routledge and Kegan Paul, 1971.

Goffman, E., *Stigma: Notes on the Management of Spoiled Identity*, Harmondsworth: Penguin, 1984.

Goldberg, J., *Rich and Poor*, New York: Random House, 1985.

Golding, P. and Middleton, S., *Images of Welfare: Press and Public Attitudes to Poverty*, Oxford: Basil Blackwell, 1982.

*Good Times*, February/March 1996.

Goode, W., *World Revolution and Family Patterns*, New York: Free Press of Glencoe, 1963.

Gorer, G., 'The pornography of death', *Encounter* 5, 4 (1955), 49–52.

Gorz, A., *Paths To Paradise: On the Liberation from Work*, London: Pluto Press, 1985.

Graebner, W., *A History of Retirement: The Meaning and Function of an American Institution, 1885–1978*, New Haven, CT: Yale University Press, 1980.

Gratton, B., 'The new history of the aged: a critique', in Van Tassel, D. and Stearns, P. N. (eds.), *Old Age in a Bureaucratic Society: The Elderly, the Experts and the State of American History*, Westport, CT: Greenwood Press, 1986, pp. 3–29.

Gray, C. *The Parents*, Edinburgh: Fotofeis Ltd, 1995.

Gray, J. and Tocher, J. F., 'The ethnology of Buchan, part III: the physical characteristics of adults and school children in East Aberdeenshire', *Transactions of the Buchan Field Club* 6 (1901), 37–68.

Green, B. S., *Gerontology and the Construction of Old Age: A Study in Discourse Analysis*, New York: Aldine de Gruyter, 1993.

Greer, G., *The Change: Women, Ageing and the Menopause*, London: Hamish Hamilton, 1991.

di Gregorio, S., 'Understanding the "management" of everyday-living', in Phillipson, Bernard, and Strang, *Dependency and Interdependency in Old Age*, pp. 327–37.

'"Managing" – a concept for contextualising how people live their later lives', in di Gregorio, S. (ed.), *Social Gerontology: New Directions*, London: Croom Helm, 1987, pp. 268–84.

Greven, P., *Four Generations: Population, Land, and Family in Colonial Andover, Massachusetts*, Ithaca, NY, and London: Cornell University Press, 1970.

Grundy, E., 'Retirement migration and its consequences in England and Wales', *Ageing and Society* 7, 2 (1987), 57–82.

Gubrium, J. F., *Individual Agency, the Ordinary and Postmodern Life*, Centre for Ageing and Biographical Studies, School of Health and Social Welfare, Open University, 24 April 1995 (printed text of inaugural lecture).

Gubrium, J. and Wallace, B., 'Who theorises age?', *Ageing and Society* 10, 2 (1990), 131–50.

Guillemard, A.-M., *La Retraite: une mort sociale*, Paris: Mouton, 1972.

'The making of old age policy in France', in Guillemard, *Old Age and the Welfare State*, pp. 75–99.

Guillemard, A.-M. (ed.), *Old Age and the Welfare State*, London: International Sociological Association/Sage, 1983.

Gullette, M. M., *Safe at Last in the Middle Years*, Berkeley and Los Angeles: University of California Press, 1988.

Gwyther, M., 'Britain bracing for the age bomb', *Independent on Sunday*, 29 March 1992, 16–17.

Haber, C., *Beyond Sixty-Five: The Dilemma of Old Age in America's Past*, Cambridge University Press, 1983.

Haber, C. and Gratton, B., *Old Age and the Search for Security: An American Social History*, Bloomington: Indiana University Press, 1994.

Habermas, J., *Towards a Rational Society*, London: Heinemann, 1971.

Halbwachs, M., *On Collective Memory*, edited, translated, and with an introduction by L. A. Coser, University of Chicago Press, 1992.

Handy, C., *Taking Stock: Being Fifty in the Eighties*, London: BBC Publications, 1983.

*The Future of Work*, Oxford: Basil Blackwell, 1984.

*The Age of Unreason*, London: Business Books Limited, 1989.

Hall, S. and Jefferson, T. (eds.), *Resistance Through Rituals*, London: Hutchinson, 1976.

Hanlon, H., Farnsworth, J. and Murray, J., 'Ageing in American comic strips: 1972–1992', *Ageing and Society* 17, 3 (1997), 293–304.

Hannah, L., *Inventing Retirement: The Development of Occupational Pensions in Britain*, Cambridge University Press, 1986.

Hannavy, J., *A Moment in Time: Scottish Contributions to Photography, 1840–1920*, Glasgow: Third Eye/Interbook Media Services, 1983.

Hareven, T. K., 'Family time and historical time', *Daedalus* 106, 2 (1977), 57–70.

'The history of the family and the complexity of social change', *American Historical Review* 96, 1 (1991), 95–124.

Hareven, T. K. (ed.), *Transitions: The Family and the Life Course in Historical Perspective*, New York: Academic Press, 1978.

Harper, S. and Thane, P., 'The consolidation of "old age" as a phase of life, 1945–1965', in Jefferys, *Growing Old*, pp. 43–61.

Harvard University Press Sociology catalogue (1994).

Harvey, D., *The Condition of Postmodernity*, Oxford: Basil Blackwell, 1989.

Harvey, P. (ed.), *The Oxford Companion to English Literature*, 3rd edn, Oxford University Press, 1946.

Harvey, S., 'Coming of age in film', *American Film* 7, 3 (1981), 52–3.

Havighurst, R. J., 'Successful aging', in Williams, R. H., Tibbitts, C. and Donahue, W. (eds.), *Processes of Aging*, 2 vols., New York: Atherton, 1963, vol. I, pp. 299–320.

Hazan, H., *From First Principles: An Experiment in Ageing*, Westport, CT, and London: Bergin and Garvey, 1996.

Hebdige, D., 'Youth culture', lecture to Birkbeck College Centre for Extra-Mural Studies Summer School, London School of Hygiene, 12 July 1989.

Hen Co-op, *Growing Old Disgracefully*, London: Judy Piatkus Publishers, 1993.

Hendrick, H., 'Constructions and reconstructions of British childhood', in James, A. and Prout, A. (eds.), *Constructing and Reconstructing Childhood*, Brighton: Falmer Press, 1991, pp. 35–59.

Hendricks, J. and Cutler, S. J., 'Leisure and the structure of our life worlds', *Ageing and Society* 10 (1990), 85–94.

Hepworth, M., 'Positive ageing and the mask of age', *Journal of Educational Gerontology* 6, 2 (1991), 93–101.

'Ageing and the emotions', *Journal of Educational Gerontology* 8, 2 (1993), 75–85.

'Positive ageing: what is the message?', in Brunton, R., Burrows, R. and Nettleton, S. (eds.), *The Sociology of Health Promotion: Critical Analyses of Consumption, Lifestyle and Risk*, London: Routledge, 1995, pp. 176–90.

'Where do grannies come from?: representations of grandmothers in Victorian paintings', *Generations Review* 5, 1 (1995), 2–4.

'Consumer culture and social gerontology', *Education and Ageing* 11, 1 (1996), 19–30.

'"William" and the old folks: notes on infantilisation', *Ageing and Society* 16 (1996), 423–41.

Hepworth, M. and Featherstone, M., *Surviving Middle Age*, Oxford: Basil Blackwell, 1982.

Hevey, D., *The Creatures Time Forgot: Photography and Disability Imagery*, London: Routledge, 1992.

Higgs, P., 'Citizenship theory and old age: from social rights to surveillance', in Jamieson, Harper, and Victor, *Critical Approaches*, pp. 118–31.

Hobman, D., *The Political Challenge of an Ageing Society*, Age Concern, Coming of Age Campaign Rights and Choices Resource Paper RC9, Mitcham: Age Concern, 1991.

Hockey, J., *Experiences of Death: An Anthropological Account*, Edinburgh University Press, 1990.

Hockey, J. and James, A., *Growing Up and Growing Old: Ageing and Dependency in the Life Course*, London: Sage, 1993.

Holdsworth, D. W. and Laws, G., 'Landscapes of old age in coastal British Columbia', *Canadian Geographer* 38, 2 (1994), 174–81.

Hopkinson, A., *Jo Spence: Matters of Concern, Collaborative Images, 1982–1992*, London: Royal Festival Hall Galleries, 1994.

'How TV stunner Carol grew old before her time', *The People*, 27 February 1993, 5.

Hummel, C. and Lalive D'Epinay, C. J. (eds.), *Images of Aging in Western Societies*, Geneva: Centre for Interdisciplinary Gerontology, 1995.

Hunt, D., 'Paupers and pensioners: past and present', *Ageing and Society* 9, 4 (1990), 407–30.

Huxley, A., *After Many a Summer*, London: Chatto and Windus, 1939.

Ignatieff, M., *The Needs of Strangers*, London: Chatto and Windus, 1984.

*The Russian Album*, Harmondsworth: Penguin, 1988.

Itzin, C., 'The double jeopardy of ageism and sexism: media images of women', in Bromley, *Gerontology*, pp. 170–84.

Jacques, E., 'Death and the mid-life crisis', *International Journal of Psychoanalysis* 46 (1965), 502–14.

Jamieson, A., Harper, S. and Victor, C. (eds.), *Critical Approaches to Ageing and Later Life*, Buckingham: Open University Press, 1997.

Jefferys, M., 'Inter-generational relationships: an autobiographical perspective', in Jamieson, Harper, and Victor, *Critical Approaches*, pp. 77–89.

Jefferys, M. (ed.), *Growing Old in the Twentieth Century*, London: Routledge, 1989.

Jerrome, D., *Good Company: An Anthropological Study of Old People in Groups*, Edinburgh University Press, 1992.

'Intimacy and sexuality amongst older women', in Bernard and Meade, *Women Come of Age*, pp. 85–105.

'Time, change and continuity in family life', *Ageing and Society* 14, 1 (1994), 1–17.

Johnson, E. S. and Williamson, J. B., *Growing Old: The Social Problems of Aging*, New York: Holt, Reinhart and Winston, 1980.

Johnson, J. and Bytheway, B., 'Illustrating care: images of care relationships with older people', in Jamieson, Harper, and Victor, *Critical Approaches*, pp. 132–42.

Johnson, J. and Slater, R. (eds.), *Ageing and Later Life*, London: Sage, 1993.

Johnson, M., 'That was your life: a biographical approach to later life', in Carver and Liddiard, *An Ageing Population*, pp. 99–113.

'Never say die', *Listener*, 23 June 1988, 21–2.

Johnson, P., *The Economics of Old Age in Britain: A Long-Run View, 1881–1981*, CEPR Discussion Paper No. 47, London: CEPR, 1985.

*The Structured Dependency of the Elderly: A Critical Note*, CEPR Discussion Paper No. 202, London: CEPR, 1988.

Johnson, P., Conrad, C. and Thomson, D. (eds.), *Workers Versus Pensioners: Intergenerational Justice in an Ageing World*, Manchester: CEPR/Manchester University Press, 1989.

Johnson, R., *What Is Cultural Studies Anyway?*, CCCS Occasional Paper General Series, SP No. 74, University of Birmingham, 1983.

Jones, S., 'The elders; a new generation', *Ageing and Society* 6 (1986), 313–31.

Jones, S. (ed.), *The Liberation of the Elders*, Stoke-on-Trent: Beth Johnson Foundation, 1976.

Jordanova, L., 'Medicine and visual culture', *Social History of Medicine* 3, 1 (1990), 88–99.

Joseph, J., *Rose in the Afternoon*, London: Dent, 1974.

Jowell, R. and Airey, C. (eds.), *British Social Attitudes: The 1984 Report*, London: Gower, 1984.

Jung, C. G., 'The transcendent function', in Read, H., Fordham, M., Adler, G. and McGuire, W. (eds.), *The Structure and Dynamics of the Psyche*, 2nd edn, vol. VIII of *The Collected Works of C. J. Jung*, 20 vols., London: Routledge and Kegan Paul, 1972.

Karn, V., *Retiring to the Seaside*, London: Routledge and Kegan Paul, 1977.

Kastenbaum, R., 'Encrusted elders: Arizona and the political spirit of post-modern aging', in Cole, T. R., Achenbaum, A., Jakobi, P. and Kastenbaum, R. (eds.), *Voices and Visions of Aging: Toward a Critical Gerontology*, New York: Springer, 1993, pp. 160–83.

*Dorian, Graying: Is Youth the Only Thing Worth Having?*, Amityville, NY: Baywood Press, 1995.

Katz, S., *Disciplining Old Age: The Formation of Gerontological Knowledge*, Charlottesville, VA, and London: University Press of Virginia, 1996.

Kaufman, S., *The Ageless Self: Sources of Meaning in Later Life*, Madison: University of Wisconsin Press, 1986.

Kelley, C. E., 'Ageism in popular song: a rhetorical analysis of American popular song lyrics, 1964–1973', Ph.D thesis, University of Oregon, 1982.

Kenny, M., 'Sex appeal has its sell-by date', *Daily Mail*, 28 February 1991, 32.

Kercher, J., 'Joan Collins: my old-fashioned values', *Yours*, April 1997, 10–12.

Kidd, D., *To See Oursels: Rural Scotland in Old Photographs*, Glasgow and Edinburgh: HarperCollins/National Museums of Scotland, 1992.

King, G. B. and Stearns, P., 'The retirement experience as a policy factor: an applied history approach', *Journal of Social History* 14 (1981), 589–625.

Kinnes, S., 'Private collection. Photography: Edinburgh International Festival Study Guide', *Scotland on Sunday*, 27 June 1993, 13.

Kitwood, T., 'The dialectics of dementia: with particular reference to Alzheimer's disease', *Ageing and Society* 10 (1990), 177–96.

Kohli, M., 'The world we forgot: a historical review of the life course', in Marshall, *Later Life*, pp. 271–303.

'Ageing as a challenge for sociological theory', *Ageing and Society* 8 (1988), 367–94.

Kundera, M., *The Book of Laughter and Forgetting*, London: Faber and Faber, 1989.

Laczko, F., 'Between work and retirement: becoming "old" in the 1980s', in Bytheway, Keil, Allatt, and Bryman, *Becoming and Being Old*, pp. 24–40.

Laczko, F., Dale, A., Arber, S. and Gilbert, G. N., 'Early retirement in a period of high unemployment', *Journal of Social Policy* 17 (1988), 313–33.

Laczko, F. and Phillipson, C., *Changing Work and Retirement: Social Policy and the Older Worker*, Buckingham: Open University Press, 1991.

Lambert, J., Laslett, P. and Clay, H., *The Image of the Elderly on TV*, Cambridge: University of the Third Age in Cambridge, 1984.

Lasch, C., *The Culture of Narcissism: American Life in an Age of Diminishing Expectations*, London: W. W. Norton, 1991.

Lash, S. and Urry, J., *Economies of Signs and Space*, London: Sage, 1994.

Laslett, P., 'The history of aging and the aged', in Laslett, P., *Family Life and Illicit Love in Earlier Generations*, Cambridge University Press, 1977, pp. 174–213.

'The significance of the past in the study of ageing', *Ageing and Society* 4 (1984), 379–89.

'Gregory King, T. R. Malthus and the origins of English social realism', *Population Studies* 39, 3 (1985), 351–62.

'The emergence of the Third Age', *Ageing and Society* 7 (1987), 113–60.

*A Fresh Map of Life: The Emergence of the Third Age*, London: Weidenfeld and Nicolson, 1989.

Laws, G., 'Spatiality and age relations', in Jamieson, Harper, and Victor, *Critical Approaches*, pp. 90–101.

Lawton, G. (ed.), *New Goals for Old Age*, New York: Columbia University Press, 1943.

Leneman, L., *Into the Foreground: A Century of Scottish Women in Photographs*, Stroud and Edinburgh: Alan Sutton/National Museums of Scotland, 1993.

Leonard, P., 'Editor's Introduction', in Phillipson, *Capitalism*, pp. xi–xiv.

Liberal Party, *The Aged and the Nation*, London: Liberal Party, 1948.

Lifebuoy Soap Series (A), The Robert Opie Collection, Museum of Advertising and Packaging, Gloucester.

Llewellyn Smith, H., *The New Survey of London Life and Labour*, 9 vols., London: P. S. King and Son, 1932, vol. III.

Longino, C. F. and Marshall, V. W., 'North American research on seasonal migration', *Ageing and Society* 10 (1990), 229–35.

Lowenthal, D., *The Past Is a Foreign Country*, Cambridge University Press, 1995.

Lubbock, T., 'At the limit of exposure', *Guardian*, 29 September 1995, 6.

Lurie, A., *The Language of Clothes*, London: Heinemann, 1981.
  *Foreign Affairs*, London: Abacus, 1986.
McArthur, E., 'Foreword', in Gray, *The Parents*.
MacAskill, E., 'A dose of the old salt', *Scotsman*, 11 June 1994, 11.
Macdonald, B. and Rich, C., *Look Me in the Eye: Old Women, Aging and Ageism*, London: Women's Press, 1982.
MacIntyre, S., 'Old age as a social problem', in Dingwall, R., Heath, C. and Stacey, M. (eds.), *Health Care and Health Knowledge*, London: Croom Helm, 1976, pp. 41–63.
McIsaac, S. J., 'How nursing home residents live while in the sub-passage of confusion: the battle of dignity and respect versus deterioration and decline', Ph.D thesis, University of Aberdeen, 1993.
Maclean, A., *Night Falls on Ardnamurchan: The Twilight of a Crofting Family*, Harmondsworth: Penguin, 1986.
Macnicol, J. and Blaikie, A., 'The politics of retirement, 1908–1948', in Jefferys, *Growing Old*, pp. 21–42.
McRobbie, A., 'Working-class girls and the culture of femininity', MA thesis, University of Birmingham, 1977.
  *Feminism and Youth Culture: From Jackie to Just Seventeen*, Basingstoke: Macmillan, 1991.
Magnusson, M., 'Foreword', in *Giles: Sunday Express & Daily Express Cartoons*, Forty-fourth Series.
Mander, A. V., 'Her story of history', in Mander, A. V. and Rush, A. K. (eds.), *Feminism as Therapy*, New York: Random House, 1974, pp. 63–88.
Mannheim, K., *Essays on the Sociology of Culture*, London: Routledge and Kegan Paul, 1956.
'Mardi Gra charges', *Independent*, 1 May 1998, 4.
Markson, E. W. and Taylor, C. A., 'Real world versus reel world: older women and the Academy Awards', in Davis, N. D., Cole, E. and Rothblum, E. D. (eds.), *Faces of Women and Aging*, New York: Haworth Press, 1993, pp. 157–72.
Marris, P., *Loss and Change*, London: Routledge and Kegan Paul, 1974.
Marshall, V. W. (ed.), *Later Life: The Social Psychology of Aging*, London: Sage, 1986.
Martell, L., *Ecology and Society: An Introduction*, Cambridge: Polity, 1994.
Martin, B., 'The cultural construction of ageing: or how long can the summer wine really last?', in Bury, M. and Macnicol, J. (eds.), *Aspects of Ageing: Essays on Social Policy and Old Age*, Egham: Department of Social Policy and Social Science, Royal Holloway and Bedford New College Social Policy Papers No. 3, 1990, pp. 53–81.
Martin, L., Gutman, H. and Hutton, P. (eds.), *Technologies of the Self: A Seminar with Michel Foucault*, London: Tavistock, 1988.
Marwick, A., 'Visual sources in twentieth-century British history', seminar at Institute of Historical Research, London, 20 November 1985.
Mass-Observation, *Bulletin*, New Series, No. 21 (1948).
Matthews, S. H., *The Social World of Old Women*, Beverly Hills: Sage, 1979.
  *Friendships Through the Life Course: Oral Biographies in Old Age*, London: Sage, 1986.

Matza, D., *Delinquency and Drift*, New York: Wiley, 1964.

Meade, C., *The Thoughts of Betty Spital: Pensioner, Activist and Radical Granny*, London: Penguin, 1989.

Means, R. and Smith, R., *The Development of Welfare Services for Elderly People*, London: Croom Helm, 1985.

*Memory Lane: A Photographic Album of Daily Life in Britain, 1930–1953*, London: J. M. Dent and Sons, Ltd, 1980.

Meyrowitz, J., 'The adultlike child and the childlike adult: socialization in an electronic age', *Daedalus* 113, 3 (1984), 19–48.

Midwinter, E., 'Workers versus pensioners?', *Social Policy and Administration* 23 (1989), 205–10.

   Review of P. Johnson, Conrad, and Thomson, *Workers Versus Pensioners*, *Ageing and Society* 9, 4 (1989), 449–50.

   *Out of Focus: Old Age, the Press and Broadcasting*, London: Centre for Policy on Ageing in association with Help the Aged, 1991.

Miles, J., 'Slow progress: why a political framework is necessary for the evaluation of pensioners' campaigns', *Generations Review* 4, 1 (1994), 4–7.

Mills, C. W., 'Situated actions and vocabularies of motive', *American Sociological Review* 5, 6 (1940), 904–13.

Minkler, M. and Cole, T. R., 'Political economy and moral economy: not such strange bedfellows', in Minkler and Estes, *Critical Perspectives on Aging*, pp. 37–49.

Minkler, M. and Estes, C. (eds.), *Critical Perspectives on Aging: The Political and Moral Economy of Growing Old*, Amityville, NY: Baywood Press, 1991.

Minois, G., *History of Old Age: From Antiquity to the Renaissance*, Cambridge: Polity Press, 1989.

Mizruchi, E., 'Abeyance processes, social policy and ageing', in Guillemard, *Old Age and the Welfare State*, pp. 45–52.

Morgan, K., 'A good time to be old', *Listener*, 8 October 1987, 5–6.

Morinis, A., 'Skid Row Indians and the politics of self', in Manning, F. R. and Philibert, J.-M. (eds.), *Customs in Conflict: The Anthropology of a Changing World*, Peterborough, Ont.: Broadview Press, 1990, pp. 361–86.

Myerhoff, B. G., *Number Our Days*, New York: Simon and Schuster, 1978.

Nahemow, L., McCluskey-Fawcett, K. A. and McGhee, P. E. (eds.), *Humor and Aging*, Orlando, FL: Academic Press, 1986.

'Naked age', *Observer Magazine*, 18 October 1992, 42–8.

National Conference on Old Age Pensions (NCOAP), Reports and Pamphlets, 4 November 1922.

   *Review of Ten Years' Progress*, London: NCOAP, n. d. [1927].

National Galleries of Scotland, *On Photography*, Edinburgh: Education Department of the National Galleries of Scotland, 1994.

National Museums of Scotland, Country Life Archive, neg. no. c. 7687.

Neugarten, B., 'Age groups in American society and the rise of the young old', *Annals of the American Academy of Political and Social Science* 415 (1974), 187–98.

*New Society* Database, *New Statesman and Society*, 24 October 1986.

*New Survey of London*, 1930–5 original MSS, British Library of Political and Economic Science, London.

Newman, J., 'Fifty something', Review of Gullette, *Safe at Last*, *The Times Higher Educational Supplement*, 14 April 1989, 14.

Noggle, A., *Anne Noggle*, London: Photographers' Gallery, 1988.

Norman, A., *Triple Jeopardy: Growing Old in a Second Homeland*, London: Centre for Policy on Ageing, 1985.

Notarangelo, R., 'Oldies' barney at the bingo!', *Scottish Daily Mirror*, 18 December 1996, 1.

Nuttall, J., *King Twist*, London: Routledge and Kegan Paul, 1978.

*Observer*, 6 July 1997.

Okely, J. M., 'Clubs for le troisième age: communitas or conflict?', in Spencer, *Anthropology and the Riddle*, pp. 194–212.

Orwell, G., *Down and out in Paris and London*, Harmondsworth: Penguin, 1971.

Ostroff, J., *Successful Marketing to the 50+ Consumer: How to Capture One of the Biggest and Fastest Growing Markets in America*, Englewood Cliffs, NJ: Prentice Hall, 1989.

Palmore, E. B., 'Attitudes toward aging shown by humor', in Nahemow, McCluskey-Fawcett, and McGhee, *Humor and Aging*, pp. 101–19.

'The Parents: Colin Gray', *Art News*, September 1995.

Parsons, T., 'Age and sex in the social structure of the United States', *American Sociological Review* 7 (1942), 604–16.

Passmore, J., 'How Maggie stays in charge', *London Evening Standard*, 18 May 1989, 3.

Pelling, M., 'Old age, poverty, and disability in early modern Norwich: work, remarriage, and other expedients', in Pelling, M. and Smith, R. M. (eds.), *Life, Death, and the Elderly: Historical Perspectives*, London: Routledge, 1991, pp. 74–101.

'Pension fraud – first conviction under new act', *News of the World*, 7 February 1909.

*People Weekly*, 27 January 1992.

Petersen, M., 'The visibility and image of older people on television', *Journalism Quarterly* 50 (1973), 569–73.

Phillipson, C., *The Emergence of Retirement*, University of Durham, Department of Sociology and Social Administration, Working Papers in Sociology No. 14, University of Durham, 1977.

*Capitalism and the Construction of Old Age*, ed. Leonard, P., London: Macmillan, 1982. Critical Texts in Social Work and the Welfare State.

'Drugs and the elderly: a critical perspective on the Opren case', *Critical Social Policy* 3, 2 (1983), 109–16.

'Inter-generational relations: conflict or consensus in the 21st century', *Policy and Politics* 19 (1991), 27–36.

Phillipson, C., Bernard, M. and Strang, P. (eds.), *Dependency and Interdependency in Old Age: Theoretical Perspectives and Policy Alternatives*, London: Croom Helm, 1986.

Photo-Poche, *Amérique. Les Années noires: Farm Security Administration, 1935–1942*, Paris: Centre National de la Photographie, 1983.

Pifer, A. and Bronte, L. (eds.), *Our Ageing Society: Paradox and Promise*, New York and London: W. W. Norton & Co., 1986.

Pilcher, J., *Age and Generation in Modern Britain*, Oxford University Press, 1995.

Pirkl, J. J., 'Transgenerational design: a design strategy whose time has arrived', *Design Management Journal* (Fall 1991), 55–60.

Plath, D., 'Resistance at forty-eight: old-age brinkmanship and Japanese life-course pathways', in Hareven, T. K. and Adams, K. J. (eds.), *Ageing and Life Course Transitions: An Interdisciplinary Perspective*, London: Tavistock Publications, 1982, pp. 109–25.

Plummer, K., *Documents of Life*, London: Allen and Unwin, 1983.

*PM*, BBC Radio 4, 15 January 1998, 21 January 1998.

Political and Economic Planning, *Population Policy in Great Britain*, London: PEP, 1948.

Pollock, G. and Orton, F., *Vincent Van Gogh: Artist of His Time*, Oxford: Phaidon, 1978.

Power, C., 'Life course influences', *Health Variations* 1 (1998), 14–15.

Pratt, H. J., *Gray Agendas*, Ann Arbor: University of Michigan Press, 1993.

Prideaux, T., *The World of Whistler, 1834–1903*, New York: Time-Life Books, 1970.

Priestley, J. B., *English Journey*, London: Gollancz, 1934.

Procacci, G., 'Social economy and the government or poverty', *Ideology and Consciousness* 4 (1978), 55–72.

Proust, M., *À la recherche du temps perdu*, Paris: Gallimard, 1919–27.

Pultz, J., *Photography and the Body*, London: Weidenfeld and Nicolson, 1995.

Q5. 'Hackney Workhouse, "H" Block, the women's ward, 1902', London Borough of Hackney Library Services, Archives Department, 1984 (postcard).

Quadagno, J., *Aging in Early Industrial Society: Work, Family and Social Policy in Nineteenth-Century England*, London: Academic Press, 1982.

Quigley, H. and Goldie, I., *Housing and Slum Clearance in London*, London: Methuen, 1934.

Range, J. and Vinovskis, M. A., 'Images of the elderly in popular magazines: a content analysis of *Littell's Living Age*, 1945–1982', *Social Science History* 5 (1981), 123–70.

Ravenscroft, G., *A Prime Passage*, Leeds: Leaf Press, 1996.

Redfoot, R., 'On the separatin' place: social class and relocation among older women', *Social Forces* 66 (1987), 486–500.

Roberts, E., *A Woman's Place: An Oral History of Working-Class Women, 1890–1940*, Oxford: Basil Blackwell, 1984.

Roberts, N., *Our Future Selves*, London: George Allen and Unwin, 1970.

Rodwell, G., Davis, S., Dennison, T., Goldsmith, C. and Whitehead, L., 'Images of old age on British television', *Generations Review* 2, 3 (1992), 6–8.

Rosenmayr, L., 'Objective and subjective perspectives in life span research', *Ageing and Society* 1 (1981), 29–49.

Rowntree, B. S., *Poverty: A Study of Town Life*, London: Nelson, 1901.

'Growing old usefully: an Easter message for the middle aged', *Birmingham Gazette*, 2 April 1931, Rowntree Papers, ART 16/2, Borthwick Institute of Historical Research, University of York.

*Poverty and Progress: A Second Social Survey of York*, London: Longmans, Green and Co., 1941.

'The care of the aged', *Industrial Welfare* (1947), 46–50.

*Old People: Report of a Survey Committee on the Problems of Ageing and the Care of Old People*, London: Nuffield Foundation/Oxford University Press, 1947.

Rubinstein, R., 'The significance of personal objects to older people', *Journal of Aging Studies* 1 (1987), 225–38.

Rupp, L. J., *Mobilizing Women for War: German and American Propaganda, 1939–1945*, Princeton University Press, 1978.

Ruth, J.-E., and Öberg, P., 'Ways of life: old age in a life history perspective', in Birren, J., Kenyon, G., Ruth, J.-E., Schroots, J. J. F. and Svensson, T. (eds.), *Aging and Biography: Explorations in Adult Development*, New York: Springer, 1996, pp. 167–86.

Sage, A., 'Six score and one', *Observer Review*, 18 February 1996, 8.

Samuel, R., 'The "eye" of history', *New Statesman and Society*, 18 December 1992–1 January 1993, 38–41.

*Theatres of Memory*, vol. I, *Past and Present in Contemporary Culture*, London: Verso, 1994.

Sarton, M., *As We Are Now*, London: Women's Press, 1983.

Saul, S., *Aging: An Album of People Growing Old*, New York: Wiley, 1974.

Sauvy, A., 'Social and economic consequences of the ageing of Western European populations', *Population Studies* 2, 2 (1948), 115–24.

Schuller, T., 'Work-ending: employment and ambiguity in later life', in Bytheway, Keil, Allatt, and Bryman, *Becoming and Being Old*, pp. 41–54.

Schuller, T. and Boston, A. M., *Learning: Education, Training and Information in the Third Age*, Dunfermline: Carnegie United Kingdom Trust, 1992.

Scott, A. (ed.), *Voices of Our Kind*, 3rd edn, Edinburgh: Chambers, 1987.

Seabrook, J. and Roberts, Y., 'Mrs Thatcher's heartland', *Observer Magazine*, 8 February 1981, 26–33.

Sealey, J., 'Whither the aged?', *Listener*, 14 June 1990, 6–8.

Sesta, H., 'Down the old, bent road . . .', *Guardian*, 12 September 1996, 6–7.

'Seuss, Dr' [Geisel, Theodore], *You're Only Old Once!*, London: Fontana, 1986.

Shakespeare, William, *Shakespeare: Complete Works*, ed. Craig, W. J., Oxford University Press, 1906.

Sharpe, R., 'Property. An A to Z of modern manors: N is for the North', *Observer Life*, 11 May 1997, 45.

Sheehy, G., *Passages: Predictable Crises of Adult Life*, New York: Dutton, 1976.

Shegog, R. F. A. (ed.), *The Impending Crisis of Old Age*, Oxford: Nuffield Provincial Hospitals Trust/Oxford University Press, 1981.

Sheldon, J. H., *The Social Medicine of Old Age*, London: Nuffield Foundation/Oxford University Press, 1948.

'Showering gifts over my dead body', *Guardian* (letters page), 14 May 1991.

Simmons, L. W., *The Role of the Aged in Primitive Societies*, New Haven, CT: Yale University Press, 1945.

Smart, R., '"Famous throughout the world": Valentine & Sons Ltd, Dundee', *Review of Scottish Culture* 4 (1988), 75–87.

Smith, J. E., 'Widowhood and ageing in traditional English society', *Ageing and Society* 4, 4 (1984), 429–49.

Smith, R. M., 'The structured dependence of the elderly as a recent development: some sceptical historical thoughts', *Ageing and Society* 4, 4 (1984),
409–28.

Sohngen, M., 'The experience of old age as depicted in contemporary novels',
*Gerontologist* 17, 1 (1977), 70–8.

Sohngen, M. and Smith, R. J., 'Images of old age in poetry', *Gerontologist* 18
(1978), 181–6.

Sontag, S., 'The double standard of aging', *Saturday Review*, 23 September
1972, 29–38.

*On Photography*, Harmondsworth: Penguin, 1979.

Spence, J. and Dennett, T., *Metamorphosis; or Do We Have the Right to Determine
Our Own Images of Ourselves After Death? A Pre- and Post-Death Collaboration*
(1991), series of photographic prints, Glasgow Gallery of Modern Art.

Spence, J. and Holland, P. (eds.), *Family Snaps: The Meanings of Domestic
Photography*, London: Virago, 1991.

Spence, J. in collaboration with Martin, R., 'Transformations', text at *New
Portraits From Old* exhibition (1986).

Spencer, P., 'The riddled course: theories of age and its transformation', in
Spencer, *Anthropology and the Riddle*, pp. 1–26.

Spencer, P. (ed.), *Anthropology and the Riddle of the Sphinx: Paradoxes of Change
in the Life Course*, London: Routledge, 1991.

Stafford, B. M., La Puma, J. and Schiedermayer, D. L., 'One face of beauty, one
picture of health: the hidden aesthetic of medical practice', *Journal of
Medicine and Philosophy* 14 (1989), 213–30.

Stearns, P. N., *Old Age in European Society*, London: Croom Helm, 1977.

Steedman, C., *Landscape for a Good Woman: A Story of Two Lives*, London:
Virago, 1986.

Stennett, M., *On-the-Ceiling*, C171 Smelt Funny, Cheltenham: Emotional
Rescue Ltd. [1997] (greeting card).

Stephens, J., *Loners, Losers and Lovers: Elderly Tenants in a Slum Hotel*, London:
University of Washington Press, 1976.

Stevenson, J., *Social Conditions in Britain Between the Wars*, Harmondsworth:
Penguin, 1977.

Stevenson, S., *David Octavius Hill and Robert Adamson: Catalogue of Their
Calotypes Taken Between 1843 and 1847 in the Collection of the Scottish
National Portrait Gallery*, Edinburgh: National Galleries of Scotland,
1981.

*Hill and Adamson's The Fishermen and Women of the Firth of Forth*, Edinburgh:
National Galleries of Scotland, 1991.

'Photography', in Scott, P. H. (ed.), *Scotland: A Concise Cultural History*,
Edinburgh and London: Mainstream, 1993, pp. 253–66.

Stoddard, K., *Saints and Shrews: Women and Aging in American Popular Film*,
Westport, CT, and London: Greenwood Press, 1983.

Stone, L., 'Walking over grandma', *New York Review of Books* 24, 8 (1977),
110–16.

Sugarman, L., *Life-Span Development: Concepts, Theories and Interventions*,
London: Methuen, 1986.

Sultan, L., *Pictures from Home*, New York: Abrams, 1992.

*Sunday Express*, 2 July 1978, 14 April 1974, 18 November 1990.

Sutton, H., *Gorleston*, London: Hodder and Stoughton, 1995.

Swift, J., *Gulliver's Travels*, Oxford: Blackwell, 1941; orig. published 1726.

Tamke, S. S., 'Human values and aging: the perspective of the Victorian nursery', in Spicker, S. F., Woodward, K. M. and Van Tassel, D. (eds.), *Aging and the Elderly: Humanistic Perspectives in Gerontology*, Atlantic Highlands, NJ: Humanities Press, 1978, pp. 60–94.

'Test-tube granny has triplets', *London Evening Standard*, 5 May 1992.

Thane, P., *Ageing and the Economy: Historical Issues*, CEPR Discussion Paper No. 16, London: CEPR, 1984.

'The cultural history of old age', *Australian Cultural History* 14 (1995), 23–39.

Review of Haber and Gratton, *Old Age*, *Generations Review* 5, 2 (1995), 16.

'Then and now', *Retirement Choice* (November 1972), 8.

Third Age Media Web Site (1997), http://www.thirdagemedia.com.

Third Age Network, 'What Is the Third Age?', *Transitions* 1 (1990), 2.

Third Age Web Site (1997), http://www.thirdage.com.

Thomas, K., 'Age and authority in early modern England', *Proceedings of the British Academy* (1976), 205–48.

Thompson, B., 'Dying by numbers', *New Statesman and Society*, 9 March 1990, 24–5.

Thompson, E. P., 'Time, work discipline and industrial capitalism', *Past and Present* 39 (1967), 56–97.

*The Poverty of Theory and Other Essays*, London: Merlin Press, 1978.

Thompson, F., *Victorian and Edwardian Scotland from Old Photographs*, Edinburgh: Tantallon Books, 1976.

Thompson, P., Itzin, C. and Abendstern, M., *I Don't Feel Old: The Experience of Later Life*, Oxford University Press, 1990.

Thompson, P., with Wailey, T. and Lummis T., *Living the Fishing*, London: Routledge and Kegan Paul, 1983.

Thomson, D., 'Workhouse to nursing home: residential care of elderly people in England since 1840', *Ageing and Society* 3 (1983), 43–69.

'The decline of social welfare: falling state support for the elderly since Victorian times', *Ageing and Society* 4, 4 (1984), 451–82.

Thomson, M., *Old Wemyss*, Ochiltree: Richard Stenlake, 1995.

*The Times*, 8 May 1995.

Timmins, N., 'John Glenn: "heroic" senator redefines space age', *Financial Times*, 17 January 1998, 2.

Titmuss, R. M. and Titmuss, K., *Parents Revolt: A Study of the Declining Birth-Rate in Acquisitive Societies*, London: Secker and Warburg, 1942.

Toffler, A., *The Third Wave*, London: Collins, 1980.

Tönnies, F., *Gemeinschaft und Gesellschaft*, Leipzig: O. R. Reinholz, 1887; trans. C. P. Loomis as *Community and Association*, London: Routledge and Kegan Paul, 1955.

Townsend, P., *The Family Life of Old People: An Inquiry in East London*, London: Routledge and Kegan Paul, 1957; Harmondsworth: Pelican, 1963.

*The Last Refuge: A Survey of Residential Institutions and Homes for the Aged in England and Wales*, London: Routledge and Kegan Paul, 1962; abridged edn, 1964.

Townsend, P. and Wedderburn, D., *The Aged in the Welfare State*, London: G. Bell and Sons, 1965.

Traynor, J., 'Musings on the place of pop records in our lives', *Generations Review* 5, 4 (1995), 7–8.

Troyansky, D., 'Historical research into ageing, old age and older people', in Jamieson, Harper, and Victor, *Critical Approaches*, pp. 49–62.

Turner, B. S., 'Ageing, status politics and sociological theory', *British Journal of Sociology* 40 (1989), 588–606.

Turney, J., 'The age of the oldie', *The Times Higher Education Supplement*, 23 May 1997, 18–19.

*Twelve Faces of Age*, 1994 calendar, London: Inquit, 1993.

Tyler, W., 'Structural ageism as a phenomenon in British society', *Journal of Educational Gerontology* 1, 2 (1986), 38–46.

*Undressed: Fashion in the Twentieth Century*, Channel 4, 22 February 1998 (television series).

United Kingdom, Central Statistical Office (CSO), *Social Trends No. 20*, London: HMSO, 1990.

United Kingdom, Department of Health and Social Security (DHSS), *A Happier Old Age*, London: HMSO, 1978.

United Kingdom, Ministry of Labour and National Service, *Employment of Older Men and Women*, London: Minister of Labour and National Service, 1952.

United Kingdom, Office of Population Censuses and Surveys (OPCS) and Central Office of Information, *Census Guide I: Britain's Elderly Population*, London: HMSO, 1984.

*General Household Survey 1994*, London: HMSO, 1995.

United Kingdom, Parliament, *Final Report of the Royal Commission on Population*, Cmd. 7695 (1949).

House of Commons Debates (Hansard), vol. 286, col. 449, 1934 (Debate on Retiring Pensions).

Unruh, D., *Invisible Lives: Social Worlds of the Aged*, Beverly Hills: Sage, 1983.

Vonnegut, K., 'Tomorrow and tomorrow and tomorrow', in Boardman, T. (ed.), *Connoisseur's Science Fiction*, Harmondsworth: Penguin, 1964, pp. 64–6, reprinted in Carver and Liddiard, *An Ageing Population*, pp. 47–9.

Wadel, C., 'The hidden work of everyday life', in Wallman, S. (ed.), *Social Anthropology of Work*, London: Academic Press, 1979, pp. 365–84.

Wadsworth, M., *The Imprint of Time: Childhood, History, and Adult Life*, Oxford: Clarendon Press, 1991.

Walker, A., 'Ageing and the social sciences: the North American way', *Ageing and Society* 7 (1982), 235–41.

Walter, T., 'Modern death: taboo or not taboo', *Sociology* 25, 2 (1991), 293–310.

Wass, H., Hawkins, L. V., Kelly, E. B., Magners, C. R and McMorrow, A. M., 'The elderly in Sunday papers, 1963–1983', *Educational Gerontology* 11 (1985), 29–39.

Waters, M., *The Nude Male: A New Perspective*, New York and London: Paddington Press, 1978.

Watson, I., *Harry Gordon 'The Laird of Inversnecky'*, Aberdeen: Aberdeen District Council, 1993.

Waugh, E., *A Little Learning*, London: Chapman and Hall, 1964.

Weintraub, S., *Whistler: A Biography*, London: Collins, 1974.

Wells, N. and Freer, C. (eds.), *The Ageing Population: Burden or Challenge?*, London: Macmillan, 1988.

Wernick, A., 'The dying of the American way of death', in Hummel and Lalive D'Epinay, *Images of Aging*, pp. 69–90.

White, L., 'The new age no age woman', *Mirabella*, 'Private View' (1991), 4–7.

Whitfield, M., 'Pensioners poised for a pivotal role', *Independent*, 21 March 1994, 8.

Wilde, O., *The Picture of Dorian Gray*, Oxford University Press, 1974; orig. London: Lippincott's Monthly Magazine, 1890.

Willcocks, D. M., Peace, S. M. and Kellaher, L. A., *Private Lives in Public Places: A Research-Based Critique of Residential Life in Local Authority Old People's Homes*, London: Tavistock, 1987.

Williams, K., *From Pauperism to Poverty*, London: Routledge, 1981.

Williams, Raymond, *Keywords*, London: Flamingo, 1983.

Williams, Rory, *A Protestant Legacy: Attitudes to Illness and Death Among Older Aberdonians*, Oxford: Clarendon Press, 1990.

Williams, V., 'Ethics of everyday life: Grace Robertson's photojournalism, 1949–1993', essay accompanying *Grace Robertson into the Nineties*, London: Watershed Touring Exhibition, 1993.

*Who's Looking at the Family?*, London: Barbican Art Gallery, 1994.

'A new age coming', *Guardian Weekend*, 21 September 1996, 38–44.

Willis, P., *Learning to Labour*, Aldershot: Saxon House, 1977.

Wilsher, P., 'Justice in an ageing world', *The Sunday Times*, 9 July 1989, Section F, 1.

Wilson, A., 'The infancy of the history of childhood: an appraisal of Philippe Ariès', *History and Theory* 19, 2 (1980), 133–53.

*Women Who Dare*, 1995 calendar, Washington: Library of Congress, 1994.

Woodward, K., *Aging and Its Discontents: Freud and Other Fictions*, Bloomington: Indiana University Press, 1991.

Wrigley, E. A., 'Reflections on the history of the family', *Daedalus* 106 (1977), 71–85.

'The year in moments: how 1996 looked to 32 *Observer* readers', *Observer Life*, 29 December 1996, 4–11.

Young, L., 'The incredible ageing woman', *Guardian*, 1 August 1989, 16–17.

Young, M. and Schuller, T., *Life After Work: The Arrival of the Ageless Society*, London: HarperCollins, 1991.

Young, M. and Willmott, P., *Family and Kinship in East London*, Harmondsworth: Pelican, 1962.

Zeilig, H., 'The uses of literature in the study of older people', in Jamieson, Harper, and Victor, *Critical Approaches*, pp. 39–48.

# Index